Caring for the Nation

A History of the Mater Misericordiae University Hospital

Caring for the Nation

A History of the Mater
Misericordiae University Hospital

Eugene Nolan, RSM

Gill & Macmillan

Gill & Macmillan
Hume Avenue
Park West
Dublin 12
with associated companies throughout the world
www.gillmacmillanbooks.ie

© Eugene Nolan, RSM 2013
Chapter 12 © Dr Peadar McGing, FRCPath
978 07171 5780 8

Print origination by Design Image
Printed by Castuera Industrias Gráficas, S.A., Spain
Index by Kate Murphy
This book is typeset in 10/14 Meridien.

A CIP catalogue record for this book is available from the British Library.

54321

Contents

Acknowledgements

Few non-fiction books are written in isolation and this one certainly wasn't. It was like a journey that I set out on about fifteen years ago. As on all journeys, people are rarely far away and are always interested in helping in any way they can. This book was my attempt to journey back in history to record not only what was happening regarding the Mater, but also in Dublin city when the hospital was being built. This meant I was forever on the move in search of information. Initially, this consisted of frequent excursions to the National Library of Ireland, Dublin City Library & Archives, or to the National Archives of Ireland. Sincere thanks to the staff of these great institutions for their help and advice.

As my research broadened, I sought help from Marianne Cosgrave, archivist, and Sr Francis Lowe at the Mercy Congregational Archives, Herbert Street; Sr Magdalena Frisby and Sr Angela Bugler, Provincial Archives, Booterstown; Angela Rice, librarian, Mater Hospital Library; and the staff of UCD Library. My thanks to each one of them for their time and the trouble they went to for me.

All research and its publication comes at a cost and this work was no exception. Very sincere thanks to Sr Peggy Collins RSM (South Central Province) Provincial Leader, and the SCP team for their interest and support, financially and otherwise, all through the project. My thanks also to Sr Mary Monica Smalle for her help. It is quite possible that without their help this book would not have been published.

In the preliminary stages of my research I became very concerned at the lack of records of any sort within the hospital dealing with developments during the first fifty years or more of the Mater. One day I mentioned this to Sr Anne Hetherington RSM from Brisbane, Australia, who was visiting the hospital. Knowing that the great Mother Vincent Whitty, who built the Mater, was transferred to Brisbane a few months before the hospital opened in 1861, Sr Anne did a bit of searching in the Brisbane Mercy Congregational archives. There she found what can only be described as a historian's treasure-trove of both annual reports and photographs of the Mater in its early years. I cannot describe how grateful I was when she sent copies of this material to me. What a help it has been in trying to piece together the activities in the early years of the hospital. I will always be grateful to Sr Anne for her help.

Writing this book started out as a spare time occupation in the old Nurses' Home. I would like to thank Anne Carrigy, Director of Nursing at the time, for her encouragement and interest in what I was trying to do. Just as I was making progress, a series of hospital building developments necessitated a number of moves over the next few years, which slowed down progress and made writing infinitely difficult. The 'big move' was in 2006 when the school of nursing on North Circular Road moved to the new Centre for Nurse Education (CNE) on Nelson Street. It was not an easy time for all involved, but help was always at hand. Special thanks to Una Marren, Deputy Director of Nursing, for her care and organisation at this time and for making sure I was provided with suitable and safe storage facilities for my archival material, notes and useful bits of paper related to this writing project. It meant a lot to me.

On 1 January 2010, I started to work full time on the book away from the CNE in the hope that I might finish it by the Mater sesquicentennial celebrations due to take place on 24 September in 2011. I did not succeed in reaching this target but I was not short of people who provided me with help and support at the time and to whom I owe a special thanks. They include Peadar McGing PhD, who agreed to write the chapter on the history of the laboratory and the service it has provided over the years. He did an excellent job. Kevin Finnan, whose help with sourcing relevant newspaper articles was a great help. Kevin also gave me a lot of useful advice from time to time. Sr Margherita Rock, who maintained an interest in what I was trying to do throughout and who agreed to read the first manuscript produced. Sr Rose Therese Corcoran, who sat beside me every evening and loved discussing aspects of ward care and hospital management during World War II. Sr Rose Therese, who came to train as a nurse in 1936, is blessed with a wonderful memory and is always worth listening to. Special thanks to Fr Alexis King OFM who translated the Latin script inserted into the foundation stone of the hospital in 1855. Thanks also to the staff of the CNE, especially Elaine Hanley and my teaching colleagues; Dr Mary Codd, Noelle Dowling and staff, Diocesan Archives; Fergus Gillen; McCann FitzGerald, solicitors; Kenneth Clear, solicitor; John Crowe, President of the Royal College of Physicians of Ireland; Harriet Wheelock, archivist; RCPI; the Mater IT department, with a special word of thanks to Siobhan Gregory, who on many occasions had to fix my computer. Special thanks to Florence Grehan, Director of Clinical Photography, who did trojan work at a difficult time for her to ensure the best photographs were made available. Her excellent pictures certainly help to make the text of the book come to life. Finally, a special word of appreciation must go to Mary Day (current *interim* Chief Executive of the Mater) for her interest in this project.

One person who deserves very special mention and thanks is John Morgan (Chairman of the Board of Directors). It would be hard to describe the many different ways John helped with this project. His advice was always excellent and very sound. When I was wandering around wondering who should publish the book, John came to the rescue and we agreed it would be best to seek the help of Gill & Macmillan. Before too long a meeting was arranged with Michael Gill, Chairman of Gill & Macmillan, John and myself. It was an excellent meeting during which the way forward was mapped out. John looked after all the business aspects of getting this book published. This freed me from the worry of something I know little or nothing about, and thus allowed me to continue writing and doing other necessary jobs associated with it. Thank you, John, for all your valuable help and thank you for agreeing to write the foreword for this book, much appreciated. Special thanks to the staff at Gill & Macmillan, especially Jen Patton, photo researcher. Thanks also to Alison Walsh for her careful editing. She has done an excellent job.

As always, my four sisters – Anne, Kay, Bernadette and Patricia – and our extended family have been a tremendous support to me in various ways throughout this project. Sincere thanks to them all. Thanks also to the Mercy Community, which I am part of here at the Mater, for their interest and support in many different ways. Thanks also to the staff in the Mater Convent. Last, but not least, a special word of thanks to all my friends, in particular Sr Martina Nolan, who made sure I got some fresh air at least once a week! And thanks to Pauline Murray and Rosemary Fox for their interest in this project and their kindness to me for many years, but particularly during the past few years.

****

This book is dedicated to the Sisters of Mercy,
especially those who have worked in the
Mater Misericordiae University Hospital.

Foreword

It is a privilege to be invited to write the foreword to a work of such importance by Sr Eugene Nolan, RSM. Here is presented the genetic code, so to speak, of Mater Misericordiae University Hospital, Dublin, namely the principles that define its identity and consequently guarantee its unity, all in the diversity of its achievements. It narrates a luminous history of significance both for Dublin and wider Irish society, far beyond the story the stones of the hospital have to tell. Constructed in 1861, within walking distance of what was then the largest tenement area in Europe, in a city which had the highest death rate in all of Europe, the hospital's story sheds unique light on important aspects of the social history of Dublin over a span of the last 150 years.

Without any fanfare or attention-seeking, it also reveals the extraordinary and dedicated contribution the Religious Sisters of Mercy have made to the benefit of Dublin and her people through the establishment of this one institution alone. This discounts any other activities of this remarkable band of women in all aspects of Irish healthcare provision, let alone their more high-profile participation in Irish education.

This book is also a timely and practical reminder of how the role and characteristics of true voluntarism, encapsulating the concept of vocationalism and active selfless service, have contributed to the building up of Irish society. These concepts are being increasingly undermined in our healthcare environment of today where a cold, cost-centred, contractual – not to say adversarial – management model has gained the upper hand in governmental treatment of the healthcare system. It cannot be underestimated how the Mater's very existence demonstrates that the active conservation and application of what is best in voluntarism is a vital and necessary ingredient for a healthy society.

This work expands the nature and scope of the author's earlier work, *One Hundred Years: A History of the School of Nursing and of Developments at Mater Misericordiae Hospital 1891–1991*. It can be distinguished in that the present study attempts to organise the full history of the Mater into a form of synthesis, similar to a musical chord composed of a large number of notes, many of which have frequently been sounded together but which, for the reader, have never before been so arranged that they can all be sounded at once.

John B Morgan
Chairperson, Mater Misericordiae University Hospital
March 2013

Introduction

Writing the history of the Mater has had a long gestation. It was an exceedingly difficult undertaking in that some of the early records and photographs had found their way out of the hospital to far-flung places such as Brisbane, Australia. In all, it has taken about fifteen years to research and write about what turned out to be an interesting period, not only within the hospital itself, but also in the country as a whole. When the Sisters of Mercy decided to build a large hospital, the city of Dublin, particularly the north side, was struggling with the after-effects of the 1800 Act of Union and in a different way, the health and economic effects of the 1845–47 Great Famine with the sick and dispossessed continuing to make their way to the city to seek help.

I came to the Mater to train as a nurse at a very difficult time in its history. I knew nothing about the place except that the School of Nursing turned out much-sought-after nurses. It became obvious to me during my training that money was scarce, but the way the sisters cared for the patients, and indeed the hospital as a whole, was for me something of a lesson in itself. I was fortunate to be a staff member by the time the centenary of the hospital was celebrated in 1961. During this time, much was recalled about the early history of the Mater at the various celebrations held at the time. Three publications on the history of the hospital were produced for the centenary – nothing had been written before that. I felt very privileged to be asked to contribute one chapter (on the hospital's nurses' badge) to the school of nursing book. Unfortunately, as I subsequently discovered, all of the publications produced failed to cover the essential reason why the Sisters of Mercy had built the hospital in 1861. In addition, little was written about the work of the nuns and the medical staff during the early years of its development and the many difficulties they encountered, locally, economically and politically, over the years.

Probably the most interesting periods of the Mater history, from the point of view of researching and writing it, were those of the various responses provided by the hospital during exceptionally difficult periods in the city itself, starting with that of recurrent epidemic diseases, largely associated with the poverty seen in the 19th century, the various outbreaks of civil strife, especially in 1913, 1916 and 1922 and of course, the impact and demands made of the Mater by the authorities during two world wars. This book includes these difficult times and also more recent tragic events such as the 1972 shooting in the hospital, the Dublin bombings in 1974 and the Stardust fire disaster in 1981.

Once the original hospital was built and ready for use in 1861, educating the medical students became a priority after patient care. Apart from the day-to-day work being done within the hospital, the amount of education provided – medical, nursing, physiotherapy, laboratory, to name but a few – are recorded in this book. The development and contribution by the Mater to the various professions down through the years is interesting, starting with the relationship between the first Medical School in Cecilia Street, founded by Cardinal Newman in 1854, and in 1908 the new National University.

All of this whetted an appetite in me to do something about recording it and making it available to those who might be interested in 'how it all began'. I had hoped for many years that it would be written at some stage by somebody, but this simply never happened. Eventually, I decided to do so myself: as St John of the Cross once said when asked by a nun who was lamenting the absence of love in society, *'Where there is no love, put love and you will find love.'* My philosophy became – where there is no written history, write it and then you will have it! Alas it was to be many years before an opportunity to do the necessary research arose. When it did I seized the opportunity with open arms and set to work to do the necessary research and writing.

The history of the Mater is almost endless. It has proved too extensive to put between two covers. Hopefully, in time, somebody will pick up a pen and fill in the gaps and move on to write about the rapidly developing history taking shape at the present time.

The first known photograph of the Mater Hospital. (Courtesy of the National Library of Ireland.)

CHAPTER 1

A Dream Becomes Reality

On 24 September 1861, the Archbishop of Dublin, Cardinal Paul Cullen, formally opened the Mater Misericordiae Hospital. A great assembly of people gathered on Eccles Street – Sisters of Mercy, clergy, dignitaries and invited guests – to admire the splendid building as they waited for the opening ceremony to begin. At midday prayers were said and the hospital was solemnly blessed, opened and dedicated 'to its high and holy purposes by His Grace the Archbishop of Dublin.'[1] The great brown door under the Ionic columns was ceremoniously unlocked and opened. The crowd then followed the Archbishop and the Sisters into the hospital through the entrance hall and to the largest room in the building – the Pillar Room. Outside, a large assembly of local people and passers-by stood in awe of the glistening granite and the two beautiful wrought iron stands at the foot of the steps supporting gas lamps.[2] This hospital would for many years be the largest in

This painting, by Sister Clare Augustine Moore, was commissioned for the opening of the Mater. The original hangs in the hospital in the top corridor outside the operating theatre.

Dublin prepared to admit anyone who was sick, irrespective of race, colour or creed. As Judge Thomas O'Hagan, a member of the council managing the development finances, said: 'Suffering is the sole condition for entry to the hospital.'[3]

Laying the Foundations

The Venerable Catherine McAuley.

The opening of the hospital, however, was the culmination of many years of planning, and was the dream of Catherine McAuley, foundress of the Sisters of Mercy. She had been anxious that the Sisters should have a hospital of their own, in which the health needs of the poor could be perfectly ministered to, and from which patients should not be compelled to leave until their health was completely re-established.[4] The reason for Catherine McAuley's concern was clear. Dublin in the 1830s was a city riven with poverty and illness. The cholera outbreak in Dublin in 1832[5] alone had claimed the lives of 5,632[6] people, many of whom had been unable to get the medical help they needed. The hospitals which existed in Dublin at the time rejected many cholera sufferers and the shame of being sick and in need of care was so great that the victims of cholera used to wait until darkness had fallen before they sought help, by which time it was often too late. All of this made a profound impression on Catherine McAuley, who determined to remedy the situation, although due to her untimely death in 1841, she would not live to see her dream realised.

The Mater might have been built much earlier if history had been shaped differently. Dublin in the early 19th century was a city in decline. After the Act of Union in 1800 the parliament in Dublin moved to London and with it went the wealthy classes who had provided so much employment in the city. They left behind them large houses that gradually deteriorated and became tenements, housing much of the city's population and producing living conditions of squalor and chronic ill health. At the time, hospitals in the city were limited in number, small in size and poorly funded, and the mainly Catholic population was often refused entry to them. Furthermore, the public viewed hospitals as places built to contain the spread of diseases rather than to treat, cure and make people well. Consequently, sick people generally felt more secure in their own homes among their loved ones, even if they were dying or starving, than in a hospital bed. Because of their negative reputation, no one wanted a hospital to be built in the locality and few ever visited one.

These three Sisters, seen here at the launch of the £5 note, with its picture of the Mater and of Catherine McAuley, gave their entire lives to the work of the hospital. From left, Sister Marie of Mercy O'Connor, Sister Rose Therese Corcoran and Sister John of the Cross Ferguson. (© Derek Speirs.)

It was the great writer Charles Dickens who drew attention to the poor conditions in hospitals in his writings[7] and society began to pay greater attention to the plight of the sick in hospitals; however, it was not until 1860 and the work of Florence Nightingale that real changes began to take place.[8] Florence Nightingale's ideas on hospital design and the training of nurses were to be hugely influential. Although the plans for the Mater would already have been drawn up by the time Nightingale's ideas took hold, they would certainly have influenced the British inspectors who came to view the hospital when it was built.

When she was consulted by St Thomas's Hospital, Nightingale's fresh thinking about the layout of wards – that there should be no corridors in ward areas, only long open spaces with beds on either side and tall windows on both sides for ventilation – greatly impressed the British administration. Her design gave rise to the term 'the Nightingale wards'.

In 1863, a Dr Bristowe and his team from London toured all of the hospitals in Ireland and England and produced a lengthy report on conditions, notably criticising the plans for the Mater hospital, which he felt offered insufficient ventilation.[9] Bristowe's concerns most likely had to do with the general problem of the odour of festering wounds. There were no disinfectants or antibiotics available at the time and there was no knowledge about how infection was transmitted: almost all wounds became infected. Pus was regarded as part of the healing process. Nineteenth-century hospitals generally stank and the public were afraid of them. The only solution seemed to be plenty of fresh air and so the only acceptable designs were those that made provision for this. Hence the reason why the Sisters later purchased the land opposite the hospital on Eccles Street, so that the wards could face open parkland and the prevailing wind.

In the decade after the death of Catherine McAuley, Ireland was to experience what was probably the most devastating period in its history, that of the Famine, which led to unprecedented morbidity and mortality. Dublin city, while it escaped the ravages of potato blight, was inundated with people who had fled or been driven from their miserable homes in the countryside. They drifted into the city and joined the thousands who were living in abysmal tenements or, worse, ended up in the North or South Dublin Poor-Law Unions, the much-feared workhouse. The Mercy Sisters, in their convent at Baggot Street, ministered to these people as best they could, but so desperate was the situation that their funds could no longer meet public needs and an appeal had to be launched in the 1840s to help them to continue to help the needy.[10]

It is hard to believe that in November 1845, the *Freeman's Journal* carried an editorial which read: 'They may starve, but they should starve contentedly'[11] – the reply given by the English Viceroy to a deputation seeking help on behalf of the poor. About nine weeks later the Sisters put an insert (one of many during those years) into the newspaper to describe the situation as they were finding it and to appeal for funds.[12] With so many people in dire need and with literally nowhere to go when they were ill, the Sisters of Mercy set about making Catherine McAuley's dream of a 'hospital of their own' a reality.[13]

The spirit and determination of Catherine McAuley lived on in the hearts of those she left behind after her death in 1841, particularly in the three nuns who would serve as Reverend Mother,[14] one after another, in Baggot Street Convent from 1844 to 1860 and who were principally responsible for the building of the Mater. All three could only be admired for their down-to-earth practicality and their prayerfulness, which in her time had characterised all of Catherine McAuley's work. Sr Cecilia Marmion, Sr Vincent Whitty and Sr Cecilia Xavier Maguire were the quintessential disciples of a great and inspiring leader. Each of them brought her enthusiasm and vision to the building of the Mater, irrespective of the difficulties she faced.

The House of Mercy

In 1844, Sr Cecilia Marmion held the position of Reverend Mother in Baggot Street Convent, the first convent established by Catherine McAuley, known as the 'Foundation House'. Being from Dublin herself, Sr Cecilia knew a lot about the hospital situation. She saw that the north side of the city was particularly badly served and the density of slum dwelling there was rapidly increasing. In addition, the North Dublin Union had a notorious reputation, labelling the needy as 'paupers'. The Sisters decided that if they were going to build a hospital, they would locate it on the north side of Dublin. Without wasting any time, Sister Cecilia wrote to Reverend Daniel Murray, then Catholic archbishop of Dublin, for permission to build a hospital.

St Catherine's Convent

Baggot Street

(handwritten and undated)

My Lord & Most Reverend Father

We beg most respectfully to submit to Your Grace the accompanying requisition requesting the establishment of an hospital at the north side of the City, and to solicit your Grace's advice as to the answer which we should return to it.

We are persuaded that an hospital such as has been proposed would be attended with incalculable advantages to the poor generally, and would be of services benefit to this establishment, as we are frequently obliged to send the young women protected in our Institute to hospital, where we cannot with such convenience administer to their comfort, as we could do if we had one under our immediate control. We have during the last season been obliged to send upwards of fifty patients from the House of Mercy. We shall therefore, in case it meets your Grace's full concurrences, willingly consent to contribute our services to so very meritorious an undertaking.

I remain, my Lord, with respect and...

Your obedient servant in Jesus Christ

(Signed) Mary Cecilia Marmion

The 'accompanying requisition' referred to in the first line of Sr Cecelia's letter has unfortunately not survived, so we cannot know what it contained or who might have drawn it up. Nonetheless, Archbishop Murray readily agreed to this request and the Sisters, with the support of a committee of 'leading gentleman of Dublin', chaired by Judge Thomas O'Hagan,[15] began work. This committee remained active for many years after the hospital opened.

Sr Cecilia Marmion contracted typhus and died rather suddenly on 15 September 1849. By this time, the search for a suitable plot of land on the north side of the city had begun. Sr Cecilia's position as Reverend Mother of the Convent at Baggot Street was soon filled by Sr Vincent Whitty, who was elected on 26 September 1849 and then re-elected in 1852, serving the maximum number of six consecutive years in office permitted by the constitution of the Mercy Order.[16] In many ways the selection of Sr Vincent Whitty was providential. She took office at a very demanding period for the Sisters and proved herself an able and energetic leader.

Sister M. Vincent Whitty

Sister M. Vincent Whitty, who took Catherine McAuley's vision forward into the building of the hospital.

Ellen Whitty was born in 1819 near Enniscorthy, Co. Wexford, of farming people. She received her education in Dublin, at what was considered one of the better schools in the city. It is known that on 6 January 1839, she met Catherine McAuley and one week later she joined the convent where she would become one of the best known of all the Baggot Street Sisters. She spent her novitiate training with Catherine McAuley, who influenced her enormously, and the benefits of this are to be seen in the courageous decisions she subsequently made on behalf of the Mercy congregation. She looked after the congregational finances for a short period and in 1844 was appointed Mistress of Novices by Mother Cecilia Marmion. Apart from taking over responsibility for building the hospital after the death of Mother Cecilia Marmion, Sr Vincent Whitty responded to a request in 1854 for a team of Sisters of Mercy to go to the Crimea to nurse the war-wounded and the sick.[17]

Even when her term of office as Reverend Mother ended, in November 1860, Sr Vincent Whitty had much to contribute to the work of the Sisters of Mercy. She received a request from Bishop James Quinn to make a Mercy foundation in Brisbane, Australia and readily set off with a small group of Sisters for Queensland, Australia in December that year. There, too, she made her mark, going on to develop a healthcare service, and in 1906 the Mater Hospital in Brisbane was opened.

Mother Vincent died in 1892. She was mourned widely, not only in Brisbane and Dublin but in all the countries in which the Sisters of Mercy were by then working, including the United States and New Zealand. In correspondence after her death, she is frequently referred to as 'our darling Mother Vincent'.[18] Her name will always live on at the Mater in Dublin, in the form of the magnificent new €284 million adult hospital development, called the Whitty Building in her honour, and opened by Minister for Health, Dr James Reilly, in April 2012.

Matters Financial

It is widely held that the person who influenced the size and splendour of the Mater building was Sr Cecilia Maguire, her vision overcoming the fact that the Sisters themselves had only limited financial resources to build the hospital.[19] They felt that they had enough money to buy the land and get the building started and after that, they would have to organise many fundraising events to see their plans come to fruition. Generally, there was a lot of goodwill around and people were anxious to pledge their support for this much-needed hospital.

Choosing a suitable site for the building was the next important undertaking. They decided to build it within the city boundary, which then extended from the Grand Canal on the south side to the Royal Canal on the north side of the city. Much of the land on the north side was owned by the famous Gardiner family. By the late 1840s, ownership of the Gardiner estate was in difficulty and it was being sold off by the Encumbered Estates Court, challenged by the family.[20] Nonetheless, in 1851, with the help of Reverend David Moriarty, President of All Hallows College, Dublin, the most prestigious plot of the whole estate – the Royal Circus as it was then known[21] – was secured as a site for the hospital. It was an amazing acquisition, given its history and the architectural proposals for it at the time.

The plot of land consisted of four acres.[22] It lay between the north side of Eccles Street and the south side of the North Circular Road. It was sold to the Sisters for £1,610,[23] although records show they were only able to pay for it three years later, in July 1854.[24, 25] When the hospital was first built, it was surrounded by a hedge, which the Sisters eventually replaced with ornate dressed granite slabs, supported on a series of sandstone balusters running along the front of the hospital.

● *Eccles Street in the early 20th century, showing the frontage of the Nursing Home and the School of Nursing.*

The lower end of Eccles Street, showing the famous no. 7, where Leopold Bloom allegedly lived.

In 1852, the Mater Misericordiae Hospital was officially founded. It is difficult nowadays to appreciate the scale of the undertaking, which some might even have called rash, as the hospital had no endowment, unlike most of the voluntary hospitals in Ireland and England at the time. No government finance was made available at any stage for this enormous development; indeed, the founding of the hospital coincided with a decision by the government gradually to cut all grants to Dublin hospitals. Instead, the Sisters of Mercy would have to trust in the support of the public. Furthermore, the hospital's great supporter, Archbishop Daniel Murray, died on 26 February 1852. Fortunately, his successor, Paul Cullen, turned out to be similarly enthusiastic.

The Sisters and the Fundraising Committee were anxious to get the building started as soon as possible, because the situation for the sick poor in Dublin was worsening. Asked in parliament on 20 May 1852 whether any arrangement had been made to extend hospital accommodation in Dublin to care for those suffering from fevers, Lord Naas merely replied that they could be accommodated in either the North or South Dublin Workhouse Unions on 'naked boards or straw pallets'. To cope with the enormous influx of sick people, sheds would be built and fitted out beside the workhouse. Many of the sick at this time were children, who were described by newspapers of the time as being accommodated 'in sheds near Glasnevin Bridge' – with a threat of them being 'stowed away while the sheds are being restored to their original use'.[26] The news that the Sisters of Mercy were about to embark on building a large hospital where sickness would be the only criterion for admission was very much welcomed by the people of Dublin.

A Modern Hospital

The well-known architect John Bourke was chosen to design the hospital, which it was hoped would eventually accommodate 500 patients, including an 80-bed children's ward. According to the newspapers of the day: 'The architect selected to design, plan, and superintend the building of this noble edifice is our young and talented fellow citizen, John Bourke Esq., many evidences of whose genius and taste are to be found in ecclesiastical structures in various parts of Ireland.'[27] Bourke was commissioned by the Sisters to travel to hospitals abroad to study the most up-to-date hospital design and construction. The Sisters felt that the hospital and its equipment should be modelled on the best features of the great European hospitals. In his design, Bourke opted for 'the corridor plan', i.e. long corridors with wards opening off them, which was considered by some to be an outmoded idea, impeding the flow of air through the wards.[28] Most hospital wards elsewhere were built with large windows at both sides and a thoroughfare down the middle. Bourke ignored that idea and in his 'corridor' plan designed small windows at intervals, high up on the internal corridor walls, to serve as air vents. All of the wards had large windows facing the park opposite the hospital to allow fresh air to flow through, and on the corridor side of the wards, the air vents faced similar large windows, through which the courtyard at the rear of the hospital could be viewed. This plan clearly had the desired effect: because the flow of air through the wards was so strong, elderly patients, especially old ladies, wore their hats in bed. Many of them also wore a warm woollen shawl around their shoulders. If it was cold, men wore their caps as they sat in bed and smoked their pipes![29]

The plans for the hospital were practical, but not without ambition, although some of the more elaborate features were later abandoned. The preliminary plan was for the hospital to be built in four sections, although the fourth section was only lightly marked on the plan because it was feared that ventilation via the courtyard might be impeded if the fourth side was built. Building it in sections would also allow for funds to be raised gradually, so that the Sisters could manage the debt. The large courtyard in the middle would contain a grand decorative campanile, complete with bells, and a series of large covered walkways for the patients was also planned: neither materialised. However, both the decorative entrance from Eccles Street, with its two sets of stone steps curving up to the front door, and the portico, featuring the great Ionic columns, were built. The entrance to the hospital was at first-floor level, through an ornate entrance hall,

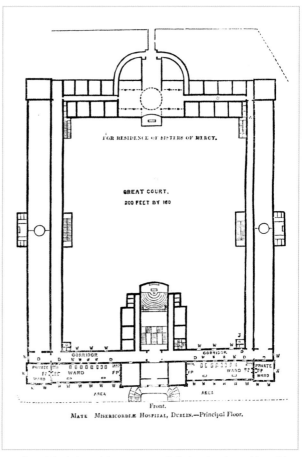

● *The original plan of the Mater Hospital, showing the position of the beds in the bottom of the plan and, at the top, what they intended to build on the North Circular Road side with a chapel opening on to the road.*

9

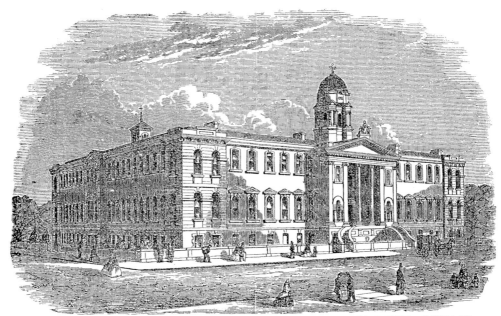

MATER MISERICORDIÆ HOSPITAL, ECCLES STREET, DUBLIN.

● *An artist's impression of the future Mater Hospital, from the 1874 Hospital Report.*

where, behind a substantial archway, a grand staircase branched left and right, to the top floor of the building. A large reception room – the Pillar Room – probably the most impressive feature of this part of the building, was situated behind the stairs. The Pillar Room was adorned with four Corinthian columns and four ceiling-height bay windows which looked out towards the northern suburbs of the city. These features still remain to this day. As per Mr Bourke's 'corridor plan' for the hospital, a long corridor ran the entire length of the building, with wards branching off it, and, at street level, there was an accident room, a dispensary and, eventually, a mortuary.[30] The pharmacy and laboratory were located beside the dispensary for outpatients. An operating theatre was located on the top floor of this section of the building, together with physicians' and surgeons' rooms, a library, museum and storerooms. It was planned that at roof level there would be a very elaborate cupola and clock tower – something of a crowning glory, which would mark the place out as a great public building. Unfortunately, due to lack of money, these features were never built.

The architect's plans provided for the building of two further sections of the hospital, leading at right angles from Eccles Street towards the North Circular Road – the east and west wings. These were eventually built, but the fourth section, in which a substantial chapel and a residence for the Sisters of Mercy were to be built, did not materialise. As things turned out, this part of the plan was completely redrafted by a new architect some years later[31] after the sudden death of Mr Bourke in 1871.

In the Public Interest

The building of the Mater provoked enormous public interest. Cardinal Cullen, who lived on Eccles Street, and who was asked about the hospital design some years later, said: 'I recollect that when it was proposed to commence this Hospital, there was a difference of opinion about the merits of the plan… Some said that the proposed building would be too expensive, that it would be too grand for the poor, and that it would be better to erect a less ornamental structure which would be more in harmony with the miserable normal conditions of our poor. Having been consulted on the question, I declared in favour of the present plan. We have palaces for guilt – we have palaces for force – we have palaces for legalised want, in which what is called pauperism is dealt with according to the principles of an unfeeling political economy. Why, then, should we not have at least one palace for the poor in which poverty would be relieved in a true spirit of charity and according to the dictates of the Gospel.'[32]

The builder chosen to build the Eccles Street frontage was a Mr John Brady of Camden Street, a friend of Catherine McAuley.[33]

It was clear that in order to serve the public well, the nursing Sisters would need to be trained, a matter which Archbishop Cullen discussed with Sr Vincent Whitty. It was arranged for some of the nuns to go to France and London to see the latest medical developments.[34] Those who would be nurses were sent to the famous Hôtel-Dieu Hospital, Paris, and those responsible for management were sent to the Hôtel-Dieu Hospital in Amiens. The hospital in Paris was particularly suitable, having been founded and run by Augustinian nuns to nurse the sick poor and to train young nuns as nurses. The Irish Sisters brought back with them new ideas, such as methods of keeping patients' ward records and recording inpatients' medications. When the Sisters returned

● *The original builder's receipt from John Brady, 1857.*

This painting, by Victorian artist Jerry Barrett, shows Florence Nightingale during the Crimean War, caring for the injured in Scutari, where the British had a hospital. The Mercy nun in the painting is Sr Clare Moore from Dublin. (© National Portrait Gallery, London.)

to Baggot Street from France in 1854, they were just in time to respond to an invitation received from the War Office, London, requesting that some nuns be made available to go to the Crimea to care for sick and injured soldiers. Sr Vincent Whitty extended this invitation to all the convents of Mercy countrywide and ultimately fifteen Sisters of Mercy set out for the Crimea from Ireland.

On 24 September 1855, a notice appeared on the front page of all of the national newspapers.

> **THE MATER MISERICORDIAE.**
> The first stone of this Hospital will be laid by His Grace the Archbishop at Twelve o'clock, on this day, the 24th instant, the Feast of Our Lady of Mercy, on the ground in Eccles Street taken for that purpose by the Sisters of Mercy.[35]

A vast number of people gathered to witness the laying of the foundation stone and the event merited half a page in the *Freeman's Journal*.

> The hour of twelve o'clock had been named for the commencement of the ceremonial, but long before that hour the enclosed space surrounding the foundation trenches was thronged to almost suffocation with an assemblage, including a large section of influential gentry and citizens of Dublin. Within the

enclosed space was a platform, erected by Mr Brady of Camden Street. Overhead a canopy of light canvass was spread in pavilion, affording at the same time openings at every point wherefrom the distinguished occupants of the platform might be heard by the vast multitude assembled. At the other side of the ground a beautiful and commodious marquee, ninety feet in circumference, was erected, within which tables, etc. were provided for the dignitaries.

Above the trench, where the corner stone of the new hospital was to be deposited, a high triangle was raised, with a pulley and tackle, from which was suspended the block of chiselled granite, especially remarkable as the first stone of the projected building. Shortly before twelve o'clock his Grace the Archbishop arrived on the ground and was received by the principal dignitaries and clergy present. Having assumed their robes in the marquee, a procession was formed, which issued forth in the usual order. The procession moved from the marquee and entered the enclosed space where the stone was to be deposited. The Archbishop, having arrived at the spot where the stone was suspended, proceeded with the preliminary ceremonies. The choir chanted the hymn 'Quam dilecta'. Prayers having been offered up, and psalms having been chanted, the first stone was lowered to its place. A hollow space was cut in the stone for the reception of a container of thick glass hermetically sealed, containing gold, silver and copper coins of the present reign and a parchment scroll on which was inscribed by Sister Maria Clare in beautifully illuminate gothic manuscript a special prayer in Latin. The stone having been laid, the choir of priests chanted a special hymn, and after a solemn prayer invoking the divine assistance for the undertaking, his Grace bestowed the pontifical benediction on the assembled multitude.[36]

From the newspaper article, it is clear that the building of the Mater was of great importance to the people of Dublin, and no detail of the ceremony was to be missed. After the stone was placed in position, the Archbishop went on to preach a lengthy sermon on the importance of building the hospital, calling on everyone to support the work of the Sisters of Mercy. He also spoke of the place of the care of the sick in the ministry of the church. The event honoured not only the sick of the city, but also the people of the city. The vision of Catherine McAuley had finally been realised.

1   Mater Misericordiae Hospital (1861), *Minutes*, pp 1–3.
2   These gas lamps disappeared when the entrance was lit by electricity. Only the mark of where they were embedded in the granite remains.
3   Carroll, A. (1881), *Leaves from the Annals of the Sisters of Mercy*. Vol. 1, New York, The Catholic Publication Society, p 60.
4   Ibid, p 56.
5   Nolan, E., 'Asiatic Cholera Outbreak in 1932'. Lecture given in 2003.
6   Lyons, J. (1991), *The Quality of Mercer's*, Dublin: Glendale.
7   Dickens C. (1843–44), *The Life and Adventures of Martin Chuzzlewit*, London.
8   It is generally thought that Nightingale's ideas, apart from her experience in the Crimea, were influenced by the so-called 'Tooting scandal' in 1849, when 200 children died of cholera at a residential childcare institution in Britain. The coroner who dealt with this tragedy said that poor ventilation was a contributing factor in the spread of the disease in the institution. (Cholera is, in fact, spread by contaminated water supplies only.) After this great attention was paid to ventilation arrangements in hospitals and much was written on the subject in the British architectural journals.
9   'Report on Hospitals of the United Kingdom', by Dr Bristowe and Mr Holmes, 1864.
10 Sisters of Mercy (1845), *Freeman's Journal*, p 1.
11 Freeman's Editorial (1845), *Freeman's Journal*, p 2.
12 House of Mercy (1846), *Freeman's Journal*, p 2.
13 Beauman, B. (1958), A *Way of Mercy; Catherine McAuley's Contribution to Nursing*, New York: Vantage Press, p 65.
14 Sullivan, M.R. (1995), *Catherine McAuley and the Tradition of Mercy*, Dublin: Four Courts Press, pp 236–241.
15 Carroll, A. (1866), *The Life of Catherine McAuley*, St Louis MO: The Vincentian Press, p 433.
16 Sullivan, M.R. (1995), *Catherine McAuley and the Tradition of Mercy*, Dublin: Four Courts Press, p 236.
17 O'Donoghue, S.M.X. (1972), *Mother Vincent Whitty – Woman and Educator in a Masculine Society*, Melbourne: Melbourne University Press.
18 Hetherington. A. & Smoothy, P. (2011), *The Correspondence of Mother Vincent Whitty 1839–1892*, University of Queensland Press, Australia, pp 354–381.
19 Beauman, B. (1958), op. cit.
20 O'Donovan, J. (1986), *Life by the Liffey: A Kaleidoscope of Dubliners*, Dublin: Gill & Macmillan, pp 139–146.
21 The Royal Circus was a plan based on Georgian architectural design.
22 Nixon, C. (1911), *Mater Misericordiae Hospital; Golden Jubilee; Speeches of the Bishop of Canea and Sir Christopher Nixon*, Dublin, *Evening Telegraph*, 1911.
23 Deeds (1855), *Registry of Deeds – Dublin No. 49 Litton (as Master) to/or Moriarty 1855.*
24 Deeds (1855), *Registry of Deeds – Dublin No. 49 Litton (as Master) to/or Moriarty 1855.*
25 Hetherington, A. & Smoothy, P. (2011), op. cit., p 125.
26 *Freeman's Journal* (1852), *The Dublin Hospitals*, Dublin.
27 *Freeman's Journal* (1855), *The Mater Misericordiae Hospital Dublin*, Dublin.
28 Bristowe and Holmes (1864), *The Hospitals of the United Kingdom*. Parliamentary Papers 1864, p 712 NL.
29 The hospital became a no-smoking zone in 2004 when the law against smoking in the workplace was introduced. In July 2010, smoking was also forbidden in the hospital grounds.
30 The mortuary was omitted in the original plans.
31 The plans for the present chapel were drawn up in 1934.
32 *Annual Report of the Mater Misericordiae Hospital Council*, 31 December 1866.
33 Mercy Srs Brisbane (2001), *Mercy Women making History*, Queensland: Sisters of Mercy.
34 Moran, C. (1898), *History of the Catholic Church in Australia* Brisbane (no date of publication).
35 *Freeman's Journal* (1855), p 1.
36 *Freeman's Journal* (1855), *Mater Misericordiae Hospital Dublin, Laying of the Foundation Stone* 25/9/1855 p 2.

CHAPTER 2

Building the Mater

fter the foundation stone was laid in 1855, building work began, progressing as and when funds became available. To raise much-needed money, the nuns organised an annual 'Grand Bazaar', which the 'great and the good' of Dublin supported. Money raised at this and at other events enabled the building to continue. The front of the hospital was built more or less as a complete unit; however, some of the facilities which might have been expected in a large hospital were missing from the plans: Bourke had made no provision for a convent, which, considering that the nuns would be providing all the nursing care and the day-to-day management of the hospital, was something of an oversight. Eventually a large room in the basement became their residence and remained so until 1886, when a convent was included as part of the west wing. A report of the hospital council (1870) noted:

> It is a sad admission for us to make, that we have been unable to provide a suitable residence for the Sisters to whom the success of this charity is due ... As a community, they have contributed more than £10,000 to the building fund, and yet the statement that we are unable to provide suitable accommodation for them is unbelievable.[1]

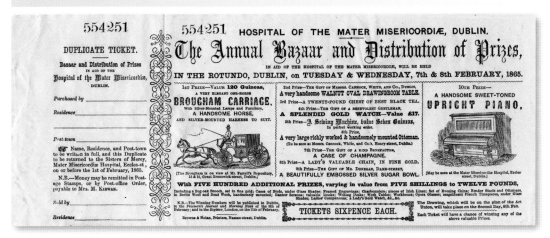

● *A ticket for the Grand Bazaar, which was held to raise funds for building the hospital.*

Another notable omission was a mortuary. Eventually a small room was made available near the west end of the building in September 1862.

All journalistic comments about the hospital at this time centre on the size of the building, its primary purpose, and the fact that it would be a building of significant architectural splendour in Dublin city, as this account in *The Dublin Builder* of 1861 notes:[2]

> The principal façade, facing Eccles Street, is nearly 300 feet in length and is divided into five compartments by slightly projecting pavilions at the ends, and by a great central projection over 70 feet in length, having in the middle portion a recessed portico, with massive Ionic columns and forming together, with four adjoining pilasters, a frontispiece crowned by a great pediment which overtops the rest of the building. Behind this will be the cupola rising 120 feet from the surface.
>
> Two approaches to the ground floor[3] lead into spacious waiting halls for out-patients; opposite these are approaches to the dispensaries and on either side are doctors' rooms, with private consulting rooms, ward dispensaries … In the rear of all is a spacious laboratory. Passing through the corridor right and left, the temporary reception wards are located together with bathrooms for patients on admission …
>
> On the wings of the ground floor will be spacious wardrobes, fumigating rooms, hospital stores, heating apparatus, entrance halls and staircases from recreation grounds, servants' rooms and refectories, together with lifts for beds and for prepared food for the patients. The rear of the ground floor will contain the great kitchen, the larder, stores, oven and bake house, laundry and drying rooms, vapour baths, together with a boiler and engine-rooms for raising water to tanks on the roof.

This account shows how much of what was being built was new and innovative at the time, for instance, 'lifts for beds and for prepared food'. Two of these lifts (described as hydraulic lifts) were built at either end of the building, 'powered' by two men employed to operate them, there being no electricity until after 1900.

The mention of 'engine-rooms' for pumping water to tanks on the hospital roof is also notable. Most hospitals in Ireland then drew their water from wells. The design of the Mater, and in particular the provision for what was at the time considered a large number of toilets – one per ward – meant that it would be consuming large amounts of water. Indeed, the provision of a toilet in each ward was criticised in the Bristowe Report[4] in 1863 as excessive, a luxury and somewhat unprecedented.

To accommodate the need for a good water supply, the hospital would have to sink a large well in the grounds, at considerable expense, but as the notion of a piped water supply for Dublin was being discussed at this time, the hospital was advised to put off digging a well. According to *The Dublin Builder*[5] things did not work out as expected. The River Vartry's supply to the city failed on a number of occasions due to drought and the Mater had to be supplied with piped water from the Royal Canal basin nearby at Blessington Street. This came at low pressure and needed to be pumped to the upper floors, and as a hospital supply, was considered likely to be impure in quality. It would be about thirty years before the Mater was supplied from a piped city supply and some years after that before a city drainage system was made available.

Although the first-floor entrance level gets little mention in any accounts, it is probably the most interesting feature of the hospital:

> The corridor, twelve feet in width, with lofty groined ceilings... Opposite the entrance hall is the grand staircase and behind it is the beautiful Pillar Room 50ft by 34ft, adorned with Corinthian columns and which is being used as a temporary chapel, to be applied in future to general public uses.
>
> In the design the operating theatres are on the top floor. Along both the east and west wing on floor 2 and 3 the plan shows large wards and a long 330ft corridor... etc. It is expected that these floors when completed will accommodate 500 beds, and which, if used in a period of calamity, could give a total accommodation of 700 beds.[6]

The Hospital is Opened

The actual building of the first section of the hospital was uneventful, the final flourish being the facing of the walls with 'dressed granite'. Before the front section was completed, building commenced on the east wing (1857), which eventually reached a height of twenty-two feet, where it stopped, due to lack of funds. It remained unfinished for many years. The available funds were directed towards the completion of the first section and towards patient care. By 1861, the Eccles Street section was ready for use and a formal opening was organised. On the day of the opening the *Freeman's Journal* carried a front-page notice as follows:

The Freeman's J[ournal]

AND DAILY COMMERCIAL ADVERTISER.

DUBLIN, TUESDAY, SEPTEMBER 24, 1861.

HOSPITAL OF THE MATER MISE-
RICORDIÆ.
On THIS DAY (Tuesday), the Feast of our Lady of Mercy, PONTIFICAL HIGH MASS will be celebrated in the CHAPEL of the HOSPITAL by his Grace the ARCHBISHOP of DUBLIN.
The FORTY HOURS' EXPOSITION of the BLESSED SACRAMENT will commence after the High Mass. Patients will be admitted to the Hospital on THURSDAY, the 26th instant.

The 'invitation to High Mass' to celebrate the opening of the hospital, from the Freeman's Journal. *(Courtesy of The National Library of Ireland.)*

17

A Hospital in Waiting

When the hospital opened, on 26 September 1861, the wards were ready to receive patients, but much of what we would now accept as standard was considered a luxury at the time, particularly for the poor. The ward beds were criticised as being too luxurious, especially the hair mattresses:[7] hospitals then generally used straw mattresses on a wooden base. The Mater beds had drapes hanging down on either side from an iron frame to keep the patient warm and free from draughts and possibly infection. Beside each bed was a warm mat, as many of the patients had no shoes. Each bed had white sheets, pillows, woollen blankets and over them a thick white counterpane, all laundered at the hospital. The emphasis was on comfort and warmth: in the early years earthenware hot water bottles were used to keep the patients warm in bed.

● *One of the earliest photographs of a hospital ward, c. 1886.*

The wards were large, accommodating about fourteen patients, with substantial space for each patient (the amount of space allotted to each patient was generally a contentious issue – because of the risk of infection).[8] There was a fireplace at either end of the ward for heat and the place was lit by gas lamps. The large windows provided plenty of daylight. At night large wooden shutters were closed over to conserve heat. The ward's one toilet was located on the opposite side of the corridor. All wards had their own kitchenette. Here food was received in containers from the main kitchen and it was served to the patients on individual trays.

The Pillar Room in 1960, showing matron Sr Concepta Greene talking to Dermot O'Flynn.

The Pillar Room, which served as a reception room for dignitaries and visitors to the hospital, was furnished with a variety of chairs and some small tables. The floor was of polished wood and large pictures decorated the walls. On either side of the room was a large fireplace, and the large windows gave on to a lawn between the hospital and the North Circular Road.

Above the Pillar Room was the main operating theatre. It was not a busy place, as surgery was in its infancy at this time, and only a small number of operations took place. One or two cases were undertaken on one day per week, usually Saturday. While the theatre occupied plenty of space, most of it was taken up by tiered seating for medical students and visiting surgeons, who might want to observe the surgery in progress or listen to a talk given by one of the surgeons. The operating table was a wooden structure on wheels and the patient was well covered with sheets and blankets for warmth during surgery. White woollen stockings were used to keep the patient's feet and legs warm. Only the part that was to be operated on was left exposed. In those days, little was known about asepsis (the prevention of infection) and surgical clothing consisted of a gown or rubber apron, to protect the surgeon's suit, and no masks or caps were worn to cover the mouth or hair. Changing rooms did not exist: any gowns or aprons used were simply hung on the back of the theatre door for further use or for laundering. A wooden towel rail, with a number of freshly laundered linen hand towels on it, was placed near the surgeon for use when needed. The place was lit by a gaslight hanging from the ceiling and air conditioning was provided through wide-open windows.

When patients were first admitted, only forty beds were available. It may seem surprising to us today, particularly given the prevalence of disease in Dublin city at the time, that there was no big influx of patients when the hospital opened, but the role of a hospital in 1861 was very different from the present day: if wealthy people became ill, they employed their own doctor to care for them, and any necessary surgery was carried out in the patient's own home. The poor were suspicious of hospitals, which they saw as places of last resort. Hence, the first patients came slowly to the Mater, but in time, word got around and the beds began to fill.

Two physicians and five surgeons were appointed when the hospital opened. Nine of the nuns undertook all the nursing duties, helped by a number of local women employed by them. Neither the nuns nor the doctors were paid for their services. At the time, doctors made their money from their private practice and from formal lectures to medical students.[9] The Mater was the first hospital in the city to remain open 24 hours a day to allow those in need of care, especially those suffering from fevers, to be admitted.[10] This may seem like an act of altruism, but the thinking was quite practical: the aim was to prevent people 'dumping' those suffering from cholera, and other fevers, on the doorstep of the hospital after dark as was the practice elsewhere in the city. Where this occurred, it was not unusual to find some of them dead in the morning.

The Next Steps

Apart from the day-to-day cost of patient care, any money over and above was used to pay off the building debt. By 1866, the last of the debt on the Eccles Street frontage was paid off. The east wing still remained unfinished – and it had been exposed to the weather since 1858. Pressure was mounting to restart construction and to try to get this section opened by 1870. Many thought that it was too large an undertaking for the Sisters to cope with financially, particularly as they now had to finance and run the Eccles Street building. A special fund was set up to enable building to recommence. In 1865, a total of £1,000 was lodged in it – nearly half of which came from a bazaar held by the nuns in aid of the hospital – but the fundraising then appears to have stalled.

On 18 February 1867, a public meeting at the hospital was organised by the hospital council, to be held in the Pillar Room, 'for the purpose of receiving a report and statement of expenditure incurred in the construction of the hospital (to December 1866) and to devise the best means for its further extension'.[11] About 70 or more people attended, including the Lord Mayor and a well-known physician, Dr William Stokes,[12] who was interested in promoting the idea of a 'fever ward' at the hospital. His Eminence Cardinal Paul Cullen, who received loud applause on arrival, took the chair.

The first to speak was the Lord Mayor. He was followed by members of the hospital council, who gave an account of the hospital's development to date. Reference was made to Mr John Bourke, the architect in charge of the original plans, and the new builder, Murphy & Son, who had recently restored St Patrick's Cathedral, and who had been commissioned to build the east wing. This new builder also agreed to receive payment for the work in instalments, which enabled the building work to start once more.

After the business of the meeting was finished, the discussion was 'thrown open' to the floor. The first to rise and address the assembly was Dr Stokes, who spoke passionately about the devastation wrought in the city by epidemics of cholera and about the care given to their patients by the Sisters in this hospital that was 'open at all times'.[13] After his address, Alderman Campbell proposed a resolution that the hospital council be empowered to adopt any measures necessary to raise at least £10,000 for the completion of the east wing within five years. Jonathan Pim, a city businessman of note and a member of parliament, seconded the proposal. After him, Cardinal Cullen rose and delivered a long speech, following which a subscription list to the building fund was opened.

The building fund was a success. Nearly three years later, on 1 November 1869, another public meeting was held in the hospital in which Sir James Power, a barrister and a member of the hospital council, announced that 'thirteen or fourteen thousand pounds'[14] had been raised over the previous three years, which he hoped would enable the east wing to be completed within ten years.

At this meeting, Dr Stokes spoke about the appointment of assistant physicians and surgeons to the hospital, including Dr Christopher Nixon (Assistant Physician) and Dr Charles Coppinger (Assistant Surgeon). In this, the Mater was following the example of some of the big London hospitals. He went on to say that 'both of these gentlemen were distinguished pupils of the hospital'.[15] Indeed, both of them went on to become renowned members of the medical staff of the Mater and of the Catholic University School of Medicine in Cecilia Street, where they became professors in their respective specialities. The next gentleman to address the meeting was Sir William Wilde, who spoke at length. In addition to his work as an eye surgeon at St Mark's Hospital, Wilde was a noted antiquarian, but is better known today as the father of Oscar Wilde.

When the building of the east wing was complete at the end of 1869, it had cost more than had been anticipated, a matter of grave concern for the Sisters. However, a city businessman, Mr Charles Egan, of High Street, came to the rescue. He 'bequeathed to the Sisters of Mercy, as the founders and owners of the hospital, four thousand pounds for building purposes, exclusive of the perpetual endowment provided by him for the annual support of twenty patients in its wards'.[16] Egan's contribution allowed the builders to proceed with the rest of the building. It is clear that practicality overcame ambition in building this section of the hospital: it is much less ornate and the stone is calp, rather than the granite which graced the front of the building. In the report of the council in December 1870[17] there is a brief account of the new wing:

> The two upper floors are occupied by eight wards, the size, lighting and ventilation of which secure the admiration of every visitor ... Each corridor terminates in an oratory and is covered by a circular groined ceiling ... In the wards upon these floors are attached still-rooms, pantries, linen stores, local pharmacies, bathrooms, closets, and ample accommodation for assistants on the ground floor.

The report mentions the splendid view from the top of this section of the building, much of which is now blocked by newer buildings and the Whitty Building.

A Deadly New Challenge

Having succeeded in the difficult task of raising funds for and building the new wing of the hospital, the Sisters now faced the prospect of raising a further £2,000 to equip the new wards, but before they could complete the process, an outbreak of smallpox presented a real challenge to the hospital. Beds had to be made available, and they had to be isolated from the rest of the hospital to prevent the spread of infection. Fifty beds were immediately made ready:

> To meet the emergency the new wing was immediately opened and separated from the rest of the hospital by temporary sealed partitions to receive cases of smallpox. The disease was courageously met and combated by the Sisters and the Medical Officers of the Hospital.[18]

There was to be no grand opening of the east wing of the Mater. The influx of smallpox patients saw to that. This table shows the sheer scale of the problem:

Year	Total number of 'fever cases' treated in the Mater	Total number of 'smallpox cases' treated in the Mater
1871	361	82
1872	288	526
1873	140	0
1874	350	0

After the smallpox epidemic it was decided to reserve the top floor of the east wing for patients with infectious fevers. Part of it remained as a fever unit until after World War I. The hope was that at some stage a fever hospital would be built on the grounds of the hospital: indeed, in 1879, the nuns purchased over six acres of land to the east of the hospital between the North Circular Road and Eccles Lane for this purpose, but local objections meant that the fever hospital never materialised. The new adult hospital is now built on most of this land.

○ *The west wing in 1886.*

Building the West Wing

As soon as the east wing was opened for use, attention then turned to building the west wing. As the original architect, John Bourke, had died (1871), a new architect, John L. Robinson from Dublin, was appointed to take over the project, and in February 1884 the foundation stone for the west wing was laid by His Eminence Cardinal Edward McCabe. This wing was built fairly quickly and was opened in 1886. Robinson followed the original design, but included a chapel and convent in his plans, along with a small extension to both the accident room and the dispensary and also an entrance from Berkeley Road. The entrance to the chapel was located to one side of the first floor, and whilst it was a long and narrow building, the chapel was ornate and beautifully decorated, particularly its gilded ceiling.

The west wing would contain a total of 100 beds, most at ground-floor level (now St Aloysius Ward) and included a children's ward. His Grace Dr William Walsh, the new Archbishop of Dublin, officially opened it on 24 September 1886. It is clear that the Sisters' dedication to the poor overcame the huge

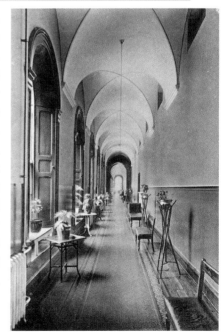

○ *St Joseph's corridor in the east wing, showing the ventilation system: the big window facing the prevailing wind and top right, an air vent through which fresh air passed into the ward. The window at the end would be replaced by a lab in 1937.*

financial considerations: the total cost of building the Mater now amounted to £68,000, an enormous burden for the Sisters of Mercy to carry and with no government grants to ease it. As a result, the north wing, which had been planned, had to be abandoned.

Changing Times for the Convent and Chapel

After the opening of the present hospital chapel in 1937, the original chapel went under many changes as the hospital adapted to developments in medicine and in critical care. Almost immediately, the space once occupied by the chapel was redefined. Wards were built on two floors – St Agatha's and St Cecilia's Wards (female surgical) on the top floor and St Gabriel's and St Agnes' Wards (female medical) on the middle floor.

President Mary McAleese with the hospital staff in St Agnes' corridor (west wing), 2011.

In the mid-1970s, St Agatha's and St Cecilia's Wards were reconstructed as an intensive care unit (ICU). A new ceiling was put in place below the ornate ceiling of the original chapel, leaving the original decorated one above it intact. In 1994, when the ICU was being refurbished, it was rediscovered and a debate ensued as to whether it should be restored to its original glory. Unfortunately, the potential cost was prohibitive, so a new ceiling was once again constructed below it. For the time being it has been consigned to history!

Almost as soon as the much-needed convent was built, it became apparent that it was too small to accommodate the numbers of nuns assigned to work in the hospital. It was a very plain building, having been built essentially for utility and service, and for ease of access to the main hospital. If anything unusual occurred, the Sisters could be on site immediately. In November 2005, the nuns moved to a new convent built near the North Circular Road and the Mercy Congregation decided to donate the old convent to the hospital. Since then, the top floor and part of the first floor have been refurbished to become an administrative and educational area for the existing ICU on the top floor and the orthopaedic wards on the middle floor. What started out with polished wooden floors throughout, and meagre gas lighting, is now lit by graceful electric chandeliers and has a red carpet underfoot. The bedrooms, originally heated by coal fires and later by hot pipes, have in recent times been turned into well-furnished offices, storerooms, overnight accommodation for medical staff, a small lecture room, and a family room for grieving relatives.

Originally the convent was such an integral part of the hospital that it had no front door to speak of, and no 'parlour' for visitors to sit and talk in. A door opened out to the courtyard, which facilitated deliveries to the convent kitchen, and there was also a door on every floor into the hospital. The Pillar Room served as a reception room for the Sisters and the main entrance to the hospital on Eccles Street was, in reality, the convent's front door. Until the 1960s, the doors to the convent on each level remained unlocked all the time and the Sisters came and went with ease, to carry out their nursing duties.

The Park and Sir William Wilde

The land opposite the hospital on Eccles Street, which had been purchased by the Sisters in 1874 to ensure a flow of fresh air for the patients in the wards, was surrounded by an untidy looking low mud wall, and, when funding became available, they decided to erect an attractive railing around it. In time, this park began to generate its own history. In 1872, Sir William Wilde was planning to erect a monument to honour the Four Masters, authors of *The Annals of the Kingdom of Ireland* (1616). He decided that a Celtic cross would be appropriate to honour them[19] and wrote to the newspapers in 1872 in search of a location for it. His suggestion was that it should be placed 'at the apex of the triangular plot of ground opposite the Mater Misericordiae Hospital'.[20] This triggered a media reaction and for weeks the public wrote to the newspapers suggesting that it should be located in Donegal, near the Franciscan Friary.[21] Wilde emphatically turned down this idea in 1875, saying that the Annals had not been written in any part of Donegal town. Sir William Wilde died before a suitable location was found. After his death, as the newspaper discussions continued, in 1876 the monument found its way

This photo of the Mater from 1980 shows the park and William Wilde's Celtic cross.

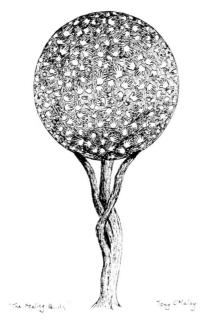

"The Healing Hands"   Tony O'Malley

● *A drawing of the Healing Hands monument by Tony O'Malley.*

to the location first suggested by Wilde – opposite the Mater Hospital. The hospital remained silent about it, as discussions continued for some time. Eventually a hedge grew around the park and obscured it. When President John F. Kennedy's visit to Ireland was announced in 1963, Dublin City Council sought permission from the Mater to landscape the park because he would be driving past it to and from Áras an Uachtaráin during his visit. They have continued to maintain it ever since.

In more recent times, a bronze monument was erected in the park to mark the beginning of the third millennium. This silicon bronze monument, designed by Tony O'Malley, symbolises God's everlasting love for his people and Christ's healing ministry to the sick. The flame at the centre symbolises the light of Christ coming into the world at the dawn of the first millennium.

1   Mater Misericordiae Hospital (1871), *Third Report of the Council of the Mater Misericordiae Hospital for the Year Ending December 31ˢᵗ 1870*. Printed at St Joseph's Cabra, Dublin, p 10.
2   *The Dublin Builder*, 1 October 1861, p 647.
3   This description is of the street level, not of Level 2 (main entrance level). There were four entrances to the 'basement' level (Level 1), two on either side of the steps up to the front door of the hospital and one at either end of the hospital.
4   Report to the Government on the Hospitals of the United Kingdom, 1863.
5   *The Dublin Builder*, 1 October 1861, p 647.
6   Ibid., p 647.
7   Report to the Government on the Hospitals of the United Kingdom, 1863.
8   Dublin Hospitals Commission: *Report of the Committee of Inquiry, 1887.*
9   The doctors received all the fees paid by the medical students who attended lectures or demonstrations at the hospital. When the hospital opened, the nuns tried to change this to allow the students to attend the lectures free, but the medics turned their suggestion down. Each of the medics also had their own private practice for which they charged fees. Some of them placed advertisements in the newspapers advertising their special skills.
10 This decision was taken by Sr Berchmans Barry, who was in charge of the hospital from 1882 to 1912.
11 Mater Misericordiae Hospital (1870), *Annual Report of the Council of the Mater Misericordiae Hospital for the Year Ending Dec 31, 1869*, Dublin, St Joseph's Cabra, p 12.
12 Dr Stokes was attached to the Meath Hospital on the south side of the city.
13 Ibid., p 9.
14 Mater Misericordiae Hospital (1871), *Second Report of the Council of the Mater Misericordiae Hospital for the Year Ending December 31, 1870*. Printed at St Joseph's Cabra, Dublin, p 16.
15 Mater Misericordiae Hospital (1871), op. cit., p 24.
16 Ibid., p 7.
17 Ibid., p 8.
18 Mater Misericordiae Hospital (1875), *Fourth Report of the Council of the Mater Misericordiae Hospital for the Year Ending December 31, 1874*, Dublin, p 1.
19 The Celtic cross in the park opposite the hospital is made of sandstone and is about 15 feet in height.
20 *Nation*, 1 January 1876, p 3.
21 *Freeman's Journal*, 12 September 1876.

CHAPTER 3

The Mater's First Patients

R ecords show that only one patient was admitted on the day the Mater opened, to the care of Mr Richard O'Reilly FRCSI, a surgeon. The unnamed patient spent 584 days in hospital until he died in May 1863. On 28 September, a 21-year-old lady from Dublin, also in the care of Mr O'Reilly, was admitted with 'acute rheumatism'. She spent twenty days in hospital and left 'cured'. A 42-year-old man arrived from Westport on 30 September suffering from a leg ulcer. He stayed for 27 days and left 'cured'. The slow drip of patients continued into early October 1861, when a 70-year-old man from Dublin was admitted with 'chronic bronchitis' and spent two days in hospital. It was clear that there was no big rush of patients to the hospital. Things soon began to change, however, and soon all the beds were in use. During October a total of 96 patients were admitted with a variety of conditions, five of whom subsequently died.

The first registry of patients to the hospital, dated 1861.

At the time the Mater opened, the population of Dublin was about 250,000, but more than half of the population were categorised as being 'poor' and with a higher than average death rate. Added to that, the city suffered from poor sanitation and regular outbreaks of disease. It had no formal water supply and sewage made its way along the streets to the River Liffey, which often had corpses floating in it, because access to cemeteries was too expensive. This in turn meant that the city's 'drinking water' was generally contaminated and so outbreaks of diseases such as cholera, typhoid and dysentery were frequent. The Mater was within walking distance of the largest tenement area in Europe, and admitted patients suffering from diseases such as tuberculosis, typhus and, from time to time, even bubonic plague. The death rate in Dublin, mostly due to infectious diseases, was the highest in all of Europe, and the problem was made worse by the fact that so little was known at the time about the spread or transmission of infection. Nonetheless, the Sisters were great believers in the benefits of good hygiene and maintained a strict regime in the hospital, preventing much infection. They also believed that good nutrition and hydration were fundamental to patient treatment.

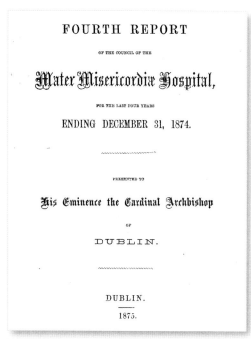

● *The Fourth Report of the council of the hospital reported on finance and patients.*

Admitting Patients to the Wards

Motorised ambulances did not appear in the city until 1914 and so getting sick people to hospital wasn't easy.[1] A horse and cart, or simply a cart pushed by an able-bodied individual had to suffice and small children were carried to the hospital in the arms of an adult. On arrival at the Mater, the admission procedure depended on how sick they were. They were greeted by the nun whose duty it was to admit them and who would endeavour to get the patient to bed as quickly as possible. Unless they were dying, patients were first taken to a bathroom near the dispensary and were given a wash. After the wash, they were helped into a white calico nightshirt or nightdress. Many of those who were admitted, especially the children, came with no shoes and wore only ragged clothes, which had to be carefully inspected for infestations and treated or burned if necessary. The patient would receive a new set of clothes when he/she left. Each year, money was put aside to buy clothing for the poor and often clothes were donated to the hospital. The hospital report of 1874 lists a number of pairs of large slippers, eighteen pairs of elastic stockings, flannel vests, several suits of clothes, boots and shoes and a dozen shirts among the donations.[2]

The front door of the hospital, dating from 1861.

The Daily Routine

Bed rest was considered important and patients spent many weeks or months in bed. Given that, by-and-large, these people were undernourished and ill, this put them at risk of 'pressure sores',[3] which required preventive treatment up to three times a day. The spiritual needs of the patients were also attended to, with the ward sister saying morning and night prayers and a morning visit from the hospital chaplain.

The patients' day started early. The gas light was lit at 6.00 a.m. and every patient was clinically checked. All patients suffering from fever had the progress of their disease observed, 'from crisis to lysis', as the expression went, meaning from the critical phase of the illness when the temperature had reached its highest, until the fever broke. At the time, given that antibiotics had yet to be invented, clinical management mainly consisted of alleviating symptoms, sponging the patient down with tepid water and giving them plenty to drink.[4] (After the modern clinical thermometer was invented,[5] a more accurate recording of the patient's temperature could be made.) Following these observations, enamel basins and water were distributed for washing face and hands. There were no bathrooms on the wards, and only a single toilet. Breakfast for patients was attended to in the ward kitchen, where the patient's trays were made ready. At 7.00 a.m., the ward sister started work and, following a report on the patients'

● *This picture of a medical ward dates from 1893. The patients are fully dressed because the only heating at this time was a coal fire. Note the lady on the left of the picture, wearing her hat.*

● *This photo shows a medical ward in around 1886. The nurse is dispensing medicine to the patients – her headdress denotes that she is a qualified nurse.*

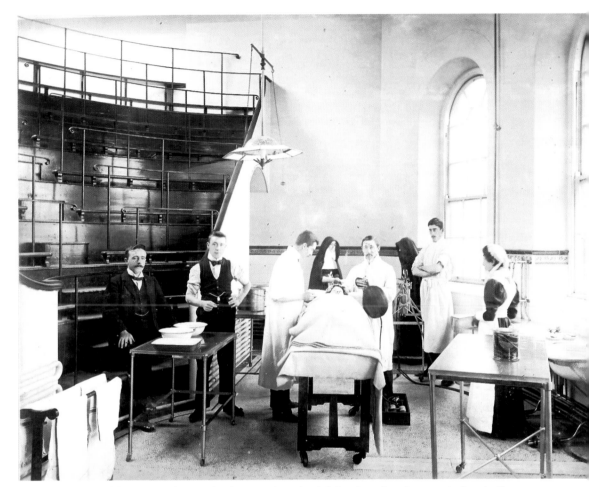

An early picture of the operating theatre, taken in 1884. The patient is being given ether: the apparatus is under the operating table, on the right. Note the surgeon's suit and the wooden towel rail for linen.

status overnight, breakfast was served. At 9 a.m., the medical staff arrived and the doctor began his ward rounds with a group of medical students. During this teaching session, the ward doors were closed and silence reigned. If the teaching was to be done by a surgeon, he had the option of taking the students to the operating theatre and conducting his lesson during his surgery with the students sitting in the tiered observation gallery.

From the beginning, the Sisters decided to delay discharging patients, even when they had recovered, so that they could care for them during their convalescence. This meant that some patients spent many weeks in the hospital, although the planned 'convalescent rooms' which were to have been built in the north wing never materialised. When weather permitted, patients were frequently wheeled outside for fresh air.

biography

A Russian Visitor to the Mater

Vladimir Pecherin

● *The hospital's first chaplain, Vladimir Pecherin.*

The most famous chaplain of all appointed to the Mater was Vladimir Pecherin, a political émigré from Russia, and a colourful figure, who was appointed as Chaplain by Cardinal Cullen in 1862. Pecherin was born in the Ukraine, near Kiev, in 1807. His father was in the military and his family belonged to the Russian Orthodox Church. He received his university education in St Petersburg and during his studies he travelled extensively in Europe, starting in Berlin. After his return to Russia in 1835, Pecherin was appointed a professor in Greek philology at Moscow University, but because of a long-held yen for freedom, he left Russia the next year on the pretext of publishing a book. He would never return. In Belgium, Pecherin became a Catholic and shortly afterwards joined the Redemptorist Order. He was ordained a priest in 1843. In 1845, he was transferred to a Redemptorist house in London, where he spent much of his time giving Missions in both England and Ireland. Controversy seemed to follow Pecherin. Shortly after his arrival in Ireland in 1855, he was wrongly accused of burning Protestant bibles, a story which captured the imagination of the international media. He was tried and acquitted in 1855, and his acquittal was celebrated in Dublin, where he was extremely popular as a preacher.

However, Pecherin's disillusionment grew – with the government, the Catholic Church and life in general. He left the Redemptorists and joined a Carthusian monastery in France but left after two months and returned to Ireland, joining the Cistercians in Mount Mellary, which he also left. It seemed that the powers that be had had enough of Pecherin, because when he applied to rejoin the Redemptorists, he was refused. However, Cardinal Paul Cullen accepted him into the diocese of Dublin and appointed him to the newly opened Mater Hospital as Chaplain, where he remained for the rest of his life. In 1885, he became a patient himself, suffering from kidney disease, and he died that year.[6] A large number of the staff of the hospital turned out for his funeral, and hundreds of people, local and otherwise, marched behind the hearse to Glasnevin Cemetery. A beautiful white monument was erected to his memory at his grave, by the Sisters of Mercy.[7]

The Cholera Outbreak of 1866

The first serious outbreak of cholera, and the first significant challenge to the Mater hospital, came in 1866. The first deaths from this disease recorded at the Mater were in August of that year, when five cholera patients died. After that, the number rose steeply. Fifty-nine patients died in the hospital in September and 53 in October. In addition to deaths in hospital, many people were dying in their homes and their relatives did not have the resources to help them. As the *Freeman's Journal* of 26 October 1866 described it:

> It would be well if some means were provided for removing cholera corpses from the place of death to the grave. I saw in Dorset Street a few boys striving to carry the remains of a victim of cholera to the grave; no surer way of spreading contagion. The Poor Law officers were only bound to provide a coffin and shroud.

The article goes on to discuss the reluctance of the hospitals to admit victims of cholera but points out that, 'The Mater Misericordiae had opened their wards to the utmost extent … In the Mater patients were at once admitted … it being ascertained that they suffered from cholera.' Although some of the other hospitals in the city claimed that they were open to receive victims too, Rev Professor Jellett FTCD, who gave an account in the papers of what was happening to the cholera victims, cast doubt on their claims. He also highlighted the difficulties of transporting patients to hospital, saying: 'There was not sufficient provision made for conveying them to the hospitals and lives were being lost owing to the delay of the cholera cart. Its job was to collect patients from the tenements and take them to hospital. There were not enough "Carts" available and when it was agreed to provide the city with two more, the suggestion was that they be painted a distinctive (yellow) colour.'

When the epidemic was at its height, a 'horror story' recounted by a Dr Speedy at a meeting of the Cholera Relief Committee came as a shock to those in charge of hospitals. Dr Speedy wished to draw the attention of the public to: 'the heroic conduct of a Police Constable towards a cholera patient. He carried a woman with cholera from Chancery Lane to the Meath Hospital [Chancery Lane lies behind St Patrick's Cathedral and the Meath Hospital is approximately 1km away]. There was no admission for her there and as the policeman could not get a cab, he had to drag and carry her to Dr Steeven's Hospital [near Heuston Station]. She was writhing in pain all the time and was vomiting.'[8]

It is hard to underestimate the climate of fear that prevailed in Dublin at the time the disease took hold, and there was great public suspicion about what happened to cholera patients in hospital. Rumour had it that they were being put into coffins before they were actually dead! To counteract this and to make those admitted to the Mater feel more secure, Sr Berchmans Barry let it be known that she would sit beside every patient who was dying and would remain with them, caring and praying for them, until they died. People were genuinely impressed with this and remembered it long

Patients suffering from cholera would often be left on the hospital steps overnight.

after the epidemic had passed. In much the same way as the hospital's 'open all hours' policy, Sr Berchmans' philosophy on the care of the sick and dying marked the Mater out as a caring hospital, dedicated to the welfare of patients. This must surely have helped to ease the suffering of those afflicted by cholera. Sadly, of the total of 143 cases of diagnosed cholera admitted to the Mater at this time, 108 patients died. During the same period, 63 cases of unclassified diarrhoeal disease were admitted and all survived.

Spreading Like Wildfire

Five years after the first outbreak of cholera, in 1871 the city was smitten yet again with an even worse epidemic. This time it was smallpox and it spread like the proverbial wildfire, starting on the north side and moving south and west of the city. The outbreak caused enormous fear beyond anything seen during previous epidemics, probably due to its ability to spread, and due to the economic as well as physical consequences of the disease. If it became known that a member of a family had the disease, anyone in employment in that family immediately lost his or her job. This brought its own problems in a city with a poverty-stricken population.

As the disease took hold, hundreds of patients found their way to the Mater and some of the other city hospitals. Unfortunately, before it was realised how infectious the disease was, it began to spread in the wards, to the consternation of the Sisters and the medical staff. The top floor of the east wing was quickly turned into an isolation unit and was sealed off from the rest of the hospital. How the patients were actually treated for the condition medically is not on record. All we know is that 'fear reigned supreme' because, apart from being an infectious disease, it was complex to treat and it lasted a long time. Because of this, there was a demand for 'convalescent beds' to be made available to patients after the acute phase of the disease, there being no real possibility that they could be discharged home. For weeks, they suffered the ravages of the disease process itself, together with all the disfigurement it left on their skin in the form of ugly pockmarks.

The Sisters faced an enormous challenge. Six to eight hundred patients were treated in the Mater during the epidemic and there was a high mortality rate – to say nothing of the staff who became infected in the course of their work. In the city as a whole, 12,000 cases were recorded. Over 2,000 or possibly more died. Because of the stigma and the potential loss of employment people were reluctant to admit that anyone close to them was suffering from the disease and the health authorities were forced to take drastic action. They withheld financial assistance from families who had refused to send their relatives with smallpox to hospital.[9] Whether this helped or hindered the situation is not known.

In 1886, the city was visited by yet another epidemic of cholera, and a further outbreak of smallpox in 1894. The Mater received a total of between 200 and 300 victims of the cholera epidemic.[10] Once again, the nuns considered the possibility of opening a dedicated fever hospital, and a plan was even drawn up to this effect, but according to Sir Charles Cameron, the city Medical Officer,[11] it was 'a vexed question' as to whether any fever patients should be admitted to or treated in a general hospital. He wrote to the city hospitals, including the Mater, in June 1894, recommending that cases of smallpox should not be admitted at this time: patients should instead be sent to the Hardwick Hospital nearby, where patients were being nursed in sheds. The 'overflow' were being transported from the North Dublin Union to more sheds in the South Dublin Union, and this caused distress and fear. Public sentiment was understandably against the building of a dedicated fever hospital, and the nuns had to reconsider their plans. By 1895, the Mater plan had been abandoned and the more immediate need for some sort of a convalescent facility was being discussed instead. According to Sir Christopher Nixon, consultant physician, speaking at the opening of the 1903 academic year:

In 1895, an attempt was made to provide a separate block for the treatment of contagious diseases, exclusive of smallpox. A very successful meeting was held in the hospital to promote this object. Plans were prepared, not alone for the fever building but also for the erection of a pathological department on a scale worthy of a great hospital. The idea, however, of building a special fever hospital seemed to upset the equilibrium of the public mind, within a proximate area, with the result that there was such opposition evoked, it had to be dropped. Those who so vehemently opposed the erection of an isolated and detached building for treating fever cases offered no objection to those cases being dealt with under less favourable conditions.[12]

THE CORPORATION.

Yesterday a special meeting of the Municipal Council was held in the City Hall.

Alderman CAMPBELL in the chair.

Aldermen—J Campbell, J P; H Tarpey, P Redmond, J M'Cann, H O'Rorke, J P; J Plunkett, J Draper, J P; W Gregg, James W Mackey, J P, and J Ryan, M D, Councillors—Sir W Carroll, J P; Sir J Barrington, D L; J Norwood, LL D, J P; G B Owens, M D, J P; H Maclean, J P; J Bolger, J P; Thomas Fry, J P; C Dennehy, J P; Hon J P Vereker, P W Long, M D; J J Redmond, W Campbell, T Dockrell, G Sykes, J Byrne, J D'C Franklin, R Callow, F Hamilton, M Carey, J French, R Keating, M Murphy, A O'Neill, W Dempsey, G P Warren, A J Moore, and Wm Meagher.

HOSPITALS.

The next item comprised the sums presented for the several hospitals, amounting to 3,641l 5s.

A report from the Public Health Committee recommended a sum of 100l for the Meath Hospital in addition to the 300l usually presented, in consequence of the increased demand made upon the hospital during the recent small-pox epidemic, and in consideration of an additional wing for the accommodation of those patients.

Mr. Byrne moved and Dr. Owens seconded the adoption of the report.

Mr. Hamilton said he should call attention to the Mater Misericordiæ Hospital, and move the same principle should be adopted in its favour. In the progress of the late small-pox epidemic it became necessary for the Public Health Committee to make certain arrangements with the several city hospitals for the accommodation of extra patients, the Council undertaking to pay for those extra patients. Amongst others the committee made arrangements with the Mater Misericordiæ Hospital that they should accommodate a number of patients above what the hospital was intended to accommodate in the usual way. That arrangement was made on the 12th April last. When the accounts came to be furnished, the Public Health Committee found that there were a considerable number of such extra patients accommodated in the Mater Misericordiæ Hospital for two months prior to that date. This entailed an additional charge on the hospital to the extent of 221l, according to the terms agreed to for the other cases. He moved that the hospital should get this 221l, in addition to the 300l, named in the schedule.

Mr Franklin—I have great pleasure in seconding that.

Mr. Norwood said he would adopt Mr. Hamilton's proposition as fair and equitable.

Mr. Maclean objected to the motion, as not being according to the agreement made with the hospital; but, if they desired to press it, he would not object, provided the same principles were applied to the other hospitals which had accommodated extra patients in like manner (hear, hear). That had been done in Hardwicke Hospital.

Mr Byrne—But Hardwicke Hospital has a Government grant.

Mr. Murphy said he thought it was legal that the hospital should be paid for the extra patients they had accommodated during the epidemic.

The Chairman—Say equitable.

Mr. Murphy—It is a most equitable and moral claim.

Mr. Byrne—That may be a different thing, but I think we will all agree that other hospitals shall have the advantage of the same principle.

Alderman Redmond considered there never was a contribution given by the citizens for which they had got better value than the contribution to the hospitals of Dublin, which had extended the most important aid to the sick poor under the most trying circumstances, and at the most trying time. He thought the amount proposed was only a small compensation for the advantages given (hear, hear). He would be ashamed to ask this for the Mater Misericordiæ Hospital without extending the same principle to the other hospitals.

The report of the Public Health Committee was adopted, with the addition of the recommendation made by Councillor Hamilton in favour of the Mater Misericordiæ Hospital, and it was agreed to increase the sums presented to each of the other hospitals, so as to bring up the difference in the sums claimed for small-pox patients.

The following presentments were agreed to without discussion:—For coroners and medical witnesses and rent of morgue, 566l 2s 6d ; Commission Court and fees on prisoners, 186l 12s 6d; costs and stationery, 117l 1s 7d; expenses of registering voters, 1,086l 18s 6d.

• *This newspaper article reports on the efforts of the authorities to deal with the smallpox epidemic which ravaged the city. (Courtesy of the National Library of Ireland.)*

Dr Nixon went on to discuss what it was then proposed to do with the funds set aside for a fever unit:

> The funds raised with administrative boldness were utilised in providing a convalescent home at Beaumont, Drumcondra, beautifully situated in rural settings... Standing in over 100 acres of pastoral land, on a high plane and in the centre of a sparsely populated district, the home should bring health and strength to many a bread-winner after such a prolonged illness... I must mention that a formal offer has been made by the Sisters of Mercy to give the site at Beaumont for the building of a sanatorium for Tuberculosis on strictly non-sectarian principles, the Sisters undertaking merely the nursing of the patients. Should the offer be availed of,[13] Dublin will be freed from the opprobrium of being one of the few cities in the United Kingdom which has no sanatorium for the poor with Tuberculosis.

Outbreak of Scarlet Fever

Dublin was to be met with wave after wave of epidemic disease in the late decades of the 19th century. 'Scarlatina' (scarlet fever) came to the city in 1896. This largely involved children, who at that time were being admitted to the Mater. The outbreak was of major concern to the city's public health department, because of the sheer number of cases and the lack of hospital accommodation, and a special meeting was called by the Superintendent Medical Officer of Health to look at the situation. The authorities feared that scarlet fever could become more widespread: 'It was a disease less influenced by unsanitary conditions than smallpox.'[14] One suggestion was that the Pigeon House Fort, at the entrance to Dublin Port, then being used as a government store for military equipment, could be turned into an isolation hospital. However, the suggestion to use this formidable building, situated on the South Bull Wall and surrounded by the tidal waters of Dublin Bay, was never taken up. With over 300 cases in the city hospitals by November 1896, the Mater and Cork Street Fever Hospital were asked to try to provide 100 beds each, the fear being that this infection would eventually exceed one thousand cases. Sir Christopher Nixon wrote on behalf of the hospital to the public health department in November that year, stating that all the beds available for contagious diseases would be devoted to scarlatina cases. On the day he wrote, the total number of 'notified cases' in the city was 630.

The Scourge of Tuberculosis

Of all the infectious diseases to sweep Ireland during this time, perhaps the most insidious was tuberculosis, a silent epidemic. Patients came to the hospital suffering from it in many forms and manifestations and equally, many names were used for it such as 'consumption', 'phthisis', 'scrofula' or even 'glands', which led to a slight distortion of medical statistics. There were no antibiotics in the early days and so treatment largely consisted of managing the presenting signs and symptoms. It more or less remained like that until the use of streptomycin began to change things in the early 1950s. However, streptomycin was a very expensive drug. Every injection had to be paid for by the patient (usually at the time they were given the injection), because there was no available subsidy. This slowed down any possible impact it could have had on the incidence of the disease. Moreover, few medics in the 19th and early 20th centuries were interested in the management of tuberculosis, probably because it was regarded as a disease of the poor and malnourished. It carried with it a social stigma – one of the reasons the Sisters of Mercy were anxious to provide some sort of a facility for sufferers and hence the suggestion that part of the land at Beaumont be set aside and used to build a TB sanatorium (it was never intended to include TB patients in the same building as those who were convalescing from other illnesses). As it turned out, a sanatorium was not built at Beaumont, probably because a place on the south side of the city was being developed for this purpose.

Development of Beaumont Convalescent Home

● *A photo of Beaumont Convalescent Home, undated.*

The purchase of Beaumont House and the surrounding 120 acres became possible largely due to a bequest to the nuns of £7,000 by a Mr Moran. When building a fever unit at the Mater proved not to be acceptable and pressure was mounting to provide convalescent beds for smallpox victims, the Sisters set about finding somewhere suitable within easy reach of the Mater. The health department did not want convalescent homes built near general hospitals.

Beaumont House became available in 1900. It had been owned by Edward O'Malley, who had bought the house and lands from Oscar Guinness in 1884. He leased it to the Dominican Sisters to use as a novitiate. When O'Malley died, the Sisters of Mercy bought the place for £6,000.[15] It was not an extension to the Mater, being what was known as a 'branch house' of the Baggot Street Convent and so the administration was located there. The staff were appointed by the Baggot Street administration and a local superior took care of the day-to-day management of the place. The number of nuns living in the convent gradually increased to meet the growing needs of this ministry.

Beaumont House, when the Sisters bought it, was in need of substantial restructuring and refurbishing to function as a convalescent home, and the total cost to the Sisters was £16,000. It was opened on 26 April 1902 and was ready to accommodate 55 patients. The first local superior was Sr M Vincent Kelly, who was succeeded by Sr Margaret Mary Malone.[16] Sr Margaret Mary faced a formidable task, because she was responsible not only for the convalescent home, but also for the development of the farm on the surrounding acres as a source of income. Later, Sr Cecilia Morgan managed the farm for many years until her retirement, helped by a small staff of farm workers. They grew vegetables for use in the convalescent home but also to be sold at the market and they also raised animals, including sheep.

Many agreements were drawn up between the Mater and Beaumont Convalescent Home regarding patient transfers. In 1905, it was agreed that on average, per day, they would have at least 21 patients from the Mater in their care. Later it was arranged that at least seven patients would be maintained free of charge: three women and four men. Although the rising cost of patient care was a continuous problem, it was hoped that the debt on the place might be paid off by about 1940. Unfortunately this was not achieved because of the cost of patient care. Sr Genevieve Bourke was determined to clear the debt, but she was faced with continuous problems with maintenance, including installing electricity, plumbing, drainage and, of course, further extensions, all of which were very costly. Nonetheless, the development of Beaumont Convalescent Home did achieve what the Sisters at the Mater had hoped for when they were struggling to manage the smallpox victims.

Beaumont House featured in hospital annual reports for many years. In 1913, the Mater report[17] gave an interesting account of its achievements and services to the hospital:

> Beaumont Convalescent Home, in connection with the Hospital, is also under the care of the Sisters of Mercy. This mansion is surrounded by acres of pasture land. The house was re-constructed and several additions made, so it can now provide for over 50 patients. Here convalescent patients are sent from the Hospital where they rapidly gain health and strength. The advantage of a place like this cannot be overestimated ... When a poor man leaves hospital he too often goes back to a dark, uncomfortable, ill-ventilated tenement, and without proper nourishment, or sufficient fuel, bedding or clothing, is likely to suffer a relapse ...

The report continues at length in the hope of encouraging financial support for the work of Beaumont House and for many years, extracts from the report appeared in daily newspapers once or twice a year as part of an advertisement seeking donations to keep the place going.

1   O'Brien, J. (1982), *Dear Dirty Dublin – A City in Distress*, California: University of California Press, p 65.
2   Fourth Report of the Council of the MMH for the last four years ending Dec 31st 1874, Dublin, p. 44.
3   Decubitus ulcers.
4   Antibiotics were not invented until 1928.
5   The modern mercury clinical thermometer was developed in the mid-1860s by the English physician Sir Thomas Clifford Allbutt.
6   He died not in the Mater, but nearby in his flat.
7   The remains of Reverend Pecherin were exhumed on 30 April 1991 and transferred to the Redemptorist burial plot in Deansgrange Cemetery.
8   This story was confirmed in the same paper by a Dr J. Banks and he went on to say that the woman had recovered.
9   *Freeman's Journal*, 7 September 1872.
10   *Report of the Mater Misericordiae Hospital for the Year 1888* (1889), Dublin: Brown & Nolan, p 5.
11   *The Irish Times*, 9 November 1896.
12   *Report of the Mater Misericordiae Hospital for the Year 1904* (1905), Dublin: Dollard Printing House, p 39.
13   There is no evidence that the Sisters of Mercy ever went ahead with this suggestion although the need existed.
14   Ibid.
15   Arthur Guinness died in Beaumont House in 1803.
16   McCormack, Sr Stella. Unpublished paper.
17   *Report of the Mater Misericordiae Hospital for the Year 1913* (1913), Dublin: Dollard Printing House, p 9.

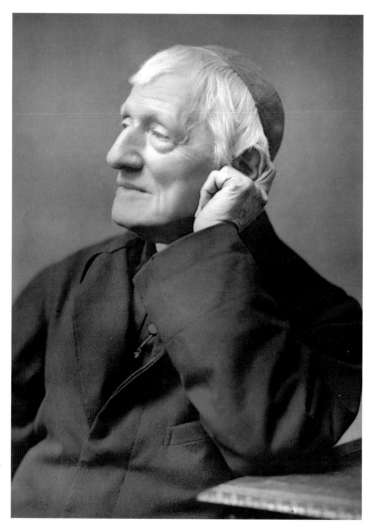

Cardinal Newman, founder of the Catholic University School of Medicine.
(© Getty Images.)

CHAPTER 4

Early Physicians and Surgeons

Until 1829 and the passing of the Roman Catholic Relief Act, Catholics were discriminated against at many levels. This had a substantial impact in Ireland, the population of which was then 80% Catholic. Catholics were denied access to certain public offices, had lesser property rights than their Protestant counterparts, and, critically, were denied access to education, particularly university education. This meant that only those who could travel abroad could obtain a university degree. Catholic Emancipation changed this for ever. Sixteen years after Emancipation, the three (nonsectarian) Queen's Colleges were opened – 'Godless Colleges' as they were referred to by Daniel O'Connell, the Liberator. They did not impress the Catholic clergy, who forbade all Catholics from attending them. The Reverend John Henry Newman was instrumental in establishing a Catholic university in Dublin, including a medical school in Cecilia Street, in 1855.

The Catholic university had the odds stacked against it from the beginning. Most of the original plans failed, largely because it never received an authorising charter or any official source of revenue, depending instead on on voluntary contributions and student fees. The one 'winner' was the medical school in Cecilia Street. Newman was determined that it, above all, should succeed. The fact that it did so was largely thanks to the help of an eminent surgeon, Andrew Ellis, a man of incalculable experience. Born in Wicklow in 1792, Ellis came to Dublin in 1815 'to be apprenticed to a surgeon, Thomas Rooney, and was enrolled in the Royal College of Surgeon's Register in 1820'.[1] He began teaching anatomy in private medical schools in Dublin. In 1850 he was invited, as Professor of Surgery, to the Apothecaries School in Cecilia Street. He was a leading Dublin surgeon and in 1848 published his *Lectures on Clinical Surgery.* In 1850, he became President of the Royal College of Surgeons, Dublin. His post as surgeon at the Mater was, unfortunately, his last appointment; he died in 1867. When Newman was told of his death he said 'he owed him a great deal of gratitude, as he in fact was the founder of the University Medical School'.

Newman's idea for this medical school was that Catholic professors and lecturers should be appointed and that the students would have access to Catholic hospitals – of which only St Vincent's Hospital existed at the time – for clinical teaching and experience. The first thing he did was to find out how many Catholic physicians and surgeons there were in Dublin. According to William Doolan,[2] quoting from Newman's Second Report to the Episcopal Board in 1856:

> Out of all the Dublin Hospitals only three have any Catholic practitioner in them at all... Out of sixty-two medical officers, the Catholics do not exceed the number of ten.
> Out of five medical schools in Dublin (excluding our University), three have no Catholic lecturers at all, and the other two have only one each. Out of forty-nine lecturers, only two are Catholic.[3]

Newman's first job was to acquire suitable premises for the medical school, and the school for apothecaries on Cecilia Street seemed ideal. However, although the building was on the market, there was no possibility that Newman himself could have purchased it: in spite of Emancipation, sectarian prejudice against Catholics was still very much in evidence. Andrew Ellis was charged with the job, one which filled him with much anxiety. According to Doolan:[4]

> Andrew Ellis bought the premises in Cecilia Street for £1,500. 'It would never have been sold to us,' Newman declared afterwards, 'if it had been known that we were trying for it, Dr Ellis told me (Newman) that for a fortnight he had not been able to sleep at night. It was a great act.'

This picture of the medical school is one of the earliest, dating from 1855.

Nobody took much notice of this purchase by Ellis, assuming that having worked there, he was buying it for his own use. However, the two men were then faced with a fresh set of problems: finance; and appointing staff to the school. The second task was probably the more difficult. They knew the people they wanted on the staff, but they did not always meet with enthusiasm or success. The very limited number of suitable people available and the difficulties they encountered threatened to derail the project before it had even begun. However, one of the important selling points was that staff would be offered posts in the new Mater Hospital, then to be the largest hospital in Ireland, when it opened.

In spite of all the problems, on 1 October 1855, Cecilia Street opened as the Catholic University Medical School. A list of the teaching staff was published in the newspapers beforehand and an announcement was made in all the Catholic churches. According to the advertisement:

> The Rector, Very Rev. Dr. J. Newman has already designated the following Professors:
>
> *Professors of Anatomy and Physiology:*
> - Thomas Hayden, FRCSI, Lecturer in Surgical Anatomy
> - Robert Cryan, LRCSI, LRQGPI. Lecturer in Anatomy and Physiology.
>
> *Professors of the Theory and Practice of Surgery:*
> - Andrew Ellis, FRCSI.
>
> *Demonstrator of Anatomy*
> - Henry Tyrrell, LRCSI.

Three of the four listed above, Hayden, Ellis and Tyrrell, would be appointed to the Mater when it opened. Robert Cryan was appointed to St Vincent's Hospital. Newman was not present at the opening of the medical school as he was away in Birmingham, and so it was left to Andrew Ellis to deliver an inaugural address to the staff and 43 students,[5] after which the work of this great institution commenced. By 1900, the Catholic University Medical School was outperforming all the other medical schools in Ireland.

In the six years between the opening of the medical school in Cecilia Street and the opening of the Mater Hospital, Andrew Ellis was kept busy, seeking staff for the medical school and making appointments to the hospital. These had to be discussed and agreed with the Sisters of Mercy, who were the owners of the hospital. Andrew Ellis was no stranger to the nuns, having been a surgeon in Jervis Street Hospital, then being managed by the Mercy Sisters. Many meetings were held, especially during 1860 and 1861, during which a formal relationship between Cecilia Street and the Mater was established. Chief among the items for discussion was the nuns' insistence that no salaries be paid to hospital medical staff. All the money that was received by the hospital was for patient care and for the development of the hospital itself. The Sisters of Mercy were not in receipt of any payment, stipend or financial support from hospital funds for themselves: as they saw it, this would be to take money from the poor and those who were ill.

During 1861, the Sisters, with the help of Ellis, decided on who should be appointed as medical officers to the hospital. A list was drawn up and the rules worked out. The following became the founding medical officers of the Mater, all of whom were linked to the new medical school:[6]

- Andrew Ellis
- Richard P. O'Reilly
- Michael H. Stapleton
- Thomas Hayden
- John Hughes
- Alexander McDonnell
- Francis Cruise

They met at the hospital on 15 September 1861 and, according to the minutes of the meeting: 'On this occasion the Reverend Mother read out for the Medical Officers the rules by which they were to be guided. The Medical Officers present signed their names at the bottom of these rules, but begged leave to dissent from one rule, which proposed, "that all matriculated students of the Catholic University should be free to the Hospital". At the discussion which ensued, no distinct resolutions were passed.'[7] Instead the discussion would appear to have centred on the duties of honorary secretary and treasurer and there would appear to have been much jostling for position. It was suggested that the junior member of the staff (Francis Cruise) should undertake both duties. This was agreed to, but not for long, because almost immediately Dr Hughes objected, saying that the roles should be separate. Before agreement was eventually reached, they had to work out which was the 'lesser' role. They decided that the post of 'secretary' should be held by a surgeon and the 'treasurer' should be a physician! This was agreed to, after Dr Hughes refused to attend further meetings and wrote a letter outlining his grievances to the Reverend Mother, Mother Mary of Mercy Norris, who was in charge from 1855 to 1864.

In particular, Dr Hughes felt that the proceedings weren't formal enough, and the Reverend Mother agreed, insisting that the minutes be brought to her before being signed. She also insisted that her approval was necessary before the board could select resident students. The discussion and rules drawn up that day apparently touched on the general governance of the hospital, patient care, education of students and the behaviour of staff, particularly relating to courtesy, loyalty and devotion to duty. On the issue that matriculated students of the Catholic University should not have to pay a fee to the hospital, the medical officers pointed out 'that while they objected to opening the Hospital free to all Matriculated Students of the Catholic University they were quite willing to offer free Hospital tickets to Scholars of the University'.[8]

Further meetings were held during the following weeks to arrange details of doctors' hours of attendance and to launch a medical staff register of attendance at the hospital, including at the dispensary. All arrangements were, to some extent, experimental at this stage. In time, a template more in keeping with national and international standards was drawn up by the medical staff, together with a teaching programme. Student lecture fees became a source of revenue for the medical officers for the purchase of equipment and in 1888 were used to employ a full-time pathologist to work and teach at the Mater. In 1867, detailed duties of the medical staff were formally drawn up.

The duties, apart from dealing with patients, had to do mainly with teaching students, resident and non-resident. They were presented to and approved by the medical board on 6 November 1867.

MEDICAL STAFF.

Consulting Physician.

SIR FRANCIS R. CRUISE, D.L., M.D., Univ. Dub.; K.S.G., F.R.C.P.; Physician to the King in Ireland; Past President R.C.P.; Member of Senate of the University of Dublin and of the Royal University of Ireland; Consulting Visitor in Lunacy under the High Court of Chancery in Ireland; Visiting Physician to St. Vincent's Lunatic Asylum, Fairview, etc.

Physicians.

SIR CHRISTOPHER NIXON, Bart., D.L., A.B., M.B., LL.D., Univ. Dub.; M.D., Hon. Causa, R.U.I.; Vice-Chancellor, National University of Ireland; Past President Royal College of Physicians; Consulting Visitor in Lunacy under the High Court of Chancery in Ireland; Consulting Physician, Central Asylum, Dundrum; Professor of Practice of Medicine in the National University of Ireland; President of the Royal Veterinary College of Ireland; Visiting Physician to St. Patrick's College, Maynooth; Member of the General Medical Council.

SIR JOSEPH REDMOND, M.D., F.R.C.P., L.R.C.S., L.M.; Past President, Royal College of Physicians; Consulting Physician to St. Michael's Hospital, Kingstown; Consulting Physician to the Coombe Hospital and Guinness Dispensary; Consulting Physician, National Hospital, Holles Street; Consulting Physician, Cottage Hospital, Drogheda.

JOHN MURPHY, F.R.C.P., L.R.C.S., L.M.; Ex-Vice-President, Royal College of Physicians; Physician to St. Vincent's Lunatic Asylum, Fairview; Late Examiner in Medicine, Conjoint Board of Examination; and Censor, Royal College of Physicians.

MARTIN DEMPSEY, B.A., M.D. (Special Gold Medal), Examiner in Materia Medica, Royal College of Physicians and Surgeons; F.R.C.P.; Professor of Materia Medica and Therapeutics, University College, Dublin; Visiting Physician, St. Patrick's Training College, Drumcondra.

Resident Physicians.

T. REYNOLDS, M.B., B.Ch., L.R.C.P., L.R.C.S.I.
F. J. BURKE, M.B., L.R.C.S.I.
S. A. M'SWEENEY, M.B., B.Ch., L.R.C.S.I.

Gynaecologist.

ROBERT P. FARNAN, M.B., B.Ch., B.A.O., Royal University of Ireland.

Assistant Physician and Medical Registrar.

JOHN O'DONNELL, M.B., B.Ch., B.A.O., R.U.I.; Leonard Gold and Silver Medallist, Mater Misericordiae Hospital; Examiner in Medicine, Apothecaries' Hall.

Physician in Charge of Electrical Department.

MAURICE R. J. HAYES, F.R.C.S.I., L.R.C.P.; Assistant Lecturer on Materia Medica, C.U.I.

Pathologist.

EDMOND J. McWEENEY, M.A., M.D., M.Ch., M.A.O., F.R.C.P., D.P.H., M.R.I.A.; Examiner in Pathology; M.o.-Sch. and Ex-University Student in Pathology, Royal University of Ireland; Pathologist to Jervis Street, Coombe, National Obstetric, and St. Michael's Hospitals; Member of the Royal Institute of Public Health; Professor of Pathology and Bacteriology, University College, Dublin; Bacteriologist to the Local Government Board for Ireland; Professor of Pathology and Bacteriology in the National University of Ireland.

Assistant Pathologist.

W. D. O'KELLY, M.B., B.Ch., B.A.O., R.U.I.

SURGICAL STAFF.

Surgeons.

SIR ARTHUR CHANCE, F.R.C.S.I., F.R.C.S.Ed. (Hon. Causa); Past President, Royal College of Surgeons; Consulting Surgeon to the Orthopaedic Hospital of Ireland, and to St. Michael's Hospital, Kingstown; Member of the General Medical Council; Surgeon-in-Ordinary to His Excellency the Lord Lieutenant of Ireland; Visitor in Lunacy under the High Court of Chancery in Ireland.

SIR JOHN LENTAIGNE, B.A., F.R.C.S., L.R.C.P., etc.; Ex-President, Royal College of Surgeons; Consulting Surgeon, Royal Hospital for Incurables, Donnybrook; Consulting Surgeon, National Maternity Hospital; Consulting Surgeon to the Allan A. Ryan Home Hospital for Consumption; Surgeon to the Household of His Excellency the Lord Lieutenant of Ireland; Visitor in Lunacy under the High Court of Chancery in Ireland.

ALEXANDER BLAYNEY, F.R.C.S., M.A. (Hons.), M.B., B.Ch., B.A.O. (Hons.), R.U.I.; Member of Council, Royal College of Surgeons; Assistant Professor in Surgery, University College, Dublin; Visiting Surgeon, St. Patrick's College, Maynooth; University Gold Medallist, Catholic University; formerly Examiner in Surgery, Royal College of Surgeons; Student and Examiner in Biology, Royal University of Ireland; and Professor in Biology, Catholic University.

Ophthalmic Surgeon.

LOUIS WERNER, M.B., B.Ch., F.R.C.S.; First Senior Moderator and Ex-Medical Scholar, University Dublin; Lecturer on Ophthalmology in University College, Dublin; Assistant Surgeon to the Royal Victoria Eye and Ear Hospital.

Assistant Surgeon.

DENIS FARNAN, M.B., B.Ch., B.A.O., Hons.; Student in Medicine, R.U.I.

Surgeon for Diseases of the Throat and Nose.

PATRICK DEMPSEY, F.R.C.S., M.R.C.S., Eng., L.R.C.P., Lond.; Leonard Gold Medallist, Mater Misericordiae Hospital.

Surgical Registrar and Anaesthetist.

PATRICK O'FARRELL, L.R.C.P., L.R.C.S., L.M.D.P.H., Extern Assistant Physician, Children's Hospital, Temple Street.

Dental Surgeon.

EDWARD SHERIDAN, L.D.S., F.R.C.S.I., Assistant Surgeon and Lecturer on Dental Materia Medica, Dental Hospital of Ireland; Examiner in Dentistry, Royal College of Surgeons; Professor of Dental Surgery, University College, Dublin.

Resident Surgeons.

JAMES STUART, M.B., B.Ch., B.A.O., N.U.I.
P. M'CARTEN, R.C.P. and S.I.
D. HIGGINS, M.B., B.Ch., B.A.O., N.U.I.
H. L. BARNIVILLE, M.B., B.Ch., B.A.O., N.U.I.
L. DOYLE, M.B., B.Ch., B.A.O., N.U.I.

Apothecary.

D. J. CHADWICK, L.P.S.I.

A list of medical staff from the 1911 hospital report.

A Loyal and Committed Staff

Although the medical staff at the Mater came from different backgrounds, they were united in their commitment to the hospital in its early years and were to prove loyal to the nuns and to the ethos of the hospital. Among the staff were also a number of colourful and distinctive characters who would make their mark on the Mater.

A key member of this early staff was Andrew Ellis. Next to be appointed was *Richard P. O'Reilly*, who was appointed as surgeon in 1861. He was on the staff of the Catholic University, Cecilia Street, in the anatomy department. He died in July 1870. *Michael Henry Stapleton* came to the Mater from Jervis Street Hospital and remained as surgeon for six years, until his retirement in 1867. He was also on the staff of Cecilia Street. He died in 1880.

Thomas Hayden came to the hospital as physician in 1861. Admired by all for his gentle approach, he earned the name of 'Gentle Thomas'. Born in Co. Tipperary in 1823, he was originally a physician at Jervis Street Hospital, and made his name as a teacher of anatomy at the Medical School, Peter Street. He obtained a fellowship from

the Royal College of Surgeons in 1852 and was appointed to the Chair of Anatomy in the Catholic University School in 1855, a position he held until 1865.[9] He obtained a licentiate of the College of Physicians 1860, became a fellow in 1867 and Vice-President of the College in 1875. He died in 1891.

John Hughes was appointed as a physician in 1861. Very little has been recorded about him, apart from his interventions at meetings of the medical board. After his objections at the first meeting, he did not attend any further meetings until the end of January the following year, having sent a letter which included the assertion, 'that a member who ventures to differ from the majority has no business being present.'[10] At the next meeting, he handed the chairman another written protest against the activities of the medical board concerning the appointment of resident students to the hospital and

Thomas Hayden. (Reproduced by kind permission of the Royal College of Physicians of Ireland.)

'dissented from agreements reached at the meeting on that particular day'. It can only be deduced that things were not as he expected when he joined the Mater staff. Nonetheless, he would remain at the hospital for 21 years.

Alexander McDonnell came to the hospital as surgeon in 1861. He died suddenly one year later, in 1862. Another surgeon to join was the eminent *Sir Francis Cruise*, who started his career at the Mater as a junior surgeon. He was 27 years of age and had just received his M.D. from Trinity College. He was born in Dublin in 1834. He did not start his career as a medic, but instead took an an arts degree at Trinity, followed by a degree in medicine in 1858. Due to overwork, his health deteriorated and so he went on a voyage to America with the Franco-Irish explorer Count Henry Russell.[11] Cruise is best remembered for his invention of the endoscope used to investigate bladder disorders. This endoscope was originally equipped with a powerful light source fuelled by paraffin. He was also much admired for his extensive contribution to medical literature on the subject of urology, but particularly endoscopy. He was President of

Sir Francis Cruise, one of the founding medical officers of the Mater. (Reproduced by kind permission of the Royal College of Physicians of Ireland.)

the Royal College of Physicians in Ireland from 1884 to 1886.[12] In 1896 he received a knighthood from Queen Victoria. He died at home in 1891.

By 1867, the hospital had lost three of its original medical staff – Ellis, Stapleton and McDonnell – so a number of new appointments had to be made. Henry Tyrrell and

Patrick Hayes were appointed as surgeons to replace Ellis and Stapleton and the role of Assistant Physician was created for the first time in Dublin when Henry Curran was appointed in the same year. Unfortunately, he died suddenly in 1872. At the end of that year, Christopher Nixon, who had served as a resident and who was by all accounts a brilliant student, was appointed to the vacancy.

biography

Christopher Nixon

Christopher Nixon served as physician at the Mater for 42 years until his death in 1914. Born in Dublin in 1849, he studied law at Trinity College and medicine at the Catholic University Medical School. He attended the Mater as a student and when he qualified, he went to Paris. In 1872, he was appointed physician at the Mater. He was Professor of Medicine in Cecilia Street for many years. He received an honorary M.D. from the Royal University of Ireland in 1885. A prolific writer, he produced a number of publications, the best known of which was *A Handbook of Hospital Practice and Physical Diagnosis*. In 1895, he was made a knight of the British Empire and in 1906 a baronet in recognition of his services to medicine. Nixon was an excellent physician, well liked by his many patients, but he is perhaps best known as an educator and was always held in high esteem by his students and his colleagues. In 1897, he was

Sir Christopher Nixon, resplendent in his academic robes. (Reproduced by kind permission of the Royal College of Physicians of Ireland.)

appointed a member of the General Medical Council, a position he held until his death in July 1914.[13] According to the *Freeman's Journal*, 'Few men performed services so thoroughly. He was President of the Royal College of Physicians, Vice-Chancellor of two great Universities, member of the Medical Council, first President of the Royal Veterinary College, which owes its existence to his zeal and enthusiasm; the holder of honorary degrees of several Universities.'[14] In 1887, along with colleagues Patrick Hayes and Thomas More Madden, Nixon represented the Mater at the committee of inquiry set up to investigate the management and working of the Dublin hospitals and the use being made by them of parliamentary grants.[15] Nixon was the main speaker for the Mater and he did his utmost to try to have some funds directed to the hospital, given that the Mater was not in receipt of any government grant. Nixon spoke at length about the financial difficulties being experienced by the hospital, but to no avail.

In 1872, the volume of work dramatically increased for the doctors with the opening of the large east wing and with the catastrophic epidemic of smallpox in Dublin city the following year. The medical and nursing staff now encountered something they had never anticipated: hundreds of patients with a 'killer disease' arriving at the hospital in a short space of time. Christopher Nixon recalled the difficulties they faced in a lecture he gave in 1904:

> In 1872, the eastern wing was opened, a considerable portion of it being utilised for the reception of contagious diseases. One year later a virulent epidemic of smallpox broke out, and, at urgent solicitation, cases of the disease were admitted – over 800 being attended to in the hospital... The results were so calamitous in the spread of the disease to the other inmates that it was determined under no circumstances will cases of smallpox be again admitted to the hospital.[16]

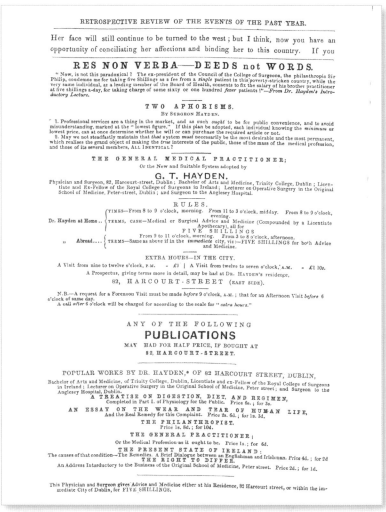

In this advertisement, surgeon Thomas Hayden promotes his services, as was common at the time, in the Dublin Pictorial Guide and Directory (1850).

Fortunately for the medics and the patients, the second half of the nineteenth century saw a rise in the knowledge of diseases. Pasteur published his famous germ theory of disease in 1861 and prior to that, Lister, an English surgeon, had studied the prevention of wound infections. However, the amount of surgery performed was still minimal because of wound infection, as can be seen from the *British Medical Journal*[17] in 1878, which published a list of 'Operation Days at the (London) Hospitals': each hospital carried out operations on only one day per week and dealt with only one or two cases. The Mater's operation day was initially on Wednesdays.

In 1878, the Mater had a total of three surgeons – Francis Cruise, Patrick Hayes and Charles Coppinger. *Patrick Hayes* was appointed as surgeon in 1867. Born in Waterford in 1838, he qualified in Edinburgh and worked at the Mater for almost 36 years. He held the position of Professor of Surgery in the Catholic University Medical School, Cecilia Street, from 1879 until his death in 1904. *Charles Coppinger* was born in Dublin in 1846. He studied arts at Trinity College, after which he went to the Catholic University Medical School in Cecilia Street to study medicine. He qualified in 1869 and was appointed to the Mater as surgeon later the same year.[18] According to J. Dowling, his house surgeon (1892), Coppinger 'was a skillful and rapid operator and was one of the first surgeons who successfully ligatured [tied off] the innominate artery[19] for a subclavian aneurism. He had practised it beforehand in the dissecting room of the Cecilia Street School of Medicine.' [20] Coppinger held a number of posts in the Catholic University Medical School, where, according to an article published in the *British Medical Journal* in 1897: 'the operations performed were operations of necessity – amputations, lithotomies,[21] removal of malignant tumours, trephinings [a surgical technique where holes are drilled or cut into the human skull – an ancient surgical practice], and ligature of arteries'.[22] The *BMJ* made reference to Coppinger as having 'done a great deal of very successful joint surgery'.[23] Coppinger worked at the Mater for 35 years. He resigned in 1904 and died in 1905.

Another physician of note at the Mater Hospital was *Thomas More Madden*, who was appointed to the Mater as an obstetric physician in 1878. His appointment was somewhat controversial in that it was made directly by the Reverend Mother, to the consternation of the medical board. Why this happened is not recorded, although it is clear that there was some disagreement about his appointment. The matter was eventually taken up with the Reverend Mother and a lengthy correspondence ensued between her and the board. Ultimately an agreement was reached following a letter from her to Dr Nixon. Dr More Madden took up his position without portfolio. He was obviously a very pleasant man and in time he 'fitted in' extremely well.

More Madden came from an exotic background, born in Cuba to an Irish father (also a medic and a famous writer) and a Jamaican mother. He studied medicine in Dublin. After he qualified, he went travelling, before returning to Dublin in 1868 and obtaining a post at the Rotunda Hospital as Assistant Master. Knowing that, as a Catholic, he could never be appointed Master of the Hospital, he sought to move to the Mater. His one ambition was to set up an obstetric unit in the hospital, but although the idea was explored many times, it simply never happened. When asked by the Dublin Hospitals Commission Committee of Inquiry 1887 about the post he was holding at the time, More Madden went on, at length, about why he thought it would be expeditious to organise an obstetric facility at the Mater. This obviously did not impress the Commissioners.

Edmund Joseph McWeeney was another of the great personalities of the Mater. A Dubliner, he had won a scholarship in 1882 to attend the Royal University to study modern languages – which would serve him well later in his career when he went to study in various parts of Europe. Then he studied medicine at the Catholic University School of Medicine, Cecilia Street, and graduated in 1887. In the two following years McWeeney went to Europe to study pathology. He was appointed to the Mater Hospital as pathologist, the first of his kind in Ireland, initially on a two-year term, being reappointed in 1890.

When McWeeney came to the Mater, no salaries were paid to the medical staff. They made their living from their private practices, but also from various university appointments. In addition, they collected and divided between them student fees for the teaching sessions they provided at the hospital. McWeeney had no private patients and did not share in the 'fees fund' arrangement and so it was decided by the medical board that he would be paid an honorarium of £50 per annum, half out of the fees fund and half from the Sisters of Mercy.

McWeeney's work and academic publications, together with his ever-growing reputation, made him a much-sought-after academic speaker. According to Meenan:

> E.J. McWeeney led the way in the organisation of bacteriological teaching in Ireland and his influence on the trend and growth of scientific medicine in all schools has been profound.[24]

He was appointed to the Catholic University Medical School, where he continued his scientific work and his teaching until, unfortunately, Parkinson's disease depleted him of his health and strength. He died in 1925. Within a decade after his death a much larger, purpose-built pathology department was nearing completion at the Mater. No doubt, Edmund McWeeney had been involved in the strategic planning of this particular development. It is sad that he did not live long enough to see his dream realised in 1936.

Maurice Richard J. Hayes's contribution to the Mater was in his work with X-ray imaging. He was born in 1878, just 17 years before the great discovery of X-rays by Röntgen in Germany. Hayes studied pharmaceutical chemistry in Dublin, following which he worked at a city dispensary in Peter Street. Obviously, this did not satisfy a yearning in him to serve suffering humanity and so he turned to the study of medicine. He pursued his medical studies in the Catholic University Medical School and, during that time, he got to know the Mater, being mentored by Ambrose Bermingham, Professor of Anatomy at the university, who had served as resident student in the Mater in 1885.

From left: (back row) D. J. Finn, P. J. Nagle, L. K. Malley, H. C. O'Rourke and J. Coffey; (front row) C. D. Kennedy *(house surgeon), T. J. O'Reilly (house physician), W. J. Roche (house surgeon), D. Murphy (house surgeon), T. J. Martin and P. J. Campbell. (The names of the two men at the front are unknown.) Nagle went on to become an anaesthetist and was present at the first cardiac surgery to be performed at the hospital. Malley became a physician and was in charge of the cardiac unit. (Reproduced by kind permission of the Royal College of Physicians of Ireland.)*

While Hayes was studying medicine, the wider world was awaiting new developments in radiology following Röntgen's famous discovery. Hayes became interested in the field and when he discussed it with John S. McArdle, Professor of Surgery, McArdle 'urged him strongly to take up and to develop the new science of radiology'.[25] In June 1907, he was appointed to the Mater. At this time, according to Doolan, 'No medical man in Dublin had then thought of radiology as a specialty.'[26] When Hayes arrived at the Mater to start to develop a department of radiology, according to Freeman he worked 'for fourteen years in a little red-tiled building on the site of the present X-ray department (East Wing), which always suggested a somewhat pretentious football pavilion'.[27] Hayes worked very hard to progress the specialism of radiology, becoming something of a pioneer in certain aspects of radiology in which he was particularly interested, particularly its role in the treatment of diseases, about which he wrote many papers and gave many lectures. His workload at the hospital progressively increased.

When World War I broke out in 1914, Hayes was in demand at the Red Cross hospital which had been established in Dublin Castle from the day it opened.[28] Eventually he went off to work as a volunteer in France at the General Base Hospital at Rouen.[29]

Referring to Hayes's work, Doolan commented that, 'No hour was too inconvenient for Hayes, no work too tedious; the claim of the wounded man, was of paramount consideration. His patience was unending, his zeal untiring … Hayes was one of the heroes of the War.'[30] Unfortunately, he returned to the Mater at the end of the war a very different man, obviously tired and traumatised by his wartime experiences. His health was rapidly failing and it was causing concern to those in charge of the hospital, particularly as his workload was continuing to rise; so he eventually agreed to the appointment of an assistant and other staff to his department. However, in May 1922, he commenced a long and difficult correspondence with various senior people in the Mater and also the Archbishop of Dublin, long and disgruntled letters, which ended in his resignation in July that year. However, his career was far from over: he went on to become Director General of the medical department of the Irish Army and died in 1930.

1   Freeman, E. (1962) *Mater Misericordiae Hospital Centenary 1861–1961*, p 15 (private publication).
2   Doolan, W. (1953) 'Newman and his Medical School: the Fateful Lustrum (1855–60)', *Studies: An Irish Quarterly Review.* Vol. 42, No. 166 (Summer), p 154.
3   Ibid.
4   Ibid., p 55.
5   Meenan, F. (1987) *Cecilia Street, The Catholic University School of Medicine, 1955–1931*, Dublin: Gill & Macmillan, p 21.
6   Freeman, E., op. cit., p 15.
7   Mater Misericordiae Hospital, Minutes of the Meetings of the Medical Board 1861–1899, pp 1–3.
8   Ibid., p 3.
9   Freeman, E., op. cit.
10   Mater Misericordiae Hospital, Minutes of the Meetings of the Medical Board 1861–1899, p 13.
11   'Sir Francis Cruise, MD', *British Medical Journal*, 9 March 1912 (2671): 586.
12   Ibid. Cruise's endoscope is still on show in the Royal College of Surgeons, Dublin.
13   *British Medical Journal*, Obituary, 'Sir Christopher Nixon, Bart., MD.', 15 July 1914, p 219.
14   *Freeman's Journal*, 'The Rt. Hon. Sir Christopher Nixon, Bart. An Appreciation', 24 July 1914.
15   Dublin Hospitals Commission, *Report of the Inquiry, 1887*, Alexander Thom & Co, p 1.
16   Report of the Mater Misericordiae Hospital, Dublin for the year 1904, Dollard Printing House, Dublin, 1905, p 38.
17   *British Medical Journal*, 20 July 1878, p 127.
18   Freeman, E., op. cit., p 21.
19   An artery in the chest that arises from the arch of the aorta and divides into the right subclavian – (supplies the arm) and right carotid artery (supplies the brain). Today it is called the *brachiocephalic artery*. The word 'innominate' means '*no name*'.
20   Dowling, J. (1955) *An Irish Doctor Remembers*, Dublin: Clonmore & Reynolds, p 42.
21   A 'lithotomy' is a surgical method for removal of stones formed inside certain hollow organs, such as the bladder.
22   'Hospital Evolution in the Victorian Era', *British Medical Journal*, 26 June 1897, p 1660.
23   'Obituary. Charles Coppinger, M.D. FRCSI, Emeritus Professor in the Catholic University Medical School, Dublin', *British Medical Journal*, 9 January 1909, p 130.
24   Meenan, F., op. cit., p 59.
25   Doolan, W., 'In Memoriam. Maurice R.J. Hayes', *Irish Journal of Medical Science*, Seventh Series No. 4, April 1930, p 163.
26   Ibid.
27   Freeman, E., op. cit., p 27.
28   During the First World War (1914–1918) parts of Dublin Castle were used as a Red Cross military hospital for British troops wounded on the front lines. When it was set up medical and nursing staff were recruited from all the Dublin hospitals to give service in it.
29   Freeman, E., op. cit.
30   Doolan, W., op. cit., p 164.

CHAPTER 5

New Departments and New Specialities

The 19th century was a time of great development, both in medicine and in the Mater. It had become clear that caring for the sick of Dublin was expensive, but that more could be offered to sick patients than just being kept comfortable in bed and well fed. Medicine and surgery had moved on and new diagnostic departments were opening in the hospital, one by one, as new surgical techniques were also being introduced.

Anaesthesia, initially using ether and later chloroform, had become somewhat safer and was being used increasingly at this time. In 1872, the Surgical Society of Ireland set up a committee to look into 'the relative safety of chloroform and ether as anaesthetics'. Surgeon Henry Tyrrell from the Mater was chosen to serve on this committee. By 1886, anaesthesia was being used more frequently at the Mater, to the extent that it was suggested by the surgeons that patients about to be operated on should be anaesthetised before being carried into the operating theatre, which differed from the earlier practice of the anaesthetic being administered by the surgeon himself in the theatre. As the apothecary was now in charge, a room close to the theatre was made available where the ether could be administered in peace and quiet.

It wasn't long before the first anaesthetist, Dr Michael O'Sullivan, was appointed to the Mater, in November 1894. He had recently qualified in general medicine. As an anaesthetist and surgical registrar, O'Sullivan was paid less than the other registrars (non-consultant hospital doctors) because the job of anaesthetist required no training then, being seen as a 'procedure' rather than a 'speciality'. At the same time, the Mater surgeons began to hear about the new surgical developments taking place in Europe and America, and were keen to update the original operating theatre which they considered to be outmoded. The one operating theatre, which was located on the top floor of the hospital, was not considered an important area of the hospital; indeed, rarely is it mentioned in any of the reports or hospital literature of the time, when it was largely used for teaching purposes. At night it closed down altogether and there were no designated night staff. In 1898, the surgeons sent a letter to the Sister Superior asking her to appoint a nurse to the operating room and not to move her from the post for at least one year. This reflected their growing concern that nurses were being sent to the operating theatre, when it was in session, to learn rather than to do valuable work. The surgeons also requested changes to the layout of the theatre to create more space. They also requested changing rooms for the theatre – until then, every surgeon took his protective clothing off at the end of surgery and hung it up on a hook until the next time he was operating!

The Mater surgeons' anxiety to improve facilities reflected the pace of change in surgery at this time. The use of anaesthesia had made it possible to operate for longer periods, increasing the amount and complexity of the surgery that could be performed. The French scientist Pasteur had put forward the new proposal that surgical instruments should be boiled in water before use. Up to that time, they were simply washed in cold water and put on a tray in readiness for use again.

In 1879, one of Pasteur's associates, Charles Chamberland, invented the first autoclave for the sterilisation of instruments, which used steam under pressure to sterilise at a much higher temperature. In Scotland, Joseph Lister was advocating hand-washing before and after surgery, using 5% carbolic liquid to prevent surgical infection. In 1884, a German surgeon, Gustav Neuber, who was studying all available knowledge and practices at the time, came up with the idea that special gowns, caps and shoe covers should be worn in the operating theatre to prevent infection. Initially it was thought that these only needed to be freshly laundered after use, but later it was considered that they should be autoclaved as well. An American surgeon, William Halsted, invented the idea of using rubber gloves during surgery in 1890. All of these developments led to much safer surgery.

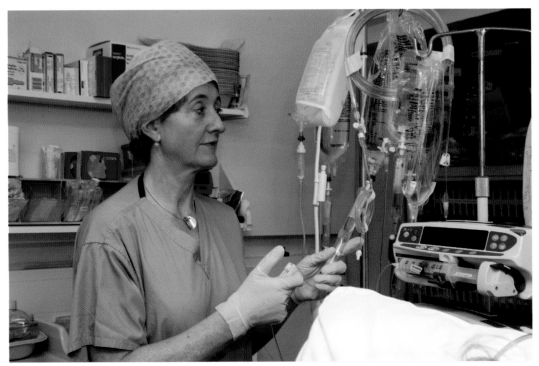

A modern anaesthetist at work.

At the Mater, the number of surgical cases gradually increased and with it the need for more theatre space. Internationally the design of operating theatres was changing. The Mater surgeons felt the time had come to bring the operating theatre facilities up to date, and they made this known to the Sister Superior, but it was easier said than done, as the hospital was struggling with an increasing debt due to the cost of patient care. In addition, the location of the existing operating theatre, three floors up in the hospital, did not favour any easy expansion. Eventually a small extension was built, at great expense, on either side of the existing theatre, from the ground up. Another small area was turned into an anaesthetic room. The operating theatre was ready for use in 1898, but for some reason, the tiered seating remained and wasn't removed until 1945.

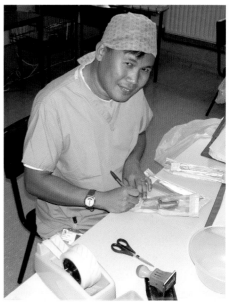

A worker in CSSD – the central sterilising unit.

Much later, the development of cardiac surgery brought about a need for two extra operating theatres. In 1970, funding was made available by the Department of Health to build them, but structural difficulties meant that the new cardiac unit was expensive and difficult to build. So expensive that Department of Health funding had to be supplemented by funds from the Mater Pools by Dr E. T. Freeman.[1] In 1972, the new theatres were formally blessed and opened.

Edmund McWeeney and the Pathology Department

The rapid developments were not just confined to surgery. The discipline of pathology was also developing apace at this time. Following his appointment to the Mater as pathologist, Edmund McWeeney became Professor of Pathology and Bacteriology at the University Medical School, Cecilia Street and later at University College Dublin. After he began work at the Mater, he immediately started setting up an appropriate pathology department. The laboratory, when McWeeney arrived, consisted of one room on the ground floor. The first thing he did was draw up a list of items he needed for the department 'to carry out Koch's treatment'.[2] Robert Koch was a German scientist who was the first to discover the mycobacterium of

Edmund McWeeney was the Mater's first pathologist, appointed in 1888.
(Original held in UCD Library, Special Collections. This digital image was created by the Irish Virtual Research Library and Archive (IVRLA) and is reproduced by kind permission of UCD Library, Special Collections and UCD Digital Library. Printed with the permission of Lafayette Photography.)

tuberculosis (known for many years as Koch's bacillus), for which he would win a Nobel Prize in 1905. McWeeney had studied at Koch's lab and had returned with many of the scientist's ideas, which were new, but expensive and ultimately not that effective. His request was referred to the Mother Superior. In 1892, the work had increased so much he made a request to the medical board for an assistant pathologist.

In 1890, Sir Christopher Nixon[3] took the opportunity to ask the Archbishop[4] for a financial contribution towards the development of the pathology department. The Archbishop was very interested in this development. Not alone did he give some money towards equipping the department, but he promised to preside at the introductory lecture to be given by McWeeney in the boardroom on 23 July 1890.

Nixon proposed to the medical board in 1894 that 'an institute for the teaching of pathology and the prosecution of research work should be established'. At a subsequent meeting it was proposed that the medical board should try to facilitate this suggestion. At the opening lecture of the 1904 medical session, Nixon talked openly about the work of McWeeney and the Mater pathology department:

> A few years ago the work of the pathologist was left to the assistant medical officers – indeed largely to the senior students. There existed the machinery for recording notes and compiling facts in connection with the pathology of disease, of comparing these with conditions found after death. But unfortunately, there were no means of pursuing inquiries into the origin of disease, nor any attempt to determine the nature of obscure conditions, which could only be investigated by the use of instruments of precision. In Dublin, the Royal University, at the instigation of Sir William Thompson and myself, made the regulation that pathology and bacteriology should be made a special subject of the medical curriculum, and, at the same time, a professorship was created in the Medical School of the Catholic University and this professor (Edmund McWeeney) was appointed pathologist to the hospital.[5]

McWeeney was a determined man, a single-minded individual whose great passion was the study and treatment of infectious diseases. At the time tuberculosis (TB) was rampant in the city and was a major public health problem. McWeeney studied the disease in the pathology laboratory and wrote numerous papers on the subject.[6] He attended conferences at home and abroad and in due course became extremely well known – as did the Mater – because of the research he was doing. According to Dr E.T. Freeman, writing in 1961,[7] McWeeney's period as pathologist marked the introduction of scientific medicine. Up to then most advances had been made by clinical observation only. The work that McWeeney did was excellent, in spite of the cramped conditions he was working in. It was he who truly established the pathology department in the hospital. He was succeeded by his assistant, Dr William D. O'Kelly.

The X-Ray / Radiology Department

● *An early photo of the X-ray department, 1906.*

If the discovery of diseases caused by microorganisms marked the middle years of the 19th century, the discovery by Röntgen of the X-ray must surely have marked the end of this same century. Röntgen's discovery of a means of diagnosing diseases other than by observing the presenting symptoms or by surgery has to be a landmark in diagnostic medicine. Röntgen took an X-ray of his wife Bertha's hand on 22 December 1895, discovering that it showed an image of all the bones. Undoubtedly, this was a 'eureka' moment, not just for him but for the entire world which would, in time, make so much use of this discovery. In 1901, Röntgen was awarded the Nobel Prize for Physics.

News of Röntgen's discovery spread rapidly. Physicians and surgeons alike began to discuss its clinical possibilities. At the Mater they were anxious to use it for the benefit of patients and in November 1896, the year after Röntgen's discovery, they were recommending to the board that 'a photographic installation' be set up. Drs Cruise, Coppinger and Lentaigne submitted a list of the equipment needed for this facility to the medical board and followed it quickly with a request for 'a room, capable of being darkened, for Röntgen Radiography'. Dr Michael O'Sullivan would become the first radiologist at the Mater.

The 1906 hospital report carries an interesting statement on the development of a radiology department: 'During the past year a heavy outlay has been caused by the purchase of Apse Coil, and fitting up a room for the X-Rays.'[8]

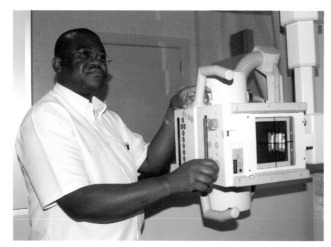

● *A modern X-ray machine.*

When Dr Maurice Richard Hayes became radiographer in 1907, the department was known as the Electricity Department and Dr Hayes as the 'Medical Electrician'. The 1911 hospital report provides an early mention of the X-ray department:

> Our very efficient X-ray department has, during the past year, proved of benefit by the increasing help it gives in the diagnosis and cure of diseases. Besides its usefulness to the intern patients, there are a great many out-patients from all parts of the city and country who attend for treatment of Lupus, Rodent Ulcer, Ringworm, etc.[9]

The 1913 annual report gives an extensive account of the work being done (probably written by McWeeney) and lists 2,784 as the total number of cases for that year.[10] Year by year the number of patients increased until eventually the department was too small to accommodate them. However, it was the early 1920s before funds became available to build a much larger department on the same site. Plans were drawn up and construction began in 1927. The 1928 annual report provides a glimpse into the new X-ray department:

● *A radiologist examines a scan.*

> Plans have been prepared for the installation of the most modern apparatus known to electrical science and for the full protection of patients and staff from the dangers of stray radiation and high-tension discharge. The whole building will be ventilated by means of warm filtered air drawn through the rooms by powerful exhaust fans. Comfortable waiting rooms, dressing rooms, and offices will be a special feature of the new department, which it is hoped will be completed at the end of 1929.[11]

Many years later, in 1981, the department was extended and the existing building reconfigured to provide for the ever-increasing numbers of patients and also to make space for new technology. The hospital annual report for that year mentions that 'the installation of a new tomographic whole-body scanner took place towards the end of the year'. This equipment was located in 38 Eccles Street, adjacent to the radiology department.

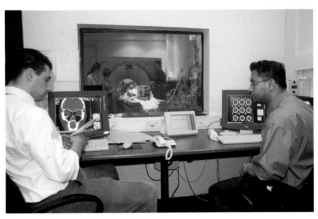

● *A CT scan in progress.*

Since then there have been further changes to the department, both to accommodate new imaging procedures and to make it a better place for the public. Some of the larger imaging equipment such as the magnetic resonance imaging (MRI) scanner and the positron emission tomography (PET) scanner have thus had to be located elsewhere within the hospital. The original department of radiology and all its various extensions is still in existence but is about to be moved to a very modern large facility on level two of the newly opened Whitty Building, on the east side of the original Mater.

The Dispensary and Outpatients Department

When the original plans for the Mater were drawn up, a small area on the ground floor was designated as 'the dispensary':

> Two approaches to the ground floor lead into spacious waiting halls for out-patients of both sexes. Opposite to these are the approaches to the dispensary for out-patients; and on either side are doctors' rooms, with private consulting rooms, ward dispensaries, etc. and in the rear of all is a spacious laboratory, with all the necessary accessories. (*Freeman's Journal*, 25 September 1861)

This area was located to the left of the original main entrance on Eccles Street and access was down a set of steps. The senior house surgeon slept in a little room beside the dispensary and the house physician slept in another room on the floor above, near the stairs. The other resident house officers and students slept in dormitories across from the dispensary, near the hospital kitchen.[12]

The Sisters saw the dispensary as a place where the sick poor could see a doctor, without the need to be admitted. This usually amounted to a medical examination, a diagnosis and a prescription for a bottle of medicine, or a dressing or splint in the case of a wound or fracture, after which they could return home. The service was free and was available six days a week from 9 a.m. There were no formalities, no appointments, no

The original entrance to the dispensary, which has since been bricked up.

triaging; every disease or problem was attended to on a 'first come, first served' basis. The doctor assigned to work in the dispensary saw everyone. If the presenting problem required hospitalisation, the patient was admitted immediately to one of the wards in the care of an appropriate physician or surgeon. There were no letters of reference from or to general practitioners and any records were rudimentary. The patient's name, address, age, occupation and disease or injury and the date of discharge were entered into a large ledger. Ward records were minimal. At a time when the better off stayed at home and employed a doctor or nurse, the dispensary served a need for the poor. Furthermore, there was no misuse of the facility because only the poor availed of it.

However, by around 1900, two changes were taking place; the label 'dispensary' was by now firmly associated with the Poor Law system, so hospitals such as the Mater moved to the more acceptable term of 'outpatients department', and this increasingly drew in the middle classes, who would previously have remained at home and called a doctor. Also, advances in medicine, such as the growth of radiology and pathology services, were changing the nature of what hospitals could provide and there was a move away from the concept of them simply being a refuge for the sick poor. The fact that the services available were free drew even more numbers to the department. Anyone could come to the Mater outpatients, which was not the case with other hospitals. (To use other hospital outpatients departments, a 'ticket' had to be obtained from a member of a 'dispensary committee' and, due to perceived discrimination, few Catholics ever looked for them.) The Mater left it open to anyone who needed care to just present themselves at the hospital. Gradually the numbers attending the outpatients department increased, in spite of the fact that the place was small and the furniture scarce. One assistant physician generally saw all the patients and the apothecary dispensed any necessary medicine. If they had been prescribed medication at a previous visit, patients were expected to bring the empty bottle back to be refilled and relabelled. The system was run as economically as possible. According to Dr Bryan Alton:

The side entrance to the dispensary, now a direct entrance to the infectious diseases unit.

> The hospital in those days held a very particular place in the life of the city. It was a monumental general practitioner for the people who lived in the north quadrant of Dublin city. The outpatients department was a place where medical aid, mild social amenities, light and warmth were all available. Its clientele was the indigenous Dubliner of every kind... There seemed to be a tremendous spirit of personal relationship – the nuns and medical staff knew the patients and their families as one would know neighbours.[13]

After the east wing of the hospital opened (1872), the dispensary moved to the North Circular Road end of this wing, to a slightly larger space. In this location it consisted of three main rooms – one for medical patients, one for surgical patients and a gynaecology

The rather cramped conditions of the 1936 pharmacy.

clinic. Who sorted the patients into the appropriate categories (given that they were self-referred) is not recorded, but it was possibly the nun in charge of the department. As in the original location, the pharmacy was located nearby, and here the outpatients department was near both the X-ray department and the laboratory.

With increasing numbers of patients attending the outpatients department, it was seen as an important place for teaching medical students. As early as 1863, the medical board laid out all the teaching duties for the visiting medical staff as follows:

> It was resolved that the accident, dispensary, and lecturing duty be represented by one surgeon at a time and be divided into periods of 10 days, the distribution for each month to be made in the order of seniority.[14]

In the decade between 1880 and 1890, the board drew up rules and regulations for new appointments made to the hospital. There is no evidence, however, that specific rules were ever drawn up for the outpatients department. It was left to evolve until eventually it bordered on the chaotic (as happened elsewhere, including the London teaching hospitals). Dr Kevin Malley, Senior Physician at the Mater, recalled the problem in his presidential address to the Medical Society, University College Dublin in 1941:

> The figures given by Burdett[15] concerning the numbers of outpatients attending the voluntary hospitals in England and Ireland in 1892 show clearly, at this time, the problem was of the first magnitude. In 1892, 160,000 patients attended as outpatients at the Dublin hospitals. Since Dublin had then a population of just 350,000, the number of outpatients per 1,000 of the population had reached the astonishing figure of 459. It need hardly be added that the Mater headed the list in this respect.[16]

Malley went on to say that because of the overcrowding, this department was not being used to the advantage of either the public or the medical staff. Here he quotes from the First General Report of the Hospitals Commission, published in 1936:

> 1. The absence of an almonry system,[17] whereby applicants to extern Departments are seen and their social conditions ascertained, favours abuse of the outpatient departments of most Irish hospitals.
> 2. The result of this abuse is usually the overcrowding of the extern departments of the hospitals and the consequent inability of the medical staff to devote the time necessary for correct diagnosis and treatment of genuine cases... etc.[18]

Malley saw the need to 'weed out' two particular groups from the attendees at this time: those who could avail of free medical services elsewhere and those who ought to be attending their general practitioner. He continued:

It is not difficult to understand the plight of the doctor in charge of an outpatient department when faced by such an ill-assorted multitude of patients. It is not unusual for him to see from fifty to one hundred patients in the three morning hours. His examination of these cases must of necessity be perfunctory; it is difficult for him to give sustained attention for more than a few minutes to any one patient. With experience he develops a 'sixth sense' in selecting those cases which need urgent attention ...[19]

This situation continued until the early 1930s, when it became obvious that a much larger building was needed at the Mater. In 1932, a large extension was planned which would open directly on to the North Circular Road, a three-storey building connected to the east wing by a corridor on the first floor. It consisted of a large outpatients area at ground-floor level, a laboratory on the first floor and a medical residence on the second floor. It was opened on 16 April 1936.

The 1936 outpatients department. The wooden benches have been replaced by more comfortable seating, but the department was very much 'of its time'.

The new outpatients department (OPD) was a welcome development, even if, from a design point of view, it was a functional building, somewhat of its time. The waiting area provided was like a very large hall with about eight clinical areas opening off it and a corridor going through it to the North Circular Road. The walls and floors were of green terrazzo and the name of the speciality was given above each clinic door. Long wooden benches were provided for the patients to sit on as they waited to be seen.

The temporary home for the outpatients clinic on Dorset Street, which has now been replaced by the new facilities in the Whitty Building.

A significant design problem was that the casualty department, or emergency department as it is now known (ED), opened off the outpatients waiting area – at a distance from the entrance. Consequently, all ambulances unloaded their stretchers on the street outside the OPD and wheeled the injured person to casualty, past all the people sitting on the benches awaiting their appointments. This lasted until 1970, when a separate emergency department entrance was built with its own ambulance bay.

From a hygiene perspective, the building was excellent, but from a comfort aspect, it was cold and uninviting. Another issue was that, as part of the development a pharmacy was built, again reflecting how outpatient departments functioned at the time: most patients went home from their visit with a medication, dispensed by the hospital pharmacist before they left, the vast expense of which quickly became unmanageable. The pharmacy served the entire hospital as well as the outpatients department.[20]

The overcrowding in the outpatients department continued until the Health Act of 1956 raised the department to consultant status. According to Dr Bryan Alton, this 'speedily diminished the patient reservoir.'[21] The OPD remained in this location until recent times when pressure for space in the emergency department meant that it needed to be relocated elsewhere. In 2007, it was decided to move the department off campus. After a difficult search, it was relocated to 81–84 Dorset Street in February 2008. The Mater Clinic, as it was called, opened on 21 July 2008. Since then, things have moved on again, and in June 2012 a beautiful new outpatients department was opened in the new Whitty Building. In this 21st-century space, each clinic is a separate self-contained unit consisting of a waiting area, a secretarial office, a number of well-equipped consulting rooms, examination areas, and a nurses' office. The emphasis is on the privacy, dignity and comfort of all patients.

The new waiting area in Whitty Building.

Twelve clinics now operate from here: all surgery clinics, oncology, neurology, respiratory, dermatology, endocrinology, cardiology, nephrology, ear, nose and throat (ENT), infectious diseases, psychiatry and all blood conditions.

The airy atrium of the outpatients department in the new Whitty Building. The colourful tapestries are by Patrick Scott. Each clinic, with its own waiting area, opens off the atrium.

The Emergency Department

The number of patients arriving to the emergency department has increased over the years. This increase is slightly more complex than in any other department in that the numbers coming through its doors (on stretchers and ambulant patients) has continued to grow year by year, especially from 1970 on, but at the same time, the 'through-put' of patients in the department has increasingly been slowed down due to the non-availability of hospital beds. This was never anticipated when

Nurses await the arrival of Princess Grace on her visit to the hospital in 1961. Note the sign for the old casualty department.

the place was extended in 1969. The large up-to-date emergency department opened on 17 February 2013. A pre-opening notice circulated in January of that year gives an outline of what will be available to patients:

The Mater Emergency Department provides a 24-hour emergency service, 365 days a year, and sees in the region of 50,000 patients annually. Approximately 21% of patients attending are maintained in hospital for in-patient treatment. The core function of the department is to provide resuscitation for critically ill and injured patients. In addition expert service is delivered to patients with lower acuity presentations including medical, surgical and traumatic cases. Patients presenting to the department undergo an initial assessment (*triage*) soon after arrival to determine the nature and severity of their problem. Thereafter they are treated according to clinical need as soon as possible.

● *Ambulances outside the 1970s emergency department.*

Accommodation in the new emergency department includes:

● A resuscitation room: the resuscitation capacity of the new department provides an increase in excess of 60% capacity compared to present capability, reflecting the increase in the number of patients attending with critical illness and injury;

● 15 new single-patient examination and treatment cubicles for patients with complex and urgent medical complaints;

● A dedicated CT/X-ray suite;

● An ambulatory care area for management of low-impact trauma cases and ambulant patients suffering from less serious medical conditions; and

● Space for liaison personnel (e.g. psychiatric liaison nurse, GP liaison nurse and a social worker).

A twelve-bay acute medical assessment unit is accommodated in the acute floor in line with clinical care programmes. Special attention has been paid to the quality of the physical environment for patients, staff and visitors, reflecting contemporary architecture and design. Great importance has been placed on maximising natural light into the facility. The design team has adopted an integrated approach to support a low-energy and sustainable design solution, which will add to this truly modern emergency department.

Another development which brings outpatient care into the 21st century is the Mater-Smithfield Rapid Injury Clinic, which opened in April 2010, about 2km south of the main hospital. This clinic, the first public clinic of its kind, was organised to offer a service to 'walk-in' patients who have minor

The reception area at the Smithfield Rapid Injury Clinic.

injuries, thereby reducing the number of these patients coming to the emergency department. The service has grown in popularity and the numbers attending are growing steadily each year.

1   Nolan, E. (1991), *One Hundred Years – a History of the School of Nursing and of Developments at the Mater Misericordiae Hospital 1891–1991*, Goldpress Ltd, p 94.
2   Medical Board Minutes, 5 December 1890.
3   Sir Christopher Nixon was responsible for bringing Edmund McWeeney to the Mater in 1890.
4   Archbishop William Walsh was Archbishop of Dublin from 1885 to 1921.
5   *Report of the Mater Misericordiae Hospital Dublin (Under the care of the Sisters of Mercy) for the year 1904*, Dublin: Dollard Limited, 1905.
6   It is said that he produced at least 55 papers. Many of these were published in journals such as the *BMJ*, *The Lancet* and the *Irish Journal of Medical Science*.
7   *Mater Misericordiae Hospital 1861–1961*, pp 25–26.
8   It is unclear what exactly an Apse Coil is, but it it is possible that 'Apse' was the name of the firm who made the coil, an essential part of an X-ray machine.
9   *Report of the Mater Misericordiae Hospital Dublin (Under the care of the Sisters of Mercy) for the year 1911*, Dublin: Browne & Nolan Ltd, 1912, p 8.
10 *Report of the Mater Misericordiae Hospital Dublin (Under the care of the Sisters of Mercy) for the year 1913*, Dublin: Dollard Limited, 1913, pp 26–29.
11 *Report of the Mater Misericordiae Hospital Dublin (Under the care of the Sisters of Mercy) for the year 1928*, Dublin: Dollard Limited, p 47.
12 The hospital kitchen is currently in the Whitty Building.
13 Alton, B. (1961), *Centenary Mater Misericordiae Hospital, Dublin 1861–1961*, private publication, p 63.
14 Minutes of the Medical Board 14 October 1863, p 5.
15 Burdett, H.C. (1893), *Hospitals and Asylums of the World*, Churchill.
16 Malley, K. (1941), 'The Out-Patient Department', *Irish Journal of Medical Science*, No. 184, April, p 154.
17 Social work department.
18 Malley, K., op. cit.
19 Malley, K., op. cit., p 156.
20 The cost of this practice, when added to the cost of medications used at ward level and those given to discharged patients going home, left the Mater with an inordinate bill, which the Hospitals Commission found hard to accept when they studied the hospital deficit, particularly in 1937.
21 Alton, B., op. cit., p 63.

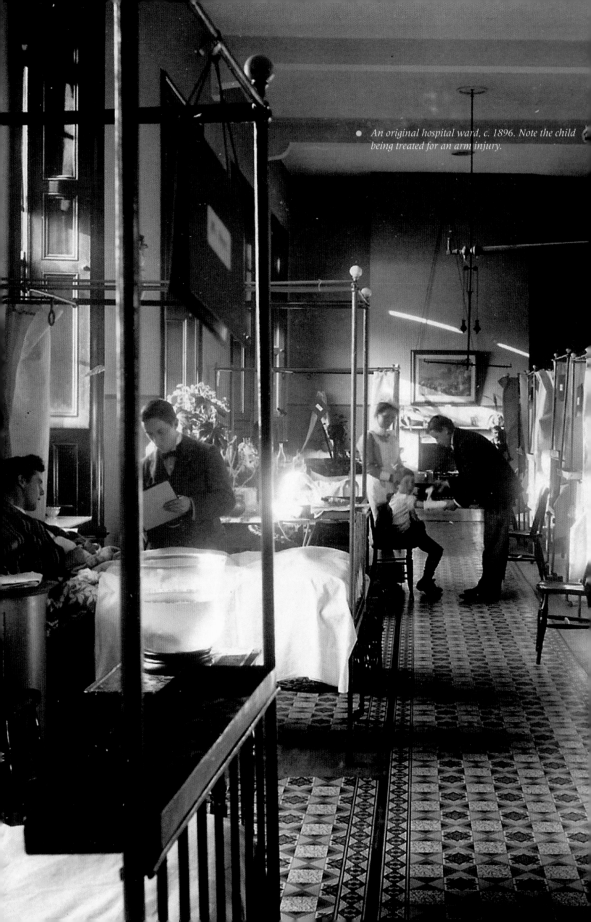

An original hospital ward, c. 1896. Note the child being treated for an arm injury.

CHAPTER 6

Poverty and Suffering in a City of Discontent: the Beginning of a New Century

ueen Victoria arrived in Dublin on 1 April 1900. This was her fourth and last visit to the city, but the response she received from the public was less enthusiastic than on previous visits. Although many thousands of people turned out to greet her each day, many stayed away, especially the Catholic clergy who felt that, as monarch, she had failed the country. Both city and country were riven with poverty, disease and discontent. The population, particularly of the cities, was malnourished and silent killers such as TB abounded. At the time, the death rate in the city was 'as bad as Calcutta, and the city's slums were amongst the worst in the world. Over 20,000 families lived in one-room dwellings. There were often more than ten families in town houses that were built for one upper-class family in the eighteenth and nineteenth centuries.'[1]

In the 20 years to come, Dublin city would be convulsed by strikes, demonstrations, and rebellion, set against the long shadow cast by World War I.

It was said that the reason for Victoria's visit was to encourage the Irish to join the British Army, then fighting the Boer War. The city of Dublin was lavishly decorated, including Eccles Street, which had a triumphal arch erected over it.[2] On Tuesday 24 April at 4.30 p.m., the Queen set off in her horse-drawn carriage from the Viceregal Lodge in the Phoenix Park to visit the Mater. She was accompanied by her youngest daughter, Princess Beatrice. According to the *Freeman's Journal*:

> The route taken was through Blackhorse Lane to Cabra Road and on to the Mater Misericordiae Hospital, the approaches to which were packed with people. In front of the main entrance to the Hospital on Eccles Street the Royal cavalcade pulled up. The front of the building was decorated with flags around the Ionic pillars, the Irish flag floating from the roof. The Hospital is the largest general hospital in Dublin[3]... The Sisters of the Community, Sisters of Mercy,

members of the medical staff, the nursing staff and others all occupied the steps. When the carriage drew up the Queen was received by the Rev. Mother, Sr Genevive Burke; Sr Liguori Keenan; the Lady Superior, Sr Berchmans Barry; Bishop Donnelly; the Very Rev. Mgr Molloy, and the following members of the Medical and Nursing staff...[4]

The presentation of medical and nursing staff followed; Sir Christopher Nixon named each as they came forward. At the close of this part of the ceremonial, three young ladies, daughters of members of the medical staff, namely Miss Phyllis Lentaigne, Miss Alice Chance, and Miss Emily Murphy, were conducted from the steps to the Royal carriage where they jointly handed to the Queen a magnificent bouquet of flowers. After this her Majesty called over Sir Christopher Nixon, and, addressing him said, 'I am greatly pleased with my visit. This is a very large hospital; how many beds have you in occupation?' Sir Christopher replied, 'There are, your Majesty, 340, but quite 500 souls sleep under the roof every night and the hospital is managed exclusively by the Sisters of Mercy and supported by voluntary contributions'. The Queen then in a few words, graciously expressed her satisfaction at finding so excellent a work in progress under the auspices of the institution, and the pleasure which the visit had afforded her. Thus was brought to a close a brief but deeply interesting ceremony, and her Majesty drove away amidst an enormous outburst of cheering which she repeatedly acknowledged by bowing to the right and left.[5]

Queen Victoria's coach pulls up to the front of the Mater on her visit in 1900, organised by Sir Christopher Nixon.

The ceremony took place on Eccles Street because the Queen was unable, due to her age and poor health, to leave her carriage.[6]

There were other occasions of good cheer in these difficult times. On 24 September 1911, the hospital celebrated its Golden Jubilee. The 'great and the good' gathered in the hospital chapel for a solemn High Mass, celebrated by Archdeacon Fricker. Bishop Nicholas Donnelly presided in place of the Archbishop, who was unavoidably absent. The music and choir were provided by St Peter's Church, Phibsborough. The organist was the famous Joseph O'Brien. Among the invited guests were the Earl and Countess of Fingall, the Lord Chancellor and Mrs Redmond Barry, Judge Doyle, President of Maynooth College, Monsignor Mannix, Sir John and Lady Ross of Bladensburg, the Lord Chief Baron and many others, including all of the medical staff and their families. A luncheon was held in the Pillar Room after the Mass. According to one newspaper of the day:

Mater Misericordiæ Hospital.

REPORT FOR THE YEAR 1911.

IN presenting to the friends and benefactors of the Hospital the Report of its progress for 1911, the Sisters of Mercy are glad to be able to state that the Hospital has efficiently carried out its mission of ministering to the wants of the sick poor, not merely of Dublin, but of the whole country.

Notwithstanding the large number of patients received within its walls, the Hospital has enjoyed complete immunity from the spread of disease of an epidemic or preventable character among its inmates.

The Sisters would call attention to the fact that the "Mater" is now 50 years founded. On the 24th of September of this year the "Golden Jubilee" of the opening of the Hospital was celebrated in a befitting manner. The celebration took the form of solemn High Mass followed by Benediction and *Te Deum* in the chapel of the Hospital. The Most Rev. Dr. Donnelly, Bishop of Canea, presided in the absence from home of His Grace the Archbishop of Dublin.

Many influential citizens were present who, during those fifty years of its existence, had watched with interest the Hospital's rise and development, and could truly say that the "Mater" has admirably carried out the ideal of Mother Catherine McAuley (Foundress of the "Mercy" Order), whose ambition it was to establish "a large Hospital where the only qualifications required of those seeking admission were poverty, sickness, and the need of that proper care which they could not receive in their poor homes." All this the "Mater" has done for half a century. It depends now for its working, as it depended for its establishment, entirely upon private charity.

The hospital's annual report for the year 1911, the Mater Hospital's Golden Jubilee year.

Bishop Donnelly, who on rising was received with applause, said: 'It is my privilege to read to you on this occasion a telegram received from the Pope, it is to the following effect:

"The Holy Father, conscious of the magnificent work done by the Mater Misericordiae Hospital for suffering humanity in Dublin during the half century of its existence, cordially imparts the Apostolic Benediction to the institution, the staff, and all the benefactors of the Hospital, to which he prays the God of Mercy may grant many years of further increasing usefulness."'

Sir Christopher Nixon, having spoken of the work of the hospital and the history of the place, conducted a tour of the wards, along with the Mother Superior and Sir Arthur Chance.[7]

The hospital was looking magnificent. It had been completely painted in the months before the Jubilee at a cost of £1,031-17s-10d. This was not the only cost incurred by the hospital in 1911: in the early years of the century, the hospital was linked in to the various city systems (water, drainage, electricity) which had reached the north side of the city by then. The hospital was lit by electricity in 1909, ending the use of gas lights. The new drainage system cost the hospital £1,171-1s-4d. Plumbing was ongoing for a number of years and was a significant expense from year to year. In addition, a new central heating system was installed. Radiators took the place of the open coal fires in the wards, corridors and departments. Modernisation came at a cost. Nonetheless, it was decided to go ahead with the repainting after the structural work: even the farmyard buildings got a coat of whitewash! This meant the place was looking clean and fresh for the Jubilee. The Sisters were very proud to be able to 'switch on the light' and show off the beautiful architecture of the Mater during the Golden Jubilee celebrations in 1911.

No Bread for the Patients

Apart from the Jubilee, there was very little cause for celebration in Dublin at this time. The strikes, which were beginning to become increasingly frequent in a city of unrest, affected the hospital in a number of ways. A week after the jubilee celebrations, the hospital faced unprecedented difficulties when they found themselves with no bread, as the two bakeries that supplied the Mater went on strike. The other city hospitals, except Jervis Street Hospital, were being supplied by non-striking bakeries. So the nuns at the Mater were in real difficulty. The convent at Baggot Street initially came to the rescue, making bread every day and delivering it to the hospital, but this was deemed to be 'strike breaking', and quite apart from that, the nuns weren't able to make enough to meet the needs of the hospital. According to one of the newspapers:

> The extent to which the city hospitals and charitable institutions have been affected by the shortage in the bread supply consequent upon the dispute in the bakery trade could scarcely be exaggerated. The Mother Superior of the Sisters of Mercy in charge of the Mater Misericordiae Hospital told our representative on Saturday that the institution was dreadfully affected by the strike. They had hardly any bread since the supply suddenly ceased. The contractors to the hospital were Sir Joseph Downes and Mr. Kennedy, and they were unable to supply their customers as their men had *'gone out'*. 'Are the patients suffering seriously from want of bread?' asked our representative. 'They certainly are,' the Rev. Mother replied. 'They are eating the crusts now,' she added with a smile. 'You see, we have over 300 persons, including nurses, to provide bread for.' 'And how are you managing?' 'Since the strike started, we have been getting a few loaves every day from Baggot Street Convent, and picking up a loaf here and there wherever we could get it, and the Sisters have been baking some cakes

in the little ovens they have (in the ward kitchens).' Our representative was informed that the Army Service Corps authorities had been making inquiries at the hospitals as to the amount of bread required for the daily consumption.[8]

This last sentence reveals that the military in the barracks at Islandbridge telephoned all the hospitals in difficulty, saying that they were prepared to bake bread in the event of any hospital shortage. It would appear that the Mater did not avail of this offer.

Rioting on O'Connell Street during the Lockout, 1913. (© Alamy.)

At this time in Dublin, morale among ordinary workers was low, due to their dismal housing conditions and poverty. Consequently anything was likely to act as tinder to spark off serious clashes within the city. This happened towards the end of August 1913, when a worker incident at the Dublin Tramways Company provoked a serious upheaval: the city's tram system ground to a halt, leading to protests which absolutely paralysed the city. It wasn't too long before serious rioting broke out, as a consequence of the 'lockout' strike.

All the city hospitals had an influx of serious casualties. Over a two-day period, Jervis Street Hospital received 320 patients.[9] No record of how many were brought to the Mater exists, but it got its share, especially as it was providing an emergency service throughout the night. When rioting broke out, people fled down side streets only to be met by baton-wielding police. In Finglas, police opened fire to disperse rioters. The lockout led to a sympathetic strike which crippled all transport including the ports. The dockers at Dublin Port refused to unload the ships. Food ran short and goods for the hospitals, including medicines, remained unloaded. This created a difficult situation for the Mater, especially at one stage when they were placed on the strike 'blacklist', and no supplies addressed to the hospital were unloaded. By January 1914, the strike, having failed, came to an end, leaving a city on the brink of starvation and with a restless workforce.

The Great War: 1914–1918

Six months after the 1913 lockout, Europe was plunged into one of the bitterest wars ever experienced. About 80,000 Irish men signed up immediately to go and fight in the British Army, mainly for employment reasons. About 27,000 to 35,000 Irish soldiers died in World War I.[10]

The war wounded were transported to the Mater and other Dublin hospitals on hospital ships, such as this one. (© Imperial War Museum.)

In October, the first of the 'hospital ships' carrying wounded soldiers back from the Front for treatment began to arrive in Ireland, to Cork (Cobh),[11] where they were met by special hospital trains.

The hospital ships formed part of the War Office plan for the care of war casualties.[12] Some of the ships took up to six weeks to reach Ireland or England. Alas, some never reached their destination, because they were torpedoed on the way. When they reached Ireland, the receiving hospitals and the names of the injured were printed in the daily newspapers, to enable relatives to find their loved ones. The majority of those who arrived in hospital ships were British soldiers. On Sunday 3 October 1915, the *Oxfordshire* arrived in Dublin with '900 men and officers on board'.[13] Most of the men had been injured during the Anglo-French offensive at Artois-Loos in September 1915. Unfortunately a serious fog prevented them from landing for 18 hours after arriving in Dublin. When eventually they did, some of the patients were sent to Belfast in two hospital trains. The Mater received 48 patients from this ship, none of whom was Irish.

During the course of the war, a total of 46 of these ships arrived in Dublin, carrying an estimated 19,255 patients.[14] This was an improvement on the 1854 Crimean post-war situation, where thousands of Irish died and thousands more were injured and on return to Ireland were ignored. This time the War Office in London arranged for hospitals in Dublin to receive the wounded, managed by the Red Cross. The best-known centre established was a hospital in Dublin Castle which looked after a total of 250 war victims. In order to provide the necessary medical staff, each of the large teaching hospitals was asked to volunteer a physician and a surgeon to work there. Dr Maurice Hayes, the Mater's radiologist and honorary secretary to the Irish Medical War Committee, served as radiologist in the Castle Hospital.[15] Many of the Mater nurses served as volunteers. Furthermore, the nuns organised for a number of nurses who wished to do some war service to travel to various battle zones. According to the 1917 Annual Report: 'About 30 of these [Mater Nurses] are now serving at various hospitals in France, Salonika, Egypt, and Palestine, as well as in England and at home. Numbers of nurses no longer in the employment of the hospital are also engaged in war service'.[16] A number of junior medical staff also took time off from the hospital to do war service.

When the pressure of work increased in the hospital due to the influx of the war wounded, senior medical staff began to complain of the staff shortages, especially in the operating theatre. In a letter from Sir Arthur Chance, surgeon, to the chairman of the medical board[17] he described his difficulties as follows: 'I have had to perform extensive and difficult operations with an inexperienced Resident Pupil as anaesthetist, and a House Surgeon as my sole assistant!'

At times, the War Office efforts to care for the wounded resulted in undue interference in the work of the hospital. On 22 November 1914, W.M. Russell, the Surgeon General, wrote to the Mother Superior the following letter, which she passed on to the medical board:

War Office,
London
22 November 1914

Sir,

With reference to the appointment of Sir Chas. Ball and Sir Thomas Myles, to be consulting Surgeons for the Army in Ireland. I am directed to inform you that it is intended that they should mutually arrange their spheres of work.

They will be authorised to visit all official and voluntary institutions where there are wounded, to ensure that the best possible surgical assistance is being afforded.

They will represent any shortcomings to you whether on the part of individuals or in the matter of stores or equipment, or in the case of urgency will take such steps as the occasions demands.

They will carry out surgery themselves in cases in which they consider such a course desirable, and will advise others engaged in operative work.

In general terms they will exercise supervision over the surgical work in connection with the Military Hospitals and other institutions in Ireland, in which wounded are treated, and will keep you informed of the results of their observations.

A copy of this communication should be sent to each of them.

I am, Sir,
Your obedient servant,

(Sd) W.M. Russell, Surg. Gen. for D.G. A.M.S.
J.M. Hearn, Lt: Col R.A.M.C. i/c Expeditionary Force Wounded[18]

This letter, read out at a medical board meeting, raised an angry response among those present and they directed that the following reply be sent to the War Office immediately:

MATER MISERICORDIAE HOSPITAL
DUBLIN

5 December 1914
Sir,

At a meeting of the Medical Board of the Mater Misericordiae Hospital held today, the following resolution was adopted unanimously:

In reply to the circular 4078, dated 'War Office, London, 22/11/14' and transmitted by Lt. Col. Hearn, the Medical Board of the Mater Misericordiae Hospital beg to inform Lt. Col. Hearn that they will not permit anyone, other than a member of the hospital staff, to supervise or criticise the treatment of, or to operate on, the patients under their care.

This resolution is in no way personal to the gentlemen appointed by the War Office.

The staff of the 'Mater' have given their services ungrudgingly to the wounded soldiers, officers and men, without thought of remuneration. Apparently their action has not earned immunity from insult.

I am, Sir,
Your obedient servant,
(Sd.) Arthur Chance

The secretary was directed to transmit a copy of the War Office letter, together with the board's reply, to the standing committee of the Dublin clinical hospitals.[19] In due course a meeting was arranged and it was agreed that the Dublin clinical hospitals would not comply with the War Office orders. This action led to a prolonged correspondence between the medical board of the Mater, the War Office in London and the Surgeon General of the Army Medical Service, with apologies and explanations being issued by the Service. However, this did not stop the Service writing to the hospital on 2 January 1915 to say they were carrying out an inspection in three days' time. The reply from the Mater to the War Office was somewhat caustic but it did assure them that:

The Resident staff will be instructed to afford you any assistance in their power; and in the event of you requiring further information, the Medical Board will, I am sure, be glad to help you in any way it can.

This letter, signed by Sir Arthur Chance on 3 January 1915, concluded as follows:

> I am glad to have the opportunity of stating to you both, that the board had the fullest confidence in your discretion, and never desired to limit your inspection. But they thought, and still think, that the rights so brusquely claimed by the War Office were the less defensible because admittedly unnecessary, and by your courtesy, inoperative.
> I am, Gentlemen,
> Yours truly
> (Sd.) Arthur Chance
> Secretary Medical Board
>
> P.S. I have sent a copy of this letter to my two surgical colleagues, and I will submit it to the next meeting of the Board so that it may be formally endorsed.[20]

The matter came before the board on 20 January 1915, to a meeting chaired by Dr John Lentaigne who, only a couple of months previously, had lost one of his sons in the first battle of Aisne in France and whose other son was still there. It cannot have been easy for him to have to deal with war issues. It obviously took its toll, for less than four months later he died suddenly, to the absolute shock of his Mater colleagues. The hospital had lost one of its best surgeons, and the Red Cross Hospital in Dublin Castle one of its main managerial advisers.

When the war casualties began to flood in, a number of serious decisions had to be taken in the Mater. Beds had to be made available for large numbers of men suffering from catastrophic injuries together with the consequences of a prolonged sea journey. The government decided that all patients in the hospital suffering from 'fevers' would be moved from the Mater to other hospitals.

Filling wards in the hospital with British army personnel suffering from appalling war injuries made enormous demands on the staff, especially the nurses. The difficulties encountered depended on the war zone the patients had come from. Some of the most difficult cases were the victims of 'trench warfare' or suffering from 'trench fever'. A consignment of soliders who had fought through the winter months and who arrived in Dublin (and the Mater) on 17 February 1915 are described as follows:

> The great majority of the soldiers were suffering from so-called 'frost bite'. The condition appears to be a neuritis brought about by prolonged standing in flooded trenches. The number of actual bullet or shell wounds is considerably smaller than in the case of the first consignment of wounded sent to Dublin.[21]

The management of wounds without the aid of antibiotics became an art in itself. Many had to be surgically debrided under anaesthetic to remove bullets and 'foreign bodies'. Another medical problem encountered was that of so-called 'shell shock'. It would appear that some soldiers suffered emotional breakdown and became exceedingly distraught due to their conflict experiences. At the time, their condition was not understood by those dealing with them. Initially their distress was thought to have an organic cause and so, in increasing numbers, they were sent to hospitals for treatment. As the war dragged on, more and more of these cases of 'shell shock' arrived to the Mater and other hospitals.[22] The treatment of it at the time was somewhat contentious in the medical literature[23] and so each doctor treated these patients as he thought best. It was many years later before the nature of this stress phenomenon was understood by the medical profession.

As each hospital ship landed, the various conditions the patients were suffering from changed little, except that the incidence of diseases such as malaria increased among those who came from places like Gallipoli. Ultimately things took a turn for the worse when the Germans began to target and sink the hospital ships.

As is clear from the above correspondence between the hospital and the War Office, the latter kept a close eye on the management of the war wounded in the Dublin hospitals, including the Mater, much to the occasional annoyance of the medical staff. For example, by the end of 1916, the War Office was concerned at the number of tetanus cases. A communication was sent to the hospitals in January 1917 advising on how tetanus should be treated. At a meeting of the Mater medical board on 15 January 1917, Dr Alexander Blayney, Secretary, recorded:

> A communication from the Military Authorities, making suggestions with regard to the treatment of wounded soldiers to prevent Tetanus, were read.
>
> The secretary was directed to reply that the members of the Board, while reserving the right to treat those under their care according to their own judgement, would be glad to receive any suggestions which the Military Authorities would wish to make.[24]

There were no cases of tetanus recorded in the report for that year or the following year in the Mater.

The war effort came at a considerable expense for the Dublin hospitals. The War Office had agreed to pay four shillings per day for each occupied bed, but there are some doubts in the literature that it actually worked out that way. The 1917 Annual Report of the Mater reveals that they received a total of £1,982-12s-0d from the 'War Office, for Maintenance, etc. of Wounded Soldiers.'[25]

On 11 November 1918, after four years of a very bloody war, an Armistice was signed in France. Ireland, by that time, was struggling with the bitter after-effects of the 1916 Easter Rising. In addition, the so-called 'Spanish flu', pandemic of 1918 had arrived to our shores, just as our troops were coming home to a very different country.

The 1916 Rising

The Easter Rising took all the hospitals in Dublin by surprise and presented them with a new problem, a sudden influx of injured people from the streets and buildings of the city. For some hospitals, like the Mater, this influx coincided with the arrival of British wounded soldiers in Dublin. Managing this situation required a careful diplomatic strategy, as did managing the political sensitivities of the staff.

The Rising commenced on 24 April 1916, but the Mater didn't receive any casualties on the first day of fighting, because the route to the Mater on that day was blocked by a cordon placed by the British Army along Parnell Street to prevent access to O'Connell Street. However, the following day, the injured began to arrive and the situation changed dramatically. According to an account given by one of the nuns:[26]

> During Easter week Mr Blayney (Surgeon) was on duty in the hospital. He never left it for the whole week. He was operating day and night. There was neither gas nor electricity and he had to operate by the light of candles brought from the sacristy. There was no sterilisation of instruments or dressings as there was no boiling water available, yet there was no case of sepsis following any of the operations. We were instructed that patients with abdominal wounds should be brought straight to the theatre without waiting to remove any clothes except the shoes and stockings.

> Tuesday was the first day that any of the wounded were brought in. Nine of these were detained and the rest were treated and discharged. One of the badly wounded, Margaret Nolan, a fore-woman in Jacob's Factory, died that day, as also did James Kelly, a schoolboy who was shot through the skull. Another schoolboy, John Healy aged 14, a member of the Fianna whose brain was hanging all over his forehead when he was brought in, died after two days. Another man, Patrick Harris, died also on Tuesday of laceration of the brain.

> Another wounded man, Patrick McCrea, was brought in. He was suffering from wounds in the hand and leg which he told me he got in the Post Office fighting. His wounds being slight, he was sent out of the G.P.O. with a dispatch. He got shelter somewhere and was brought to the hospital for treatment covered up in a cart load of cabbages. Almost immediately a G man called McIntyre came to the hospital. He identified McCrea and took up his position on the corridor outside the ward to keep him under observation. He did not even go out to get his meals and I was unwilling to supply him with any. One of the nuns thought it a pity not to give him something to eat and brought him to the kitchenette.

A medical student made various suggestions for dealing with McIntyre, including chloroforming him! In spite of McIntyre's vigilance, McCrea managed to get away safely on the 4th May. While McIntyre was in the kitchenette having his dinner, one of the Sisters who had made all the necessary preparations beforehand, got the key leading from the pathology department to the street.[27] She took a nurse, called M.O'C from Kerry into her confidence. The latter brought McCrea along the corridor through the mortuary to the exit door, let him out and locked the door behind him. The whole thing did not take five minutes and the Sister replaced the key in its lock without its having been missed. McCrea was afterwards an active Volunteer and I heard he was in the armoured car that tried to rescue Sean MacEoin from gaol.

On Wednesday, the number of wounded increased, twenty-one being detained. Two of them were already dead when brought in and six died in the course of the day. Twenty-one wounded were detained for treatment on Thursday. Seven of them died within a week and another on the 14th May. Eight of the nine wounded brought in on the Friday and who were detained for treatment died in the hospital. Only eight were detained on Saturday. One of these was already dead and another insane. The latter was removed to the Richmond Lunatic Asylum after a few days. Only one wounded man was detained for treatment on Sunday. Practically all the wounded men who were brought in were Volunteers, but very few of them were in uniform. There was at least one looter brought in. He was very drunk and was found wearing a couple of suits of clothes and was in possession of many other accessories including a toy revolver which was large enough to be taken for a real one.

This was a particularly difficult week for the hospital. Like all the other hospitals in Dublin, food ran short during the week, but once the citizens of the city realised this, they rallied round and helped to transport food to the various hospitals. Another problem was the number of dead now filling the mortuary, and the many distraught relatives searching for their loved ones. Communication systems were not developed enough at the time to be of much help, so the newspapers came to the rescue, daily printing lists of the dead and injured and what hospitals they had been taken to. Again, because of space difficulties at the city morgue, many inquests were held at the hospitals where the victims had been treated. In the case of the Mater, the inquests were held in the Pillar Room. Most of them were short and little more than a formality.

The Death of Thomas Ashe

Thomas Ashe was one of the 1916 leaders and a well-known member of the Irish Volunteers, of which he was Commanding Officer of the 5th batallion. This batallion had fought at Ashbourne, Co. Meath, in a battle which resulted in the death of eleven RIC

This corridor runs the length of the front of the building. It was along this corridor that the crowds filed to view the remains of IRA man Thomas Ashe.

officers. Ashe escaped execution in the immediate aftermath of the rebellion and was released from prison in June 1917 as part of an amnesty on prisoners. He was rearrested later that year, following a 'seditious' speech, and sentenced to two years in prison. Eventually Ashe and six of his fellow prisoners went on hunger strike. Ashe was put into a straitjacket and forced-fed by the authorities.[28] Unfortunately this was mismanaged and he had to be admitted as an emergency patient to the Mater, where he died on 25 September 1917.

After his death, word quickly went around and about thirty to forty members of the Volunteers assembled outside the hospital on Eccles Street. That night a number of them acted as a guard of honour beside his remains in the ward where he was laid out in the uniform which he had worn during the Easter Rising. They also formed a guard of honour in front of the hospital on Eccles Street and another on the North Circular Road.

The following morning, crowds gathered on Eccles Street. Towards 8.00 a.m., the Volunteers moved the people into a formal queue, four deep, and they began to file up the steps to St Raphael's Ward. In silence, the crowd moved past the remains with its guard of honour. Twelve hours later, the Mother Superior thought it was time to close the hospital, by which time, it was calculated, about 15,000 people had filed past to pay their respects. There were as many more still waiting out on Eccles Street. The hospital was opened again at eight o'clock the following morning and the people resumed filing past.

On the morning of 27 September the coroner requested that the hospital pathologist, Professor McWeeney, carry out a post-mortem examination. Because of the manner of Ashe's death, a number of significant people either requested or were instructed by the coroner to attend the procedure. Among them were Sir Thomas Myles (RAMC), Sir Arthur Chance (Mater), Dr Dowdall (for Mountjoy Prison), Surgeon P. Hayes (Mater), Dr O'Kelly and Dr Kathleen Lynn. After the post mortem, McWeeney prepared his statement for the inquest, which was to take place in the Pillar Room in the hospital at noon. The death of Ashe was a big news story, and all the newspapers sent staff to cover it, but the number of others who turned up, cramming into the Pillar Room was unprecedented. Many of them were there in an official capacity but some came just to watch and listen to the proceedings.[29] At the end of the morning, the inquest was adjourned and arrangements were made to transport the remains to the Pro Cathedral for Requiem Mass the following morning.

> The body was borne to the hearse outside the hospital under the directions of Mr Eamonn de Valera MP in his capacity as Commandant of the Irish Volunteers. The coffin was draped in the Republican colours. The procession was headed by a number of picked volunteers... Upwards of fifty Catholic clergymen, several of whom had travelled long distances from the country, formed a striking feature in the procession... The procession was swelled by two hundred National School teachers, large numbers of University students, the Boy Scouts and thousands of different classes of the public...[30]

Thomas Ashe, who died in the Mater while receiving medical treatment following a hunger strike. (Courtesy of the National Library of Ireland.)

The funeral at Glasnevin Cemetery the following day, organised by Ashe's friend Michael Collins, once again brought thousands out on to the streets of Dublin to bid Ashe farewell. The funeral oration was delivered by Michael Collins. Thomas Ashe was buried in the Republican plot in the cemetery.

The 1918–1919 Influenza Pandemic

While people were mourning the death of their loved ones on the battlefields, or waiting anxiously for their return home, another 'enemy' made its appearance in Ireland – the 'Spanish flu' or 'black flu'. The reason for the latter name was that the skin of sufferers turned black and ultimately made the bodies of victims unrecognisable. Early in 1918, this flu made its appearance in the north-east of the country and quickly spread.

The 'Spanish flu' pandemic is considered to have caused more deaths over a shorter period of time than World War I. Closer to home, this flu gave rise to a number of problems for the Mater (and other hospitals as well). The Mater beds were already filled with war-wounded soldiers, some who also had the flu, and then very quickly, especially in late 1918, large numbers of patients began to arrive to the hospital. These patients were dying with pneumonia or simply of the flu. The mortality rate was so high that some of them never even needed a bed. On 23 October 1918 the Assistant Medical Officer at the Department of Health came to review the situation at the Mater and to see what could be done about it. He announced that he had come to:

> ascertain how far the accommodation was interfered with by the occupancy of the wards by the military. The intention is to request the authorities to relieve the hospitals of soldier patients by providing for them in military institutions. If not, the Government has power to commandeer institutions which would serve as such. The death toll is growing daily. Travelling in trains, tramway cars and buses should be avoided as much as possible.[31]

The following day, Sir Charles Cameron, Chief Medical Officer, sent a message to the Mater saying that 'the military authorities had informed him that they would send no more patients to the civil hospitals during the epidemic.'[32] The wounded soldiers were to be accommodated instead in a makeshift hospital in Glasnevin, a mile from the Mater.[33]

In an attempt to curb the spread of infection, the city medical officer ordered that all schools, cinemas, churches and any place people might congregate should be closed. He ordered that:

> Flushing of the whole of the city with carbolic acid should start on Saturday… Washing down of the streets to be continued until the epidemic abated.[34]

Eventually all trams and buses were taken out of service twice a day for disinfection. The number of transport crews gradually diminished, as did the police, due to absenteeism.

At the Mater, the incidence of the disease and the death rate among staff became a concern. There was a serious shortage of nurses; indeed, nurses and doctors throughout the country became flu victims. Some of them died. Requests were being received daily by the hospital for the loan of both doctors and nurses, but particularly for doctors. On 25 October the Chaplain, Reverend Thomas Murray, died. He was very popular and the newspapers wrote a lengthy obituary about him.[35]

The death rate continued to rise exponentially. Soon the hospital mortuary filled and couldn't be emptied, because the option for families to bring the body home was not advisable. The city faced an enormous crisis. At Glasnevin Cemetery approximately 50–70 flu victims per day were arriving for burial. By November, coffins were in short supply and many of the gravediggers were sick with the flu too. The only solution the authorities could think of, according to the *Freeman's Journal*, was to open some of the vaults in the cemetery and store the bodies there until the situation improved. The paper went on to say:

> No diminution has taken place in the numbers of funerals to the city cemeteries. There were 35 burials at Glasnevin yesterday, and ten bodies had to be placed in the vaults...

> Forty burials took place early yesterday and 18 bodies were laid in the vaults. During the afternoon there were 27 other funerals to the cemetery and the remains were also transferred to the vaults awaiting interment. Fourteen funerals took place to Mount Jerome Cemetery on Monday and 11 yesterday.[36]

This flu pandemic presented in three waves worldwide and lasted until 1920. The mortality rate in Ireland was extremely high and thought to be in excess of 20,000 due directly to the flu, with many others dying as a result of of pneumonia or complications of the illness.

1   UCC Multitext Project in Irish History: Dublin 1913, Strike and Lockout, www.multitext.ucc.ie.
2   Cappock, M. (1999), *The Royal visits to Dublin*, Dublin, Historical Record, Vol. 52, No. 2, p 98. Available at: http://www.jstor.org/stable/30101221.
3   The *Freeman's Journal* here gives an account of the history of the building of the hospital.
4   Every member of staff (and their relatives who were present) was listed.
5   *Freeman's Journal*, 25 April 1900.
6   She died nine months later, in January 1901, at the age of 81.
7   *Weekly Irish Times*, 30 September 1911, p 15.
8   *Irish Independent*, 2 October 1911, p 5.
9   *Freeman's Journal*, Monday 1 September 1913, p 7.
10   Horne, J. (2008), *Our War, Ireland and the Great War*, p 6, citing Jeffery, *Ireland and the Great War*, pp 33–35.
11   Pennell. C. (2008), *Our War, Ireland and the Great War*: the 2008 Thomas Davis Lecture series, Royal Irish Academy, p 44.
12   There is no indication on the lists of patients from these hospital ships as to how they were selected or why they were chosen to be sent to the Mater.
13   *British Medical Journal*, Correspondence, 16 October 1915, p 585.
14   Waterford County Museum (2004), *The First World War and Ireland – Hospitals, Nursing, & Relief Organisations*, p 3 [online] http://www.waterfordcountymuseum.org/exhibit/web.
15   *British Medical Journal*, Correspondence, 23 December 1916, p 888.
16   *Mater Misericordiae Hospital, Dublin*, Report for the Year 1917, Dollard Printing House, Dublin, p 46.
17   A. Chance to A. Blayney, letter dated 13 February 1917.
18   Board Minutes, 5 December 1914, pp 395–396.
19   Ibid, p 397.
20   Ibid, p 402.

21   *British Medical Journal*, 'Notes: Sick and Wounded Soldiers in Dublin', 27 February 1915, p 395.

22   It was called 'combat fatigue' in World War II.

23   Jones, E. *et al.* (2007). 'Shell Shock and Mild Traumatic Brain Injury: A Historical Review', *American Journal of Psychiatry*, Vol. 164, No. 11.

24   Board Minutes 1915–19.

25   *Mater Misericordiae Hospital, Dublin*, 1917, op. cit., p 20.

26   Bureau of Military History [BMH] Witness Statement [WS] 463, *Statement of a Member of the Community of the Mater Hospital*, pp 2–4.

27   This would have been in the vicinity of the (current) Infectious Diseases Unit. This door opened directly on to Berkeley Road.

28   Famous Dingle Peninsula People [online]. Available at http://www.dodingle.com/pages/famous peninsula_people_2.html.

29   The result of the inquest was asphyxia, due to the forced feeding being inhaled into the lungs. The cause of death, cardiac arrest due to asphyxia.

30   *The Irish Times*, 'Death of Thomas Ashe, Coroner's Inquest Opened', 28 September 1917, p 3.

31   *Freeman's Journal*, 'Toll of the Flu – More Hospital Accommodation Necessary', Thursday 24 October 1918, p 4.

32   Op. cit., 25 October, 'Influenza Ravages', p 4.

33   Op. cit., 30 October, 'Fighting the Epidemic – measures which should hasten its decline', p 3.

34   Op. cit., 28 October, 'The Influenza Scourge', p 5.

35   Op. cit., 26 October, 'No Abatement Yet', p 5.

36   Ibid, p 5.

CHAPTER 7

The Years of Civil Strife

The years following the 1916 Rising were difficult for the hospital, but nothing could prepare them for the War of Independence (1921–22) and the Civil War that followed it. From 1919 onwards, it was evident that the political mood of the Irish nation was rapidly changing as assassinations and retaliations became regular occurrences. As a Dublin city hospital, the Mater was at the front line of the trouble: increasingly, injured rebels were finding their way to the hospital for treatment. The British administration in Dublin Castle began to view this with some concern. In 1920, a special file on the hospital's activities was opened by the Castle authorities with the intention of monitoring admissions and discharges, especially of any possible 'suspects'. By then, it would appear, they viewed the hospital as a hotbed of intrigue.[1] Long communications were sent by the police to Dublin Castle complaining about foiled attempts to find 'wanted' individuals thought to have been admitted to the Mater. One exasperated police officer wrote to the British Under-Secretary of State as follows:

> There is little doubt that Brett[2] was brought to the Mater Hospital and I understand that he is very seriously wounded and not likely to recover...[3]

> The Community of nuns who manage this hospital, the majority of the medical staff, the nurses and practically all the students are Sinn Féiners or Sinn Féin sympathisers. The Superioress is definitely hostile to the Police.

> It is a difficult matter to ascertain for certain if this man Brett is in the hospital or not, and if there, in what ward. A search of the hospital in order to locate him would be big business. It is a huge building (400 beds) with private homes adjoining and attached to it. Such a search should manifestly be carried out under the supervision of a Medical man. There is some objection to the employment of RAMC Officers[4] in such cases and I feel sure no civilian practitioner would undertake a duty of this nature.

> The Mater Hospital is a semi-religious institution, the management being entirely in the hands of the nuns. A forcible search by police and military would therefore create much popular feeling and excitement. Such a search would have to be undertaken by a strong force as a small party would very likely be attacked.[5]

An Auxiliary stands guard outside the Mater during the Civil War. The Auxiliaries and Black and Tans were convinced that the Mater was a hotbed of IRA activities and raided the place many times.

This document, whilst making a few sweeping statements about the hospital and its personnel, certainly reflects the thinking of the officers of the Metropolitan Police Office at Dublin Castle.[6] However, if one pauses to think about this particular time of civil unrest and an institution whose staff was more than likely all Irish nationals, it is not difficult to see how the Mater could house 'hostile' individuals. Following the Brett incident, the police were even more suspicious of the place and so increasingly 'raids' were carried out in the hospital, without any warning, by the feared Black and Tans.[7] These raids isolated the place for many hours at a time and were very disruptive. Some of the staff sought to fight back, but this was not condoned by the hospital authorities. Nonetheless, stories abound about 'wanted' individuals being protected, concealed, abruptly admitted, discharged or pronounced dead and hastily put in a coffin, to be spirited out of the hospital. In so many creative ways, staff managed to outwit 'the Tans', much to the chagrin of the British administration in Dublin Castle, who had perhaps been right about hostility in the Mater. In time, the police would 'hit back' in unexpected ways![8]

Croke Park and 'Bloody Sunday' 1920

On Sunday 21 August 1920, two incidents took place in Dublin which led to appalling loss of life. Early that morning, in reprisal for earlier raids, a group of IRA activists entered the homes of British officials and shot them in their beds. Fifteen were killed. That afternoon, during a Gaelic football match in Croke Park, Crown forces opened fire on the spectators, using rifles and automatic fire.[9] People were crushed in the stampede which ensued when they tried to escape. Some were shot as they attempted to climb over the wall to nearby streets. As a result, thirteen people were killed and over fifty sustained serious wounds.

● *The* Evening Herald *report on Bloody Sunday, Croke Park. (© Getty Images.)*

The two hospitals that received the injured and the dead were Jervis Street and the Mater. Of those brought to the Mater, over thirty were treated and discharged. A number were dead on arrival and many with serious injuries were admitted, some of whom died later – all were young people. According to the newspapers of the time, a large crowd of people gathered outside the hospital the following morning in search of loved ones who had failed to return home. There were also large numbers of people awaiting treatment for their injuries at the dispensary: they had gone home to escape from the mêlée and returned in the morning to have their wounds attended to. On 23 November 1920, a military court of inquiry into the massacre was held in the Pillar Room of the hospital.[10]

The situation grew progressively worse through 1921 as the death rate soared. People were burned out of their homes and gun battles were commonplace. The injured and the dead arrived to the Mater every hour of the day and night. The night of 3 February 1921 was an appalling night of violence in O'Connell Street, as civilians were mowed down with tanks and guns.[11] The wounded found their way to the Mater, where they felt safe and were cared for immediately. They were always admitted directly to the wards because if they were delayed, there was a risk that the Black and Tans would arrive and take them outside and shoot them dead. This was not mere rumour: it had happened in the Cork Union Workhouse when they learned that their 'wanted man'

THE WOUNDED

Hospitals to Give Particulars of Patients

MILITARY ORDER

Details of Persons Injured by Bullets and Explosives

It now transpires that notices have been served on the authorities of all Dublin hospitals requiring them to furnish, daily, to the military authorities, a list of patients who were admitted suffering from bullet wounds, etc.

The hospital authorities are very reticent in regard to the matter, but, from inquiries made by a FREEMAN'S JOURNAL representative, it transpired that the order was sent to the secretary of the Committee of Management of each of the hospitals, and it would also appear that the terms of demand, which has been made under the Restoration of Order Act, are being complied with in some of the hospitals, at least where such cases have since been admitted.

"NO OPTION."

The onus of supplying the necessary information is thrown on the secretary and the Committee of Management and the medical staffs take no direct part in compiling the returns. In many of the hospitals the position in which they are placed by this new order of things is keenly felt, but the hospital authorities appear to think that they have no option but to comply with the order.

It was pointed out to our representative that, in the existing state of things, the Crown forces can enter the hospitals at any time, day or night—and that they have been doing so—and, in face of this fact, there appears to be very little reason for compelling the hospital authorities to furnish this particular return.

The following is the text of the order:—

To the Secretary, —— Hospital.

By virtue of the powers conferred on me under Regulation 53 of the Restoration of Order in Ireland, Regulation 1, the under-signed, being a Competent Military Authority under the said regulations, do hereby order you, the secretary, being the person in charge of the —— hospital, to furnish to me (in writing) the names and descriptions of all persons admitted to your hospital who are or are suspected to be suffering from wounds caused by bullets, gunfire or other explosives, together with such particulars and information concerning them as may be within your knowledge.

Such information is to be furnished by you daily to me at Headquarters, Dublin District, Lower Castle Yard, Dublin.

Failure to comply with this order will render you liable to be proceeded against for an offence against the Restoration of Order in Ireland Regulations.

R. D. F. OLDMAN, Colonel Commandant, Commanding Dublin District. Competent Military Authority.

Lower Castle Yard, Dublin.

"A REQUEST, NOT AN ORDER."

The Secretary of Mercer's Hospital told a FREEMAN'S JOURNAL reporter that they, in common with the other hospitals, had received a circular from the military authorities asking for this return. He had not the circular by him at the moment, but, as far as he recollected, it was worded as a request, and not as an order. The order, or request, was being complied with, so far as his hospital was concerned, but the medical staffs had nothing to do with the return.

The procedure adopted was that each day the admission books were sent to the secretary's office. These books contained the names of patients admitted the previous day, and if, on going through the books, the secretary found there was a man admitted suffering from bullet wounds, he would report to the authorities the fact, together with the name which the man gave.

The house surgeon at the Meath Hospital told our reporter that he had no information to give on the matter, which was one altogether for the secretary and the committee.

The Secretary, subsequently interviewed, admitted that he had received the document, which he described as an order, but declined to go any further than that.

---

was a patient there. They demanded to be taken to St Francis Ward and although the man was seriously injured, reports tell us that they 'ordered him to dress and come with them .... The party proceeded out by the back entrance, ordering the officials to close the gate and go back. A few minutes afterwards shots were heard, and subsequently the dead body was found lying in a pool of blood just outside the gate'.[12] A similar case occurred a few days later in Cork Infirmary, when an unconscious patient who had been shot in the head the day before was carried out on to the road and shot dead.[13]

The Hospitals Order – January 1921

After it became known that the Mater had treated a number of 'wanted men', the military authorities became more determined than ever to do something about it. In January 1921 they served this notice to the Mater and to all the Dublin hospitals:

To the Secretary, Mater Misericordiae Hospital.

By virtue of the powers conferred on me under Regulation 53 of the Restoration of Order in Ireland... the under-signed, being a Competent Military Authority under the said regulations, do hereby order you ... to furnish to me (in writing) the names and descriptions of all persons admitted to your hospital who are or are suspected to be suffering from wounds caused by bullets, gunfire or other explosives, together with such particulars and information concerning them as may be within your knowledge.

Such information is to be furnished by you daily to me at headquarters, Dublin District, Lower Castle Yard, Dublin.

Failure to comply with this order will render you liable to be proceeded against for an offence against the Restoration of Order in Ireland Regulations.

R.D.F. OLDMAN, Colonel Commandant, Commanding Dublin District.

● Increasingly worried about the Mater's role in 'sheltering' IRA activists, the military authorities sent them this warning in 1920. (Courtesy of the National Library of Ireland.)

The newspapers quickly set to work to find out how the Dublin hospitals were responding to this order. The smaller city hospitals indicated that they would have to comply with it, or they simply had no comment to make. The larger hospitals took a different approach, placing the welfare of their patients before politics. Professor John McArdle, a surgeon at St Vincent's Hospital, was interviewed and he spoke of the evil of being expected to betray patient confidences and the doctor's responsibilities to his patients. Dr Louis Byrne, a senior surgeon in Jervis Street Hospital, said that he was only interested in patients' ailments and not their names or politics. The Mater made no comment at all, but there is no doubt that this 'order' caused grave concern to all the hospitals: a group of doctors took the matter to the Royal Colleges of Physicians and Surgeons asking them to intervene, but got little help from either organisation.

However, the IRA response was swift. It issued a warning that if any doctor or member of staff disclosed information about a patient to the military authorities, they would be treated as 'spies' and dealt with accordingly. The *Freeman's Journal* discussed the issue in an editorial on 23 March 1921, saying: 'Militarism directly challenged the medical profession – that is the only interpretation of the hospital order.' The paper went on to say that the order had been strongly denounced at a meeting of the Irish Bar Council. All the time pressure was being put on the Royal College of Surgeons to take issue with the administration in Dublin Castle. Eventually an official statement was issued from Dublin Castle:

In answer to a question as to the meaning of the order recently issued to hospitals requesting them to furnish details of wounded patients admitted, it was officially stated today that the smuggling into public hospitals and subsequent medical treatment in secret of gunmen injured in street attacks on Crown forces has been a considered policy on the part of Sinn Féin.

This is clearly shown in documents recently captured... But in serious cases, wounded Republicans have been got into public hospitals, often under assumed names and there is ground for stating that in many cases both their presence and the nature of their wounds have been wilfully concealed.

It was with a view to checking the use of public institutions for the hiding and harbouring of evil-doers that the military order was issued requesting daily particulars of the wounded admitted for treatment.

The recent protest against this order by the Council of the Royal College of Surgeons, Ireland, who contend that it entails a disclosure of information obtained in the discharge of their professional duties is surprising in view of the fact that the details sought by the authorities are no more than those which are entered in the porter's admission book of any well-regulated hospital.[14]

The pillar room in the early 20th century. Note the birdcages at the rear, which so frightened the Black and Tans.

It is not difficult to see which hospital the authorities were referring to in this statement. The Mater made no statements, but the hospital continued to admit large numbers of the victims of shootings, beatings and burnings. The patients were admitted under pseudonyms, treated in the wards and discharged as soon as possible. Little was written in their medical notes. All the time the Auxiliaries or Black and Tans were never far from the place, keeping an eye on people as they came and went. Periodically they blocked Eccles Street with wooden fencing, barbed wire and other contraptions. They did this in order to search nearby houses, the hospital itself, or the various delivery vehicles bringing goods such as bread, milk, vegetables or medical supplies to the hospital. The blockades meant that at times the hospital was left short of supplies such as milk for the patients. The patients never complained. Life at the hospital went on and the Black and Tan 'raids' continued. In an undated account of events at the Mater at this time, one of the nuns gives an insight into a Black and Tan raid and a rare lighthearted moment:

> We were raided here by the Black and Tans on various occasions. One evening when they came to the hospital, they went into the reception room, known as the Pillar Room, and were searching under the couches and in every corner of the room. There was a parrot in a cage in the room which was usually covered at night with a cloth. When it was disturbed by the light and the noise, it gave a dreadful shriek and all the 'Black and Tans' threw themselves on the floor thinking it was the signal for an attack. Everyone in the place thought it a huge joke and the Black and Tans left shamefaced.[15]

Searching the Hospital for 'Wanted Men'

• The Black and Tans were looking for Dan Breen, who was a patient at the Mater, having sustained gunshot wounds during a raid. (© Topfoto.)

Probably the most dramatic raid at the hospital took place on 12 October 1921. On that day, IRA volunteers Dan Breen and Sean Treacy, both 'wanted men', had sought refuge in the house of Professor John Carolan[16] in Drumcondra, north Dublin. Somehow the police discovered where they were and after a gun battle, during which Carolan was mortally wounded, Breen and Treacy managed to escape. Breen had sustained a number of gunshot wounds. A day or two later, Michael Collins negotiated his admission to the Mater for treatment. The nuns, in their wisdom, decided that he would be safer in the private nursing home on Eccles Street.

In due course, the Black and Tans arrived to search the hospital for him. According to Desmond Ryan in *Dublin's Fighting Story 1916–21*:

> The raid on the Mater was the longest and most elaborate of them all. The Black and Tans, the Auxiliary force, and a force of military threw cordons round the building and its approaches, and for nearly three hours carried out a methodical search of every ward... An armoured car was stationed on duty outside the Mater while other armoured cars patrolled the neighbourhood. Breen saw the Auxiliaries on guard as he looked down from the window of the nursing home on Eccles Street. The search did not extend to the home, but it lasted long enough to rouse concern in Breen's friends outside. The alarm spread through the city, and something like a general mobilisation of all available Volunteers began.[17]

The death rate from the violence continued to soar and by the middle of the year had reached over a thousand. However, at a political level, things were changing somewhat and a truce was agreed by 9 June 1921. This led to peace negotiations between Ireland and Britain. On 6 December 1921, the Treaty which would create the Irish Free State was signed, after which British troops, including the Auxiliaries and the Black and Tans, began to disappear from the streets of Dublin. For the first time in two years, the hospital was free from the worry of raids and the human consequences of the fierce gun battles which had punctuated city life.

The Siege of the Four Courts

However, peace at the Mater was to be short-lived. The politics around the Treaty quickly polarised people, and by the middle of 1922 a vicious civil war had broken out between supporters and opponents of the Treaty, bringing large numbers of dead and wounded to the hospital once again. In Dublin, the anti-Treaty people (also known as Irregulars) seized the Four Courts on 14 April 1922 to set up their headquarters there. In June of that year, following pressure from the British government, the National Army laid siege to the building, and those within the building mounted a formidable defence. Obviously they were concerned about the injuries resulting from the fighting and so they negotiated with the Mater Hospital for a small team of medical and nursing personnel to be made available on 28 June 1922.[18] Serious fighting broke out the following day when the National Army shelled the building with the aid of 18-pounder field artillery guns. This led to enormous loss of life and a long list of wounded arriving to both Jervis Street Hospital and the Mater Hospital.

The siege of the Four Courts lasted approximately 60 hours, by which time the place was on fire, following two massive explosions on 29 June. Thirty-six people were killed and ninety wounded. Many of the injured admitted to the Mater were suffering from chest injuries. Shortly after midday on 30 June, the fire from the Four Courts, described by the *Irish Independent* as 'a roaring furnace', began to spread rapidly. Explosion after explosion was heard, from mines laid within the building, and a continuous bombardment from outside the building shook the city. Soon, all the buildings in central Dublin were on fire and shooting all over the city led to an enormous death toll and hundreds wounded.

On that day, 20 people with bullet wounds were admitted to the Mater from the city centre and 16 with bullet wounds were brought to the hospital from the Four Courts. According to *The Irish Times*:[19]

> The number of wounded persons admitted to the Mater Misericordiae Hospital was very high. Three of them were firemen, who courageously carried out their duties at the Four Courts under great difficulties, and ran a great deal of risk.

As the fighting went on, conditions deteriorated at the Mater. As the city could no longer function, food ran short in the hospital. Sporadic gunfire could be heard outside the hospital and the streets were not safe. The staff worked extremely hard, most of them not leaving the place for almost two weeks. The wards and the operating theatres were busy 24 hours a day, and the mortuary area was too small to deal with the number of bodies arriving. As one burial after another took place at Glasnevin Cemetery the newspapers referred to this period as 'Dublin's Holocaust'.[20]

Post-War Financial Difficulties

Although the years of bloodshed finally ended in 1923, the Mater was in crisis. The years of civil conflict had depleted the hospital finances and the only reason the hospital survived was because the nuns and senior medical staff received no salary. It was difficult to fundraise in the 1920s, but the nuns and the medical staff realised that this is what they would have to do. A number of fundraising events, including a 'monster carnival', were planned for the following year. One of the more immediate things they decided to organise was a sweep on the 1921 Grand National horse race in aid of the hospital.

A very dedicated group came together during the year to contribute to the fundraising effort. As part of this effort, a public meeting was held on 16 July 1920. It was presided over by Lord Mayor Laurence O'Neill and most of Dublin's notable citizens attended. The Lord Mayor brought it to everyone's attention that the 1921–22 Civil War had brought the hospital to the verge of bankruptcy. He also pointed out that the Mater, unlike other hospitals, had no government grant and that while they had done their best to raise funds, it was not enough to keep the place going and to meet the existing debt. There and then some of those present made a donation to the cause. Dr Henry Barniville, Secretary of the medical board, announced the receipt of £1,000 from the Archbishop[21] and £100 from an anonymous donor. Barniville went on to say that they had set up a new fundraising organisation, which went by the considerable name of the Mater Misericordiae Hospital National Exhibition and Carnival Organisation. Joseph C. Rock was appointed General Secretary and a dedicated office was opened in Prosperity Chambers, O'Connell Street to organise ongoing fundraising.

The Four Courts in flames during the siege of the building. (© Corbis)

At the time the streets of the city, especially at night, were anything but safe and because of this and night-time curfews, it was difficult to arrange evening events and hope that people would come to them. But come they did. The first in a number of fundraising events, a series of orchestral concerts in aid of the hospital, began on Sunday afternoon, 8 November 1920, at La Scala Theatre in central Dublin, organised with the help and advice of Vincent O'Brien, conductor of the Dublin Symphony Orchestra. The concert hall was packed to capacity. At least twenty of these concerts were held over the next few months.

In the autumn of 1920, word reached the great tenor Count John McCormack that concerts were being held in Dublin to raise funds for the Mater Hospital. He wrote from London to the fundraising committee in early December:

Count John McCormack during his visit to Ireland, when he organised a fundraising concert in aid of the Mater. (Courtesy of the National Library of Ireland.)

> I have heard with the deepest regret of the unfortunate circumstances in which the great Mater finds itself. As soon as I return to New York, I intend to arrange a concert solely on its behalf…. God Bless the Mater. It is a gift to the Nation.[22]

In March 1921, the Rathmines and Rathgar Musical Society put on eight performances of the Gilbert and Sullivan opera *Yeomen of the Guard* at the Gaiety Theatre in aid of the hospital. Some months later, a very special and spectacular event was organised. Joseph Rock decided to invite the Vatican Choir to Dublin for a special performance in aid of the hospital. The director of the choir, Maestro Raffaele Casimiri, agreed after much assurance that they would be safe in 'war-torn' Dublin! Comprising of choristers from St Peter's Basilica and St John Lateran in Rome, the choir gave two performances at La Scala Theatre, both of which were packed to capacity. At the first performance, members of the Provisional Government attended, together with members of the clergy and other dignitaries.

In January 1923, John McCormack fulfilled his promise to give a concert in aid of the Mater, and another in aid of the St Vincent de Paul Society. President W.T. Cosgrave wrote to him to say how pleased everyone was that he had chosen to appear and his visit generated enormous public enthusiasm. He came in early January with his wife and four-year-old (adopted) son. The concerts were held in the Theatre Royal,

Dublin, which had a seating capacity of 3,850. At the request of the great maestro himself, special excursion trains, at reduced rates, were laid on from much of the country, but especially from the west of Ireland. His opening concert commenced with two great arias composed by Handel. After the concert performances, he left Dublin for Monte Carlo to give some more concerts. During an interview while he was in Dublin, he was asked for his views on the political situation compared with what it was like when he last visited Ireland. His answer was quick and to the point:

> It is like this, I am a man of harmony, and my purpose in life is to promote the cause of harmony. I am now engaged in a work of charity which is dear to my heart in order to show my affection for my native country. I am greatly gratified at the success of my efforts so far, as I have been informed that the booking includes not only all parts of Ireland, but Glasgow, Greenock, Manchester and Liverpool.[23]

LA SCALA BALL.

A most successful ball, which inaugurated the Mater Misericordiæ Hospital National Exhibition and Carnival, to be held next year, took place in, the splendid ballrom of the La Scala Theatre last Friday, and was attended by upwards of four hundred people, many of whom came from remote parts of the country. The ballroom was tastefully decorated with palms, and its panelled Grecian pillars lent it a most artistic appearance. The well-polished floor, with its patent spring and corner slides, was found by the dancers to be excellent for their purpose, and, with the changing lights and colour effect of the ladies' dresses, the scene was a brilliant one. The secretaries—Lady Redmond and Mrs. Barneville, and Messrs. Shiel, Hatch, and J. C. Rock—are to be congratulated on the result of their elaborate arrangements. There were musical items from the stage by Mr. Schwiller during the dance, and Mr. Clarke-Barry's orchestra, personally conducted, supplied the dance music. Messrs. John Shields and Joseph Kenny acted as masters of ceremonies, and the catering was in the hands of Mr. Mills. Dancing was kept up until after "Curfew" hour.

● *This newspaper report celebrates the successful fundraising concert at the La Scala Theatre. (Courtesy of* The Irish Times.*)*

The Civil War continued until about May of 1923, but the visit of Count John McCormack had an enormous 'mood-lifting' effect on the population as a whole. Everyone talked about it, especially the staff at the Mater. Before he left the country, the singer paid a quick visit to the Mater to greet the nuns and all the staff. Whether he sang for them during this visit is not on record, but he created great joy and excitement.

The Hospital Sweep

The Mater's first attempt to make money on a sweepstake on the Aintree Grand National in 1921 had yielded less than expected so the fundraising committee was advised to contact Richard Duggan, a bookmaker with an extraordinary interest in and ability to make money through sweeps on various horse races:

> The Executive Committee of the Mater Hospital approached him with a view to obtaining his help and influence, as their efforts on previous occasions to raise money by means of sweepstakes for small prizes had not met with marked success. Duggan suggested that the Executive Committee should promote a sweepstake on a larger scale than heretofore, and offer prizes to the amount

of £10,000. The Executive Committee could not see their way to embark on a venture of this magnitude, and Duggan thereupon declared his willingness to accept full responsibility for the promotion and carrying through of a sweepstake on the lines he had suggested.

The Executive Committee agreed to accept Duggan's offer, upon the understanding that the sweep should be run in aid of the Mater Misericordiae Hospital; that, whatever the result of the sweepstake, the Executive Committee should receive £10,000, but no more, for the purposes of the hospital; that any surplus in excess of £10,000 should belong to Duggan; and that for the purposes of the sweepstake, Dublin should be fixed as headquarters, the staff employed should be of Irish birth, and Duggan should be solely responsible for the cost of the staff employed, the printing, posting, and all other expenses or liabilities incurred, etc.[24]

The executive committee of the Mater had sought permission to hold the sweep from the President of the Provisional Government early in 1922 and a formal agreement was signed in August 1922. Tickets went on sale for the first time at a special stall at the Mater carnival in September of that year, at ten shillings per ticket.

Richard Duggan's first hospital sweep was run on the Manchester November Handicap in 1922. Before the draw even took place, people were greatly exercised by the size of the draw and the amount of money that was flowing in to the new sweep offices in Dame Street, not only from Ireland but from England and America. However, some questioned the ethics of the undertaking. They wondered whether the new State would benefit in some way from Richard Duggan's profits from the sale of what turned out to be millions of tickets worldwide.[25] Of course, the Mater sweep also caught the attention of the other cash-strapped hospitals and some charities, not to mention the Revenue Commissioners and some members of government. The issue was raised in the Dáil on 10 October 1922 by Thomas Carter, who asked Kevin O'Higgins, the Minister for Home Affairs, if he was aware of the sweep (which contravened the 1823 Lotteries Act) in aid of the Mater Hospital. Carter wondered if the promoters would be obliged in due course to have these activities audited and published and whether the Minister would take steps to ensure that the entire net proceeds would be handed over to the hospital.[26] The Minister referred the question to the President, who merely said that the Mater carnival committee had sought permission from him and that he had granted it.

But the debate did not stop there. A month later, the question was raised again in the Dáil, this time by Piaras Béaslaí. He wondered if Duggan's accounts would be properly audited and whether he would pay tax on his profits, to which the President replied that he had nothing to add to what he had said the last time. It was the duty of the income tax commissioners to deal with the payment of any tax due. He went on to say that he had been informed that it had been proposed to hold one other sweep of a similar nature. Following this, Béaslaí went on to ask if the government intended to legalise sweeps, to which the President replied that the government had not considered it.[27]

Lotteries, in Ireland and England, had been good fundraisers from the mid-1600s on, because they were always popular. However, the authorities didn't share the public's enthusiasm and in 1823, the Lotteries Act forbade the sale of lottery tickets on the grounds that lotteries were 'a nuisance'. However, it would appear that when charitable organisations held a lottery, the 'powers that be' simply ignored the legalities of it. When Duggan became involved with his sweep and large sums of money flowed in to him, the Inspector of Taxes took him (and the Mater) to court, the case ultimately ending up in the Supreme Court in 1928. There it was decided that the 'Profits [where Duggan was concerned] derived from carrying out a sweepstake, being profits derived from a criminal enterprise, are not accessible to income tax.' The judge fined Duggan a small amount of money and more or less wished the Mater well in the work they were doing.[28]

On 23 November 1922, the draw took place and the race was held. The winner of the first prize (£5,000) was from Derry. The second and third prizes went to England. The rest was divided into small prizes for those who had drawn horses. The event was recorded in the newspapers and included an appreciation released by the Mater Carnival Executive of the work done by Richard J. Duggan. Publishing the note of appreciation was probably ill advised, because by that time the government was beginning to review the work of Duggan, particularly in relation to the 1823 Lottery Act. This did not seem to be of any real concern to Duggan, who was pleased with what he had achieved. What he did not take into account was the ensuing public discussion.

The following year Duggan ran another sweep to raise funds for a parish church and also in aid of the Dublin Skin and Cancer Hospital. He organised it as he had the Mater Sweep in 1922: he gave each organisation £5,000 in advance of the 1923 Aintree Grand National. Eventually Richard Duggan had to deal with the Inspector of Taxes, who had decided to tax him on a sum of £40,000 for the year 1922–23. He disputed his case with them and fought it through the courts on the grounds that 'The profits in question are not assessable to income tax, on the ground that such profits were derived from a source prohibited by law.'[29]

Ultimately he was fined £50 for his activities in 1924 and was bound over to keep the peace for 12 months and not become involved in any further sweepstakes.[30] His inactivity was short-lived. There were no further sweeps held in aid of the Mater, but Duggan organised a number in aid of some of the smaller Dublin hospitals. Eventually, in 1929 the government of the day began to investigate the possibility of using sweeps as a means of financing the post-war 'cash-strapped' voluntary hospitals. Unfortunately, due to a change of government, it was 1931 before the 'Hospitals Sweepstake' came into existence. While it was of some help to most of the hospitals, the Mater's relationship with them was, at times, very difficult. The downside of introducing the Sweepstake for financing all the voluntary hospitals was that charitable donations disappeared and in time the hospitals became totally dependent on the Hospitals Sweepstake to finance them.

1   McGarry, F. (2006), 'Keeping an Eye on the Usual Suspects: Dublin Castle's 'Personality Files', 1899–1921. *History Ireland* 14 (6), pp 44–49.
2   Thomas Brett was involved in a shooting incident in Thurles in which a British police officer was shot dead.
3   Brett died from his injuries at the end of June 1920.
4   RAMC – Royal Army Medical Corps.
5   British National Archives, CO 904/194/26, p 2.
6   This particular statement was made by W.G. Johnstone, Chief Commissioner of the Police on 14 June 1920 and he addressed it to the Under-Secretary of State. Five days later, a note was added by a D. Barrett to the effect that Brett had died at the Mater Hospital, and he included information on the 'verdict of the Coroner's Jury'. British National Archives, CO 904/194/26, p 2.
7   The 'Black and Tans' were a large force of police who arrived in Ireland in March 1920 to supplement the existing force. They wore khaki army uniforms and were greatly feared because of their brutality. They were joined by another force in August 1920, who were known as the Auxiliaries.
8   See *Freeman's Journal*, 26 March 1921, p 4, 'Dublin Castle Defence of the Hospital Order'.
9   Subsequently named 'Croke Park Bloody Sunday'. Dublin and Tipperary were playing in a GAA football match, which had to be called off.
10   See: http://goliath.ecnext.com/coms2/gi_0199-2980828/Death-in-the-afternoon-the.html accessed 04/09/2010.
11   According to the *Freeman's Journal*, February 1921, 'Night of tragedy: Blood shed in Dublin Streets': One man shot in the back in O'Connell St and a wheel went over his face... In Nth Earl St, a youngster named ...was seriously injured. The second victim, Miss Mary ... (21) was wounded by three bullets, and now lies in the Mater Hosp.' The accounts in all the newspapers of the time make disturbing reading.
12   *Freeman's Journal*, 19 February 1921, p 3.
13   Op. cit., 1 April 1921, p 3.
14   Op. cit., 26 March 1921, p 4.
15   Bureau of Military History 1918–21, No. W.S. 463, p 6.
16   Professor Carolan was a lecturer in St Patrick's Teacher Training College, Drumcondra, almost beside his house.
17   Conchubhair, B. (2009), *Dublin's Fighting Story 1916–21, Told by the Men who Made it*, Cork: Mercier Press, p 270.
18   *Irish Independent*, 29 June 1922.
19   *The Irish Times*, 1 July 1922, p 3.
20   *Freeman's Journal*, 8 July 1922, p 4.
21   Archbishop William Walsh, Archbishop of Dublin 1885–1921.
22   *Freeman's Journal*, 18 December 1920, p 3.
23   Ibid.
24   *C. Hayes, Inspector of Taxes, Appellant, v. R.J. Duggan, Respondent (1) [1929].* In *The Irish Reports*, p 406.
25   Doyle, J. (2009), available at: http://www.irishtimes.com/newspaper/opinion/2009/1211/1224260511592_pf.html.
26   *The Irish Times*, 14 October 1922, p 4.
27   *Freeman's Journal*, 18 November 1922, p 9.
28   [1932] T.I.T.R. 388 R.G. Davis (Inspector of Taxes) v. The Superioress, Mater M. Hospital, Dublin.
29   *C. Hayes, Inspector of Taxes, Appellant, v. R.J. Duggan, Respondent (1) [1929].* In *The Irish Reports*, p 413.
30   Coleman, M. (2009), *The Irish Sweep – A History of the Irish Hospital's Sweepstake 1930–87*, University College Dublin Press, p 7.

CHAPTER 8

A Time of Turbulence: the Years between the Wars

The £10,000 from the Mater Sweep of 1922 solved the hospital's existing debt problem, but it did not provide the Sisters with enough money to enable them to undertake any of their ambitious list of refurbishments to the hospital, including building a new operating theatre in the private nursing home, an extension to the opthalmic department and two new lifts.

Of course, even though the Sisters considered these improvements to be essential, they incurred substantial debts in the process. The main source of hospital revenue at the time (1917)[1] was as follows:

	£.	s.	d.
Subscriptions and Donations	4,408	6	5
Anonymous Donation, 'For the Sick Poor'	600	0	0
Bequests	697	10	11
Boards of Guardians (Maintenance of Patients)	504	9	3
City of Dublin War Pensions Committee (for Discharged Soldiers)	44	16	0
Corporation Grant	475	0	0
Dividends and Interests (Invested Bequests)	2,578	19	7
Earnings from private nurses and student nurses' fees	1,402	13	2
Farm Produce	416	9	6
Insurance Committees and County Councils	260	18	5
Private Patients	2,903	5	5
Refund of Income Tax	661	8	4
Rents	563	13	11
Subscriptions received through Collectors	336	6	1
War Office, for Maintenance of Wounded Soldiers	1,982	12	0
X-Ray Fees	167	5	6
Securities realised	2,760	0	0

Whether the Sisters quietly hoped that another sweep might provide them with the necessary finance to meet capital expenses is not on record. The days of holding elaborate events to raise funds would appear to have ended as the public, by this time, viewed sweepstakes as the answer to all the hospital's financial difficulties. Furthermore, the Sisters and their advisers weren't willing to risk the legal consequences of another sweepstake. So the Sisters would have to find another way to raise funds. This was all the more important because the bathroom facilities on the wards needed urgent attention, even though, with one toilet per ward, the Mater hospital was, in fact, doing better than many other city hospitals, which only provided one toilet for the entire hospital. (This 'luxury' had earned it some criticism when the hospital was built.) The Sisters judged that proper bathrooms were needed. However, the Mater wasn't alone in seeking funds. Many other hospitals were in similar financial straits, at a time when the government could least afford to help them.

An Investigation Begins

● *Nurses draw tickets in the Hospital Sweep, Ballsbridge, 1940. (Courtesy of the National Library of Ireland.)*

When the Revenue Commissioners focused their attention on Richard Duggan's (untaxed) profits from the sweepstakes, they also turned their attention to the Mater. They decided to investigate all sources of revenue within the hospital and for this purpose, a tax inspector was dispatched to the hospital in 1923. He reported that:

As distinct from the public hospital, there was a portion of the hospital known as the Mater Private Nursing Home, that annual profits arose or accrued to the Superioress from a trade of carrying on a private nursing home, and that the Superioress was properly chargeable for income tax upon such annual profits or gains.[2]

The Sisters appealed against this finding, holding that the nursing home was not 'a trade' and even if it were, it was certainly not a profitable one. They went on to state that there was no demarcation between the public and the private hospitals and so it was unfair that this section of the hospital should be taxed on non-existent 'annual profits or gains'.

The matter eventually, in 1932, went all the way to the Supreme Court, which found in favour of the Sisters, stating that:

There was no evidence to support the findings of the Commissioners, and, alternatively, that the Commissioners misdirected themselves in forming the opinion upon which the finding was based.[3]

While the Supreme Court did accept that that the private nursing home was not a separate entity and that all its activities and control were part of the general hospital administration, the matter would return to haunt the Sisters some years later.

The Irish Hospitals Sweepstake, 1930

The sweepstakes issue rumbled on through the 1920s, with various arguments being advanced for and against and the voluntary hospitals continuing to struggle with their debts. Ultimately, the Public Hospitals Act of 1930 enabled funds to be raised by means of sweepstakes, and a three-man 'committee of reference' would be responsible for seeing that the sweepstake money 'would be distributed fairly and equitably' between all the voluntary hospitals. The Act also provided for an assessment of the needs of the individual hospitals regarding:

- Structural alterations
- Repayment of loans
- Furniture (beds/bedside lockers, etc.)
- Provision of medical equipment and patient appliances
- Investment.

The Act decreed that any available surplus should be divided as follows:

- Two-thirds to be divided between the voluntary hospitals according to their needs.
- One-third of the funds to go the Minister for his use, which it was expected would be for the funding of county hospitals and county homes, then being funded from the local rates.[4]

The use of these funds for non-voluntary hospital purposes would, in time, become a somewhat contentious issue, but the Sweepstake as a source of revenue was a great boost to the collective morale of the voluntary hospitals. As large amounts of money became available, they were able to 'make the most of it' in the early days. The 1932 Finance Act, however, limited its impact by imposing a stamp duty of one-fourth of each of the voluntary hospital's share of the sweepstake fund, to be paid before any money would reach them and in addition, the remaining money was to be taxed. It became a dwindling blessing.

In the following year, a new Hospital Bill was introduced in the Dáil and on 27 July 1933 the Public Hospitals Act (1933) was passed. This addressed the whole subject of the Sweepstake and the funding of hospitals from its proceeds. It was not liked by the voluntary hospitals, including the Mater, the instigator of sweepstake funding!

A committee of reference would examine individual hospital applications and decide if they would qualify under rules laid down by the Hospitals Trust for the dispersal of funds. Hospitals which wished to apply for funds were obliged to set up a committee of three within the hospital, who would make applications for funds and be answerable to the Hospitals Trust in due course for the use of these funds. At the Mater, this responsibility was assigned to the medical board,[5] which appointed surgeon Henry Barniville, Professor Henry Moore and Dr P.J. Smyth to form the necessary committee (known in the hospital as the *building committee*).

The first application for funding under this new arrangement was made in early 1931. In that year, plans were drawn up for the much-needed ward bathroom amenities[6] and for installing hand basins in the wards for staff use. In November 1931, a further list of needs for the Mater was drawn up and submitted to the committee of reference.[7] It included:

1. New outpatients department (OPD), accident room, and an observation ward near the accident room.
2. A new mortuary and post mortem room.
3. Residential quarters for resident medical staff and medical students.
4. New accommodation for nursing staff.
5. A unit, separate from the main hospital, for patients suffering from tuberculosis or other infectious diseases.
6. A social services department, together with at least two trained social workers and an endowment fund of at least £10,000.

The bathroom and ward hand basins received the committee's approval, but the cost of the development of the outpatients block was later the subject of much discussion between the hospital and the Hospitals Commission, who had taken over from the committee of reference, and who had set a ceiling of £40,000: in 1934, the architects estimated that the building would cost £45,000. In 1936, the OPD building[8] was complete and was formally opened on 16 April 1936.

● *The entrance to the 1937 outpatients department.*

The Hospitals Commission and the Central Bed Bureau

Another task of the Hospitals Commission, which had been created by the 1933 Act, was to establish the Central Bed Bureau in Dublin, centralising the control of hospital beds and opening up something of a 'can of worms' in the hospital sector. The intention was that it would facilitate admission to hospital of people who could not contribute financially towards their hospital care: increasingly, as their financial difficulties had taken hold, voluntary hospitals had been admitting patients who could afford some payment towards their care or had some sort of insurance to pay for at least some of their care, and the poor often found it hard to get admitted.[9]

The hospitals targeted initially by the Bureau were those in receipt of sweepstake funds. By then the Hospitals Commission had all the operational details of the various hospitals and so it was in a position to demand cooperation with the scheme. In June 1941, it became operational. It was hugely contentious where many of the voluntary hospitals were concerned. They saw it as erosion of their independence and of their right to admit patients as they saw fit, i.e. those who could pay. The 1933 Act also made it mandatory for hospitals who sought funds from the sweepstakes to produce evidence that at least 25 per cent of their patients were 'free', or at least not paying (or being paid for) more than ten shillings[10] per week. This caused no difficulty for the Mater, because a large percentage of the patients in the hospital wards were in that category.

The establishment of the Hospital Commission marked an important power shift in the running of some of Dublin's voluntary hospitals, notably the Mater and St Vincent's (and to a lesser extent the Adelaide Hospital).[11] Up to this point, all power had rested with the Sisters of Mercy and the Sisters of Charity. They held ultimate control over the services provided, the staff appointed, the buildings erected, even the patients admitted.[12] They set their own standards of patient care and could act independently of the government (within the law of the land). This power began to be eroded after the Public Hospitals Act and also when the sweepstakes became a crucial source of revenue, when other 'players' became important, and power struggles within the Department of Health began to play a role. In addition, patients who would have paid a little towards their upkeep while in hospital now saw no reason to do so, because they felt that financially the hospitals were doing well because of the sweepstakes.

In May 1936, the Mater received a communication from the Department of Local Government and Public Health, addressed to the Mother Superior and outlining two proposals from the 'Report of the Hospitals Commission Regarding the Provision for Poor Patients in the City of Dublin':

1. That four large voluntary hospitals (or St Kevin's Hospital) should be developed as the chief clinical centres;
2. That the four hospitals should devise a scheme to control and regulate the admission of poor persons to hospital and that a small committee should be constituted from the hospitals to examine their position and formulate a suitable scheme.[13]

Needless to say, this sense of control being exerted on voluntary hospitals by a new body caused considerable concern. It was suggested that a meeting with medical representatives of the hospitals listed should be held. Representatives from the Richmond Hospital, Sir Patrick Dun's, Mercer's and the Royal City of Dublin Hospitals were invited to attend, along with delegates from the Mater and St Vincent's. In the meantime, the matter of the Commission report was communicated to the Archbishop of Dublin, Dr Edward Byrne, who became gravely concerned, mainly around the issue of voluntary hospital autonomy, particularly that of the Mater, St Vincent's Hospital and the National Maternity Hospital, Holles Street. He wrote to the chairmen of the medical boards of the respective hospitals and suggested that they set up a permanent committee to deal with the matter.

The hospitals drew up what they considered was a suitable arrangement and sent it to the Commission. Prolonged discussions took place over many months on the subject of the Central Bed Bureau, not only at the hospitals but within the Hospitals Commission itself, and also in the Dáil and Seanad Éireann. It was eventually decided that only those hospitals in receipt of sweepstakes funds were to be asked to participate in the system. The Commission also tied stringent supervisory regulations into the system, entitling the Bed Bureau not alone to request beds, but to inspect any hospital that refused to provide a requested bed and to take the matter to the Minister for Health, who was given the right to set up a public inquiry if necessary.

In 1940, the Dublin Hospitals Bed Bureau Order was enacted. It provided for every kind of bed needed, except beds for psychiatric patients, and listed 30 medical institutions in Dublin and county as participants in the scheme, limiting them to those in receipt of hospital sweepstake funds.

The scheme was well thought out. It worked on a rota system and was operated from its headquarters in Upper Mount Street, Dublin. The hospitals particularly affected were the acute general hospitals and the children's hospitals. As far as the Mater was concerned, it immediately led to overcrowding in the wards, because when the hospital was 'on call' for the Bed Bureau, eight beds had to be vacated and left ready, two each in the male and female medical and surgical wards. When the Bed Bureau beds were occupied, other patients (those at the pre-discharge stage of their treatment) had to be moved. This sometimes meant setting up temporary beds in the wards, which was not a good idea, but one of the rules associated with Bed Bureau admissions was that the patients were not to be delayed or kept waiting for a bed.

The system started on the morning of 3 June 1941. Five hours after it commenced (the Mater being the on-call hospital) the bombing of the North Strand, nearby, took place. By 10 p.m. that evening, the hospital had admitted twelve patients through the Bed Bureau, not accounting for the large numbers of bomb victims who were brought directly to the casualty department of the Mater on that night rather than being sent through the Bureau.

A Fraught Relationship

The Mater's relationship with the Hospitals Commission was an uneasy one. Every hospital was obliged to submit a copy of its audited accounts to the Commission before funds were paid out. The Mater seemed to have difficulty doing this, especially in providing information about the actual hospital itself, its management and the format of its financial returns. When they did submit the requested accounts and the supplementary information, the question of the private nursing home raised its head once more. The Commission objected to its inclusion in the general hospital accounts and requested a copy of the audited accounts (which did not exist) in respect of the year 1933 for the private nursing home on its own, as it was argued that the nursing home was not a separate entity, but an integral part of the hospital. The Commission repeatedly requested that expenses for the home be removed from the general hospital accounts and the ensuing debate delayed funding from the sweepstakes until eventually a compromise was reached. The accounting system would have to change.[14]

However, when the Commission studied the Mater accounts, they realised that the private nursing home was not self-sufficient and that it depended on the main hospital for practically everything, bar the beds the patients lay on. In their desire to separate the nursing home from the hospital, the Commission embarked on something of a witch hunt, at one stage requesting that the nurses and domestic staff who worked in the nursing home be excluded from any residence in the hospital. In those days, it was unthinkable that staff nurses be obliged to live away from the hospital, because they were so poorly paid. The problem reached a climax in 1938, when the hospital submitted a claim for a deficit of twice what it had been the year before.

There were many possible reasons for the steep rise: for example, the hospital had opened a new outpatients department, pathology lab, and medical residence in 1936; the number of patients attending the outpatients department had risen substantially during 1937 and consequently the pharmacy and surgical dressings bill had dramatically increased. But what is clear is that the correspondence between the Mater and the Commission had became somewhat fraught, to say the least. One gets a feeling that an enormous level of animosity by now existed between the two sides.

Eventually, the Superior of the hospital, Mother Brigid, on the advice of auditors, wrote a lengthy letter to the Secretary of the Department of Local Government[15] defending the management and the accountancy system of the hospital.[16] She specifically refuted allegations that the Mater was irresponsible in regard to the purchase of drugs, surgical items and the general day-to-day provisions in use in the hospital. She also made it very clear that the system had been changed with regard to the private nursing home and that 'the public hospital renders no service to the private home that is not paid for on a monthly basis and accounts are furnished in detail'. Mother Brigid concluded by reminding the Secretary that, 'the members of the Community, numbering 38 Sisters of Mercy, give their services free and devote their entire lives to the work of the hospital. The hospital work is carried out as conscientiously and efficiently as has been the practice for the 70 years previous to 1931.'[17]

Sister Brigid was not alone in her protests. On 21 November 1938, Professor Henry

Henry Moore's letter to The Irish Times *expressing his frustration at the situation with the Hospitals Commission. (Courtesy of* The Irish Times.*)*

Moore, chairman of the hospital medical board,[18] covered many column inches in *The Irish Times*[19] with his grievances against the Hospitals Commission and their treatment of the Mater and of the Sisters of Mercy, itemising each issue that had been the subject of correspondence between the Commission and the Mater. About a week later[20] even more newspaper space was taken up with a response to his article from Sean T. O'Kelly, Minister for Local Government and Public Health. He took each of the allegations made by Professor Moore and either refuted them or explained the reason behind them. The debate gathered momentum as *The Irish Times* discussed the issue in its editorial and carried comments from a number of Dublin hospital consultants, all of whom were more or less in agreement with Professor Moore.

In the meantime, the funds (outstanding since 1 January of that year) were paid in full by the Commission to the Mater on 28 October, accompanied by a note of warning that the hospital need not think that in future years it would automatically get the full amount requested. This warning obviously annoyed Professor Moore once more, as he published an even longer article in *The Irish Times*,[21] in which he dealt with the Commission's threat in a formidable exposé of the frustrations being felt by a number of the hospitals at the time.

A Chapel at Last

On a happier note, the hospital chapel, which had been part of the original 1860 plans, would at last come into existence, but not before another encounter with the Commission. Up to 1934, the chapel had been located in the west wing and was much too small. According to Professor Moore, it held about 150 people and about 400 wished to attend Mass on Sundays.[22] By 1934, the decision was taken to build a new chapel, and architects W.H. Byrne & Sons were employed to design it. The builders selected were Fitzgerald & Leonard. The design for the chapel was large and ornate and it was going to cost a lot of money. An application was made to the Hospitals Commission for a special grant, on the grounds that it was a facility for both the patients and staff of the hospital, but this

The chapel in 1937, before the marble angels were removed to bring the altar closer to the congregation.

was refused. In order to get the building started, the Sisters of Mercy in Carysfort Park, Blackrock, made a large sum of money available. The rest of the money came – somewhat ironically – from the profits of the private nursing home, as well as from fundraising.

The original plans for the chapel had the nave in a north–south position and the transept east–west. In the new plan this was changed and the building was set much further back from the North Circular Road. The space between the chapel and the east wing was used to build a new operating theatre for gynaecological surgery.[23] On the other side, and linking it to the west wing, additional living accommodation was built for the Sisters, including a convent infirmary for sick Sisters.

The building commenced in late 1935 and was finished in 1937. On 22 September 1937, the solemn opening and dedication by the Archbishop of Dublin, Edward Byrne, took place. A large number of clergy were present at the ceremony as well as the nuns from the Mater Convent, from Carysfort Park, and from many other convents. All of the medical and nursing staff, past and present, attended. The government was represented by Sean T. O'Kelly, W.W. Doran, Chairman of the Hospitals Commission, and W.T Cosgrave and Mrs Cosgrave. Representatives from University College Dublin and many others associated with the Mater also attended.

The chapel was beautifully designed and constructed. On the outside, it is built of Wicklow granite and limestone. Inside, there is lavish use of marble, some from Ireland but much of it, especially the white marble pillars, imported at considerable cost from Italy. The woodwork is of Austrian oak and the mosaic work was done by Irish craftsmen. A local sculptor, Albert Power, did all the beautiful sculpture work: when the chapel was opened there were two magnificent life-sized marble angels on either side of the altar, but 35 years later, following Vatican II, they had to be removed in order to bring the altar closer to the congregation. Over the altar is a very beautiful mosaic representation of Calvary. The altar and some of the stained glass windows were made by Messrs Early & Co. The cost of the building was £38,000.

Today, the chapel is still very much at the heart of hospital life. Two special interdenominational liturgies are held before Christmas each year, one for those who have died in the intensive care unit and the other for those who have died in the emergency department. On 14 February or thereabouts every year, heart transplant patients and their relatives attend a special interdenominational liturgy in the chapel. This particular event has, on occasions, been attended by the president of Ireland or other dignitaries. The following verse seems to sum up the spirit of the Mater chapel:

Lord –
We thank Thee for the lights that we have kindled,
The light of altar and of sanctuary;
Small lights of those who meditate at midnight
And lights directed through the panes of windows
The Rock, T.S. Eliot

1   Mater Misericordiae Hospital, Dublin (1917), *Report for the Year 1917*, Dollard Printing House, Dublin, p 20.
2   T.I.T.R. [1932] 388, p 7.
3   Ibid., p 7.
4   See http://historical-debates.oireachtas.ie/S/0014/S.0014.193106170004.html.
5   Medical Board Minutes, 22 April 1931.
6   There were no bathrooms in any of the wards – a feature of all the older hospitals.
7   Medical Board Minutes, 13 November 1931.
8   The outpatients department was built by Fitzgerald & Leonard Builders.
9   All admissions under this scheme were emergencies and made at the request of a GP.
10   Ten shillings was a substantial amount of money at the time.
11   The Adelaide Hospital (Church of Ireland) refused on moral grounds to accept money from the proceeds of the sweepstakes until about 1960.
12   The name and address, diagnosis and name of the referring consultant or GP were submitted to the Superioress of the Hospital or her deputy, before a patient could be admitted to one of the wards. This system remained in place until the 1970s, when an admission unit was put in place.
13   Medical Board Minutes, 23 May 1936.
14   Letter to the Rev. Mother from R. Ryan, Solicitor, 25 December 1934.
15   Sr M. Brigid Brennan to the Secretary, Department of Local Government and Public Health, 8 November 1938, NAI, DH A04/1 (Vol. 1).
16   From 1924 Sr M. Claude Meegan, worked (full-time) as Hospital Secretary and Accountant. She was extremely meticulous in all her work. She retired in 1972.
17   Ibid., p 3.
18   Professor Henry Moore was senior physician in the Mater. He was one of the three appointed to represent the hospital when the Committee of Reference was set up by the government. He was Professor of Medicine in UCD and was very well known as an academic both nationally and internationally.
19   Moore, H. 'The Obstruction of Medical Development in Ireland', *The Irish Times*, 21 Nov 1938, p 3.
20   *The Irish Times*, 29 November 1938, p 7.
21   Ibid., 19 December 1938, p 5.
22   Moore, H. op. cit., p 3.
23   This operating theatre is currently being used for day surgery.

The devastation caused by the bombing of the North Strand. (Courtesy of Dublin City Council.)

CHAPTER 9

The War Years

At the beginning of September 1939, World War II was declared. Ireland announced that it intended to remain 'neutral' throughout. On 2 September, the Irish government declared a state of emergency; the Emergency Powers Order was enacted and with it came compulsory legislation that was to affect the entire population for the next seven years. This legislation included provision for media and postal censorship, compulsory cultivation of land and a range of other measures. Because this war was virtually 'on our doorstep', a lot of precautionary measures had to be taken, such as building air raid shelters in the city and also in the hospitals. Air raid shelters were constructed along the middle of O'Connell Street and the Mater built a long shelter on the ground floor of the hospital. It was built according to the specifications laid down by the authorities but it was a crude-looking building, periodically inspected by the local air-raid precaution (ARP) officer. In addition, all the hospital windows were covered with wire netting to protect them in the event of bomb blast. The hospital was also obliged to fit all the windows with blackout facilities. These were to be used at night when the lights were on. On the roof of the hospital, two large circular signs with a big H in the middle of them, visible from the air, were painted in red to warn reconnaissance aircraft of the nature of the building.

The use of the beds, should the war be extended to Ireland, became the subject of much discussion. It was generally felt that the total number of hospital beds in Dublin was inadequate. With the city facing an uncertain situation, arrangements needed to be made to allow for a sudden influx of patients into one or all of the hospitals. At the Mater, the space previously occupied by the old chapel in the west wing was converted into large wards on two floors, thus adding fifty new beds to the overall bed complement in 1939. In addition, more space within the hospital became available when the resident medical staff moved from various residential areas of the hospital to the new medical residence in 1936. Nevertheless, many were worried that the number of beds would still fall far short of what might be needed.

In February 1939, when the prospect of war looked likely, some of the medical staff attended a special planning meeting at the Department of Local Government and Public Health, at which the city's chief engineering inspector and chief architect, as well as the assistant secretary to the Minister were present. The proposals submitted to increase the bed complement at the Mater were ambitious: they ranged from building two floors above the existing operating theatres to provide 150 new surgical beds to building a new 450-bed hospital beside the existing hospital on Eccles Street.[1] The plan was agreed to by the hospital representatives, only if the Minister would sanction the building of a new much-needed nurses' home. The plans got as far as preliminary-sketch stage, but would seem to have then been shelved.

On 12 September 1939, a special meeting was held in the Royal College of Surgeons to discuss the role the hospitals would play if the city was bombed. After much discussion it was decided that the hospitals would consider the following arrangements:

1. That the city hospitals would be turned into casualty clearing stations and that a hospital of 400 beds would be built a short distance outside the city to receive civilian patients from the designated city evacuation hospitals.
2. That provision was to be made for adequate, but simple, operating theatre facilities in the 'outlying' hospital.
3. That the necessary equipment for the treatment of post-operative trauma cases would be made available by the government.
4. That enough nurses, supported by voluntary help from the Red Cross, would be provided.
5. That a minimum resident medical staff of two house surgeons and two house physicians would be in charge of the hospital at all times.
6. That the visiting medical staffs from the Dublin hospitals should attend their own patients.

They went on to list how many beds each of the city hospitals would be obliged to make available. The Mater and Richmond hospitals would provide 100 beds, St Vincent's, the Meath and the Royal City of Dublin hospitals 50 beds each, and Adelaide and Mercer's hospitals 25 beds each. It is interesting to note that Jervis Street Hospital is not mentioned at all and no reason for this is indicated.

The meeting went on to discuss the logistics of how injured patients would be admitted to the hospitals and what protection should be taken in the event of air raids. The government issued a warning to the hospitals that it would not be responsible financially for protection, equipment, or other necessary supplies. Any decontamination required was to be the responsibility of the St John's Ambulance Brigade.

Some officials became somewhat carried away in exercising their duties. In December 1940, the Mother Superior received a request from the local ARP warden requesting the use of the roof of the hospital for the purpose of establishing an observation post. This proposal was refused. Some months later, the ARP authorities wrote an apology to the hospital, saying that they had never sanctioned this proposal.

A Night of Bombs, 1941

The aftermath of the bombing of the North Strand. (Courtesy of Dublin City Council.)

The hospital's emergency plans were soon to be put to the test. Before midnight on 30 May 1941, the drone of an aircraft could be heard over the city, and at 12.04 a.m., the anti-aircraft searchlights over the city were switched on.[2] The first bomb was dropped at 1.28 a.m. and it landed on the North Circular Road, near North Richmond Street. The only person injured was a Brother McKenna from the Christian Brothers School, North Richmond Street, who was caught in the blast. He was taken to the Mater. By the time he reached the hospital, another bomb had fallen nearby on a shop in Summerhill Parade. The owner of the shop was buried in the rubble and it took some hours to rescue her. She was critically injured and was quickly transported to the Mater, as was her next-door neighbour, who was also injured. A third bomb fell in the Phoenix Park, after which there was a lull, but not for long. At 2.05 a.m. a large bomb fell on the North Strand. The blast from this bomb was widespread because it hit the tram tracks, which prevented it sinking into the ground.

The Mater responded immediately. All of the resident staff who were in bed got up and prepared to receive the injured. Some medics and nurses set off to join the Red Cross mobile trauma unit to render on-site help to the injured.[3] Meanwhile, the Matron (Sister Emmanuel O'Connor) assembled all the available nurses, including student nurses, and sent them to where they would be needed most. According to Miss Mai Connolly, then a nurse at the hospital,[4] there was a class of junior nurses who also donned their uniforms but were disappointed when the Matron decided that they did not have the necessary knowledge or experience and would only be in the way. The following day An Taoiseach Éamon de Valera called to the hospital to see the bomb victims and the staff. A total of 28 people were killed in the bombing of the North Strand, and 11 more would later die of their injuries.

The bomb site, according to the Mater staff was a shocking sight. 'Limbless bodies lay close to where the bomb had dropped,' as one reported. The injured were given first aid and dispatched to the hospitals. The Mater received 28 injured that night, including two babies. The worst cases were those who had lost limbs or eyes. Many were suffering from crush injuries and fractures, having been hit by masonry. Some had been hit by flying glass and a few were suffering from burns. Injured people kept coming throughout the night and into daylight hours and began to fill the casualty department, while bodies were arriving at the hospital mortuary, including one entire family of seven, killed in their beds. They were brought in a lorry to the Mater mortuary, where they remained until the day of the inquest at the city morgue. According to the *Irish Independent*, 'Tragic scenes were witnessed at all the hospitals during the week-end as distraught people sought missing relatives.'[5] In total, 39 people were killed, 90 were injured and 300 homes were destroyed by the German bombs.

Struggles during the War Years

The bombing of the North Strand was to be the last in Ireland during World War II, but the country had many desperate problems at this time. Under the shadow cast by the Civil War, Ireland was plagued with high levels of poverty and people suffered from a low standard of health. Perhaps more important, Ireland was still dependent on Britain for supplies, especially of food and fuel. It wasn't too long before rationing came to the country. Early in the war, Britain had introduced a system of rationing food, petrol, clothing and other items and towards the end of 1941 the Irish population was obliged to follow suit. People had to register for ration books for items such as tea, sugar, butter, flour and bread.[6] Petrol was rationed and eventually only supplied to doctors and the emergency services. Cars went off the roads. Clothing was rationed, which became a problem where nurse's uniforms were concerned. Coal, gas and electricity were also rationed. Rationing extended to hospitals, but somehow the Mater was able to supply enough food to both patients and staff, albeit in meagre amounts, without running into serious difficulties; but this required skill and effort. Government regulations meant that the hospital staff had to submit their food coupons to the hospital authorities and the hospital had to register with food suppliers to ensure that rationing was observed. Thankfully, the Mater was able to supplement the rations with vegetables grown on the vacant land to the east of the hospital (now occupied by the adult hospital) and all linen was laundered and repaired in the hospital laundry room.

● *This aerial photo of the Mater, taken in 1959, shows the extensive vegetable garden on the upper right hand side, below the large new nurses' home.*

The Problem of Tuberculosis

Chief among the problems dogging the country at this time was TB, a silent plague hidden in the population, which was made worse by the effects of food rationing. Furthermore, the large slum areas which had filled the city remained breeding grounds for diseases like rickets, caused by a deficiency in Vitamin D, and TB. Tuberculosis has probably always existed in Ireland to some extent. In records[7] held at the Mater, there is evidence that during a five-month period in 1866, 19 people from one residence in the city died in the hospital.[8] Eight of these were young people who died a few days after being admitted with tuberculosis. The others died from heart disease and scarlatina or scarlet fever.

As the incidence of tuberculosis continued to rise during the war years, various committees were set up in Dublin. Probably the best known of these was the Dublin Hospitals' Tuberculosis Committee, on which sat medical representatives from the larger hospitals. The Mater was represented by Sir Arthur Chance, a senior surgeon at the hospital, who worked towards making it a notifiable disease.[9] The committee's work was very much encouraged by Lady Isabel Aberdeen, wife of the Viceroy. Lady Aberdeen founded the Women's National Health Association, which did a considerable amount of good work in health education about TB.

However, in spite of the efforts of many, gradually the hospitals were filling up with long-stay cases of tuberculosis and so the need for secondary treatment facilities became critical. In 1914, the Sisters of Mercy had purchased a mansion in Dún Laoghaire, called The Cedars, on sixty acres of land. Before they actually bought the place they had asked Sir Christopher Nixon to visit and advise them as to whether it would be suitable for development as a sanatorium. There were only two sanatoria in Dublin at the time and it was difficult to get patients admitted to either of them.

Nixon visited on 2 July 1914 and wrote a report indicating that it would be ideal for development as a sanatorium. The sisters duly purchased it and extensive renovations were carried out. It was officially opened and named Our Lady of Lourdes Hospital on 11 February 1918. Patients with TB were transferred to it from the Mater and the medical staff provided all the expertise needed in their treatment.

When World War II began, the three main killer diseases in Ireland were heart disease, cancer and tuberculosis, in that order; however, it is likely that if every case of tuberculosis in the country was correctly identified, it would undoubtedly have been listed as the number one disease. TB was generally hard to identify as a single entity because of the number of names it was called: in the hospital it was generally referred to as *phthisis*[10] (pulmonary tuberculosis), *consumption* or any of its less obvious manifestations such as 'glands', 'Potts caries' (tuberculosis affecting the spine), etc. Frequently, patients arrived with some other medical or surgical condition and were found to have tuberculosis as a co-existing disease or as a contributing factor.

The problem for all the hospitals was the risk it posed for the staff, especially the nursing staff. Statistically it was found that approximately 9.9% of all hospital nurses became infected in the course of their work. They were three times more likely to develop the condition than medical students, who were considered to be the next most 'at risk' group within the system. This began to cause concern not only within the hospitals, but also at government level.

A whole national programme of providing accommodation for those suffering from tuberculosis was drawn up in the 1940s. At the end of July 1942, the Medical Officer of Health wrote to the Mater requesting increased facilities for the treatment of tuberculosis and suggesting that the hospital might consider erecting wooden huts in the hospital grounds for patients it was known would be long-term cases. E.T. Freeman, then Secretary of the Medical Board, replied:

13 November 1942

Dear Sir,

Your letter of the 25th July has been duly considered by the Medical Board, whose view it is, that increased facilities for treatment of tuberculosis in clinical hospitals are desirable.

The Board, however, is not in favour of wooden huts as such, as properly ventilated and solidly constructed wards are much better. We would not either view with favour, the establishment in city hospitals of units where advanced cases might be left for indefinite periods.

A hospital unit should be one where doubtful cases of tuberculous infection could be diagnosed, and the degree of activity estimated; where active treatment, either by pneumothorax or surgical methods of lung collapse, could be carried out on suitable patients, whilst awaiting admission to a sanatorium.

In this connection, I would like to point out that the Mater Misericordiae Hospital has been doing this work on a considerable scale for the past ten years.

Yours truly,

E.T. Freeman

Secretary to the Medical Board

During the war years, as the problem of TB became alarmingly widespread, the Irish Red Cross became involved in dealing with the problem in a number of ways, including sponsoring nurses' training. In 1948, with over a thousand patients awaiting admission to sanatoria, the government embarked on a major building programme of multiple small sanatoria throughout the country, with the help of funds from the Hospitals Trust. Before they reached the end of this scheme, however, the incidence of tuberculosis in Ireland was beginning to decline. This was largely due to the development of streptomycin, which, at long last, proved a useful weapon against the disease.

The Dawn of Specialisation at the Mater

From the time of the appointment of Thomas More Madden as an obstetric physician in 1878, the idea of treating patients with similar medical conditions together and in the care of a 'specialist' came into existence. In the late 1800s, patients suffering from skin conditions were treated at a special dermatology clinic and were the responsibility of the assistant physician in charge of what was then known as the dispensary (outpatients). The other group of patients who were cohorted for treatment purposes were those with eye conditions. They were in the care of one of the senior medical staff with a special interest in eye diseases. When the dispensary and pharmacy moved from the ground-floor area, two wards were developed for all eye cases admitted and another two wards for ear, nose and throat (ENT) cases. Some years later a small operating theatre was built beside the 'eye ward' (St Anthony's Theatre) for both eye surgery and ENT surgery. When the Phase 1A ward block opened (1989), both eye cases and ENT patients transferred to new wards. The area vacated was reorganised and eventually opened as an infectious diseases unit. Further restructuring of this unit commenced in 2006 in order to install special air-handling equipment in the isolation rooms. In December 2008, the unit was formally opened as St Bernard's Ward. It is categorised as a National Isolation Facility.

The growth of specialisation took hold after World War II, and in the Mater, this could clearly be seen in the reorganisation of the hospital's east wing. Up to 1945, all staff, except the senior medical staff, were in residence in the hospital, a large number being accommodated in the east wing, in a series of dormitories for the kitchen, cleaning and laundry staff. After the new nurses' home opened in 1954, they were moved to the old nurses' home, then named Rosary House. Once the place was emptied the medical staff began to actively discuss possibilities for the space. They were anxious that the hospital should respond to the growing interest in cardiology after the war and they were anxious to set up a specialist unit for patients suffering from heart disease (statistically the most prevalent disease in Ireland at the time). There was also a need for a larger physiotherapy department and it was decided to include it in this section.

A Cardiac Unit

Some years before the east wing became available, discussions had been taking place with the Minister for Health[11] regarding the possible development of a cardiac unit at the Mater for both medical and surgical conditions. In this regard, the sisters were responding to the great medical advances taking place in cardiac treament at the time. However, the minister made it known that he was against the hospital undertaking cardiac surgery and would not fund anything to do with it. He also disputed the wisdom of undertaking cardiac catheterisations in the proposed unit.[12] The correspondence relating to this was very protracted and eventually John Charles McQuaid, Archbishop of Dublin, became involved (in support of the Sisters' request for the proposed cardiac unit).

When the east wing was vacated in January 1956, construction commenced. The plan was to locate the cardiac unit at one end of the wing and a physiotherapy department at the other, with a corridor leading to the X-ray department forming the 'dividing line' between the two departments. Unfortunately, the estimated cost caused delays well beyond anything expected by the Sisters, who were the driving force in this development. The cardiac unit consisted of male and female wards. Between the wards a special cardiac outpatients department was built, an ECG (electrocardiograph) room and an X-ray room. The X-ray room was equipped to provide chest X-rays as

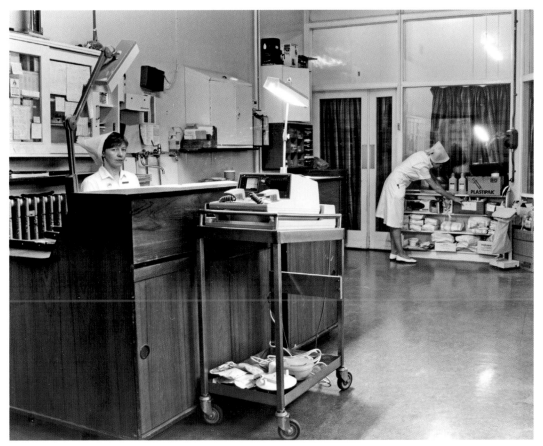

An early photo of the Coronary Care Unit, taken in the 1970s.

well as cardiac screening and cardiac catheterisation procedures. It was built as a self-contained unit, using all the available knowledge and experience of the 1950s. The whole place was put into the care of Sister John of the Cross (Ferguson) who had trained as a nurse at the Mater and then as a radiographer. She spent many years working as a radiographer in the cardiac X-ray unit.

The sisters' foresight in building the cardiac unit was proved right. As will be seen in the next chapter on surgery, specialist treatment of heart disease began to develop at the Mater more or less at the same time as the cardiac unit opened. The seed was sown by Mother Madeline McCormack,[13] who as Reverend Mother, felt that the Mater should provide for young patients suffering from rheumatic heart disease, and the consequent problems of chronic carditis and cardiac valve stenosis,[14] leading ultimately to congestive cardiac failure in relatively young adults.

The Physiotherapy Department

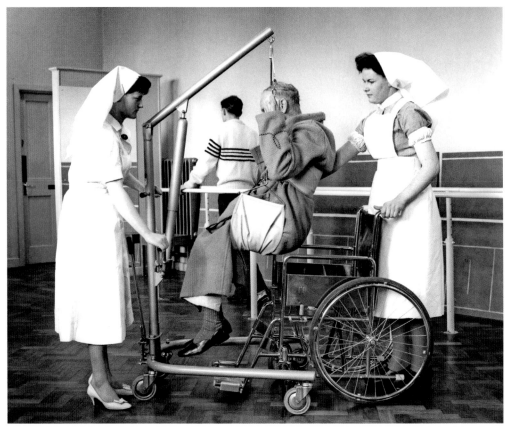

● *This patient is being lowered into a wheelchair to be taken for physiotherapy treatment.*

At the other end of the east wing, the physiotherapy department was constructed. It, too, was based on the available knowledge of the 1950s and it served the hospital well until a large new department was built as part of the Phase 1A development in 1989. The 1950s' department consisted of a treatment area, a small gymnasium, a doctor's consulting room and an office. Sr Concepta Greene was appointed physiotherapist in charge of the department and became Matron of the Hospital in 1943.[15]

Of course, the use of physiotherapy in the treatment of the sick and injured is probably as old as humanity itself. However, it is in more recent times that its function and many applications have been clinically defined. Records show that, in the Mater, physiotherapy was being used as far back as 1898, when 'massage', given by a designated nurse, was offered to the private patients, for which they were charged two guineas per week or five shillings per session. In 1913, the patients could have 'electricity' added at a total cost of seven shillings and six pence per session.[16] But the true value of physiotherapy became clear in the 20th century, and the Mater physiotherapy department now offers a full range of services for both musculoskeletal and cardiorespiratory problems. In addition, a rehabilitation service is provided for

A class of physiotherapy students at a prizegiving ceremony in 1959. They are all sitting on the hard benches of the outpatients department.

those present following trauma such as spinal injury, head injury or stroke. It offers such assistance as 'chest clearance techniques, progressive exercise and controlled mobilisation... in order to prevent and treat many of the complications associated with respiratory conditions and surgical procedures.'[17]

When the east wing plans were being discussed in the late 1940s, the subject of staff for the physiotherapy department became an important issue, mainly because physiotherapy were scarce and difficult to recruit in Ireland. John Charles McQuaid, then Archbishop of Dublin, took up the issue, focusing on the particular difficulty that Catholics in Ireland were having in accessing physiotherapy training.[18] The Archbishop decided that the only way this problem could be solved was by opening a school for physiotherapy in association with University College Dublin (UCD). He invited his friend, Dr Dermot Roden, Director of the Physiotherapy Department at the Richmond Hospital, to discuss it with Dr Michael Tierney, President of UCD, and it was agreed on the need for a school. The Archbishop saw that the Mater might be able to help, particularly as it had just opened a new physiotherapy department. At the Mater, Dr Roden met with nothing but enthusiasm for the suggestion. Mother Gabriel was anxious to help in any way she could, which Dr Roden found very encouraging, especially as she was prepared to provide him immediately with a possible location for the school. Without delay, Mother Gabriel consulted with the architects and soon the development was on its way.

The staff of the physiotherapy department in 1959. The lady at the centre is Pauline Walsh, who was in charge of the department.

The hospital centenary celebrations, featuring, from left, Dr E.T. Freeman; Prof. Michael Tierney, President of UCD; Dr Dermot Roden, Head of the School of Physiotherapy; and Prof. E. Keenan, Dean of the Faculty of Medicine.

In the meantime, Dr Roden set off to recruit someone for the post of principal of the physiotherapy school. With some difficulty, he eventually managed to make contact with Sr Kevin Reynolds, a nun in Birmingham, who had been the principal of a physiotherapy school that had recently closed. Sr Kevin agreed to fill the post on a temporary basis. She arrived at the Mater in 1955. In the same year, Dr Roden was appointed Medical Director of the physiotherapy department and of the School of Physiotherapy.

Sr Kevin's biggest difficulty was a shortage of physiotherapy teachers, which made establishing a school difficult, Nonetheless, the school started in October 1955, with an intake of 23 students. It had been agreed by then that UCD would award a university diploma to students who qualified in the Chartered Society of Physiotherapist examination (UK), which had been organised by Sr Kevin. Some months after the school opened, Eileen Riordan joined the teaching staff, followed in 1959 by Mairead Lynch. In the meantime, Mother Gabriel selected two of the Sisters, Sr Gemma Byrne and Sr Reparata Hanly and arranged for them to train first as physiotherapists and later as physiotherapy teachers. They both became members of the school staff.

In 1961, Sr Kevin, feeling that her work was done, returned to her community in Birmingham and her place was taken by Ann Curran and then in 1962 by Betty Jones. Miss Jones held the post at the Mater until 1988 when she retired and was succeeded by Dr Mary Garrett. In 1982, physiotherapy became a degree course and was incorporated into the medical school of University College Dublin. On 9 February 2005, the Mater hosted a special event to mark the transfer of the School of Physiotherapy at the Mater to its current location in the School of Health Sciences at UCD's Belfield Campus.

The head of the physiotherapy department, Dr Mary Garrett, stands with Prof. Bill Powderly, and on the right, Prof. Conor O'Keane.

The Child Guidance Clinic

The Child Guidance Clinic.

In 1962, a very significant building development reached completion and was formally opened on 7 October: the Child Guidance Clinic, a purpose-built, child-friendly unit to address the needs of a very vulnerable group in society, children with difficulties and their families. The founding professional team at the clinic were:

Dr Seán Malone (neuropsychiatrist) as Medical Director
Dr Maureen Walsh (child psychiatrist)
Sr Jo Kennedy (speech therapist) and administrator for many years
Pia Kasteel (psychologist)
Anita Thompson (psychiatric social worker)
Sr Margherita Rock (psychiatric social worker)

At the end of 1964, Dr Paul McQuaid joined the staff and was appointed to the position of Medical Director. Dr Nuala Healy (child psychiatrist) deputised for him in 1969. In 1972, she was appointed to a permanent position on the staff of the clinic where she worked for many years. In 1965, the clinic was accredited for the training of social workers. This was to be the beginning of similar arrangements for other academic

Child Guidance Clinic – Sr Margherita Rock with children and staff.

disciplines, such as psychology and speech therapy. In 1970, two satellite facilities were opened: St Paul's Hospital and special school for autistic children, which opened at Beaumont Woods and a clinic in Ballymun. Four teams from the clinic provided services to the inner-city area, along with Darndale, Swords and Balbriggan.

By 2008, new developments on the Mater campus necessitated the demolition of a number of buildings, including the Child Guidance Clinic, to make way for the construction of the new Whitty Building. To facilitate this, the entire department was moved to an inner-city location on James Joyce Street. In 2012, the Golden Jubilee of the clinic was celebrated.

Dr Paul McQuaid, Medical Director of the Child Guidance Clinic.

1   Where the Breast Check and Symptomatic Breast Care units are now.
2   Kearns, Kevin C. (2009), *The Bombing of Dublin's North Strand, 1941 – the Untold Story*, Dublin: Gill & Macmillan, p 3.
3   *The Irish Times*, 2 June 1941.
4   Mary Josephine Connolly qualified as a nurse in the Mater and went on to become a Sister of Mercy. She worked for many years in St Kevin's Hospital, James Street; St Michael's Hospital, Dun Laoghaire; Jervis Street Hospital and eventually the Mater Hospital, where she became Matron. She retired from that position when her health declined and took on the job of nurse adviser to the design team when Phase 1A was being designed/built and eventually opened. For many years after her eventual retirement from active service, she worked as Convent Bursar. She died suddenly on the night of 8 November 2005, when all the Sisters were busy getting ready to move from the convent in the west wing of the hospital to the new convent on the North Circular Road.
5   *Irish Independent*, 2 June 1941, p 3.
6   Bread was rationed for a short time only.
7   Death Certs. Form D (19 November 1866 – 2 June 1867).
8   The address of these people is given as Merrion Square – by no means a slum area.
9   In 1942, notification of TB as an infectious disease was restricted to infective cases only. There was a fear within the government that if it made all cases of TB notifiable it would increase the reluctance of the population to seek medical advice at the outset of the disease. See: http://historical-debates.oireachtas.ie/D/0087.194206030015.html.
10 According to T.P. Kilfeather, writing in the *Sunday Independent*, 12 April 1964, p 2, 'The struggle against tuberculosis has been long. Homer knew about its dreadful progress within the human body. Hippocrates described it and he called it "phthisis" (from a Greek verb meaning "to dry up"). This was the description applied to the disease until the nineteenth century by the medical men.'
11 The Minister for Health was Mr T.F. O'Higgins.
12 The minister insisted that cardiac catheterisation should be undertaken in the X-ray department only.
13 Mother Madeline McCormack trained as a nurse in the Mater and worked for many years as a ward sister. She was much loved by everyone. There is no record extant as to how she became interested in this particular group of patients.
14 Inflammation of the heart. Mitral valve problems associated with rheumatic fever usually occur because the leaflets/cusps of the valves eventually sick together and compromise the flow of blood – valve stenosis.
15 Sr Concepta Greene trained as a nurse before becoming a physiotherapist.
16 *Mater Misericordiae Hospital Dublin, Thirty Seventh Session 1898–99*, p 13, and *Report of the Mater Misericordiae Hospital, Dublin, for the year 1913* (1913), Dollard Printing House, Dublin, p 34.
17 http://www.mater.ie/services/depts/p/physiotherapy
18 This was part of a wider problem experienced at the time of Catholics accessing any third-level education (apart from the National University of Ireland colleges), not only in this country, but also in Britain.

CHAPTER 10

'A Plant of Slow Growth': the Development of Surgery

A s this quote from George Washington suggests, surgery did not play a significant role in 19th-century hospitals. The four surgeons appointed to the Mater in 1861 when it opened[1] were all probably selected for academic reasons, rather than need, as surgery during the first few years was minimal. According to the annual report of 1866,[2] most of the surgical cases treated were limb fractures and there were three cases of bullet wounds.

When John Bristowe visited the Mater in 1863 on behalf of the British government, he discovered that, 'Of the 32 surgical cases, six might be regarded as acute, including two of simple fracture, one compound fracture, a case of erysipelas, and a burn; 26 were chronic or trivial cases, including ulcers of the leg, diseases of the eye, and chronic inflammation of joints. There were two cases operated on that day, both doing well, vis., a case of amputation of the leg, and one of a purely trivial nature.'[3]

Furthermore, whilst the number of surgical cases gradually increased, the welfare of surgical patients was hardly a priority. Year after year, until about 1900, the same statement appeared in the hospital's annual report:

> In the surgical department the number of operations successfully performed has been greater than in any previous year and we are assured by our Medical Staff that the very great measure of success attending these operations is, to a large extent, to be attributed to the excellent hygienic conditions as regards air-space, ventilation, diet, and general surroundings which our patients, as compared with those of other metropolitan hospitals, enjoy.[4]

And, without the benefit of electricity, technological developments were slow, apart from Francis Cruise's notable discovery of the endoscope.[5] Cruise's invention was so notable it was written about in the medical journals of the time, including the *British Medical Journal*.[6]

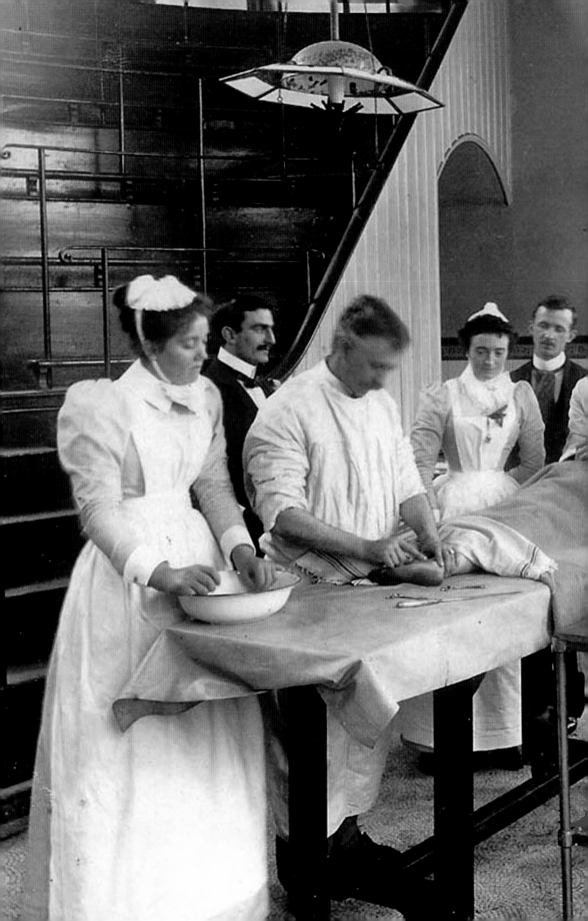

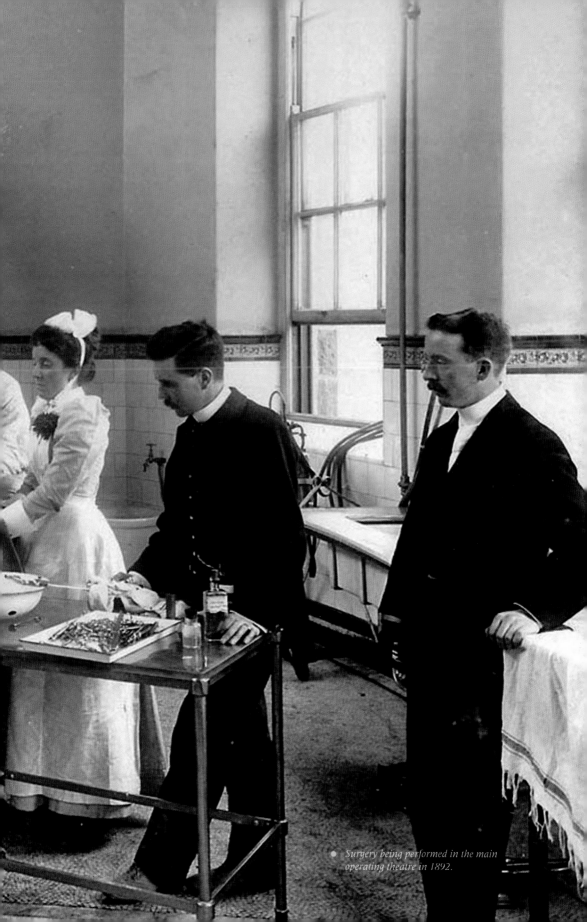

Surgery being performed in the main operating theatre in 1892.

In the early years of surgery, it was dangerous and often fatal. Surgeons and hospital staff had yet to understand the concept of wound infection, and infections were often widespread in hospitals. In 1889, J. Dowling, who, as we saw in Chapter 4, witnessed surgeon Charles Coppinger operating, wrote of his experience as an assistant to Coppinger:

> I began to take an interest in surgery and attended regularly in the operating theatre. The days were long past in which the surgeon when operating wore an old frock-coat which had seen much service in the operating theatre. Though antiseptic methods had been in use for some years in the Mater, modern antiseptic technique had not been developed and sterilised gowns, masks[7] and rubber gloves were not worn. Instruments were sterilised by being immersed for half an hour in a solution of carbolic acid, but soon afterwards, a water steriliser was provided in which they were boiled. The surgeon's preparations were simple. Having removed his coat, he put on a waterproof apron, turned up his shirt sleeves, thoroughly scrubbed his hands and forearms, disinfected them in an antiseptic solution and was ready to begin his work.
>
> Many of the operations were of a minor nature, because owing to the want of facilities for surgical work in most of the country infirmaries, a large proportion of the cases were sent to the city hospitals. Emergency operations were rare and during my eighteen months' residence in hospital, which terminated in 1892, I had never seen an operation for appendicitis... Patients suffering from perforation of gastric or duodenal ulcers were operated on, invariably with fatal results, when peritonitis had developed.[8]

The concept of sepsis and antisepsis became more widely understood as the century progressed, and this, with better understanding of the science of the human body, meant that surgery could finally be effective in the treatment of injury and disease.

The next 'stepping stone' in the development of successful surgery was anaesthesia. In the early days, ether and chloroform were the anaesthetics used, and they were not without their hazards – one of them being that it was assigned to the 'junior' in the theatre to act as anaesthetist![9] Sometimes the junior was only a student, but usually the task fell to the medical intern. (There is no mention in any of the surgical records in the Mater of any mishaps or fatalities.) The anaesthetic equipment sat on the floor, a small wooden box with a container of ether or chloroform standing in it and a rubber tube connecting it to a rubber mask, which was placed over the patient's face. As surgery became more complex and prolonged, the role of the anaesthetist evolved into a speciality in its own right with a qualified anaesthetist in charge.

The Mater appointed its first anaesthetist in 1899, a Dr Michael O'Sullivan, who had just qualified as a medical doctor. Even in his part-time role, he started making changes in order to make things easier for patients undergoing anaesthesia. O'Sullivan was succeeded in 1904 by Dr James Hayes. His successor, Dr Patrick J. O'Farrell, who remained in the post for thirty years until his death in 1936, would undoubtedly have witnessed the great progressions in surgery at the time, brought about by the traumas of World War I, the Easter Rising and the Civil War. Indeed, a second anaesthetist was appointed in 1918, Dr Hugh Kelly, who gave many years of sterling service to the hospital. The appointment of Dr Patrick Drury-Byrne in 1931 increased the number of anaesthetists to three. By 1960, there were five anaesthetists, together with one anaesthetic registrar and one house doctor.[10]

It is said that the work of dealing with war-wounded individuals and the victims of civil strife advanced medical science and surgical techniques at this time. It's certainly true that by the turn of the century, surgery had become safer, because of developments in understanding infection and in anaesthesia. However, the world had to wait for the discoveries of Austrian-American scientist Karl Landsteiner in 1902 before safe blood transfusions became a possibility. Landsteiner defined the ABO blood-group system, which meant that blood transfusions became much safer. By the end of World War II, medical science began to move at a remarkable rate. The antibiotics penicillin and streptomycin were in clinical use by 1945, developments which would change the whole field of surgery and make it a great deal safer.

A New Era

So rapid were developments in the second half of the 20th century that by 1953, malfunctions of the heart could be surgically corrected. The first case of cardiac surgery in the Mater was carried out in that year, when surgery was performed on a young girl suffering from mitral stenosis. Stenosis occurs because the leaflets/cusps of the valves eventually stick together, harden and compromise the flow of blood, i.e. *valve stenosis*. Mitral valve problems at this time were usually associated with rheumatic heart disease. John Corcoran, who was known for his excellent surgery, decided to perform a 'closed' mitral valvotomy on the young patient. He skilfully inserted a special blade through the atrium and severed the stenotic adhesions to allow the blood to flow more freely through the heart. He did this without stopping the heart beating. He was assisted by Mr Eoin O'Malley, who would go on to be one of the most dedicated and successful surgeons of his generation, anaesthetists Dr Alex Blayney, Dr Hugh Raftery and Dr Patrick Nagle, and Dr Kevin Malley (physician-in-charge, cardiac unit). The surgery was carried out successfully. The patient made a quick recovery and was sent to Beaumont convalescent home to recover.

In 1957, as equipment and knowledge were advancing, Eoin O'Malley, now Professor of Surgery, began to explore the possibility of performing more advanced cardiac surgery, so that more patients could be helped. The first cases he dealt with were adult cases of mitral valve stenosis in 1959, followed by the even more challenging area of congenital heart abnormalities, commencing with cases of patent ductus arteriosis (PDA) in children. This is a congenital heart defect in which the ductus arteriosis does not close after birth, which can lead to heart failure in time. Surgical treatment involves

The first heart surgery performed in the Mater Hospital, a mitral valvotomy, in 1953. Surgeon John Corcoran is assisted by Eoin O'Malley.

open heart surgery, which at the time posed its own challenge – that of trying to open and operate on a pumping heart. O'Malley embarked on what was then the accepted technique – 'controlled hypothermia', in which the patient's core body temperature was reduced and in turn this reduced the oxygen requirement of the body for a short period of time, long enough to allow surgery to be performed. The first open heart paediatric cases that O'Malley and his team undertook, on 17 December 1957, consisted of repairing congenital atrial septal defects (ASDs),[11] i.e. 'hole-in-the-heart' cases.[12] The burden of this pioneering work for O'Malley and the surgical team was enormous. It was not unusual to find him pacing the corridor outside St Anne's Ward late into the night until he was satisfied that some child's condition was stable after surgery. By February 1960, according to *The Irish Times*:

> At the Mater, 100 cases of congenital heart disease and 68 cases of acquired heart disease have been operated on, using many of the most complicated techniques of modern heart surgery, many of which have only been developed within the last few years.[13]

A Technological Breakthrough

However, it was to be the arrival of the heart–lung machine that would change cardiac surgery significantly. This machine, which would take over the functions of the heart and lungs whilst the patient was undergoing surgery, held enormous potential. The Mater's first heart–lung machine arrived on 3 March 1961 and the first priority for the surgical team was to familiarise themselves with the machine and what it could do. They set up a research laboratory in a small building in the hospital grounds, testing the machine first on dogs. Only when the team was proficient did they undertake cardiac surgery on patients and the procedures they were able to do were, on the whole, very successful. The team was able to undertake a number of operations that would have previously been considered too dangerous, such as replacing heart valves, patching holes in the heart and operating on 'blue babies' (those suffering from the heart condition Fallot's tetralogy). The technology was truly revolutionary.

The heart–lung machine – also known as a 'pump', was a specialist piece of equipment and needed a specialist to operate it. The Mater's first pump technician, or perfusionist, was a Ms Eileen McCabe. Today, a

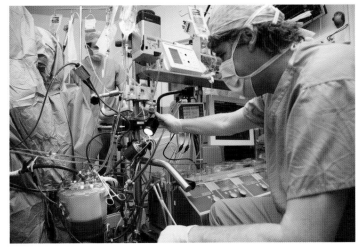

● *A perfusionist at work.*

team of perfusionists perform all the necessary work associated with these life-saving machines, including cleaning and sterilisation.

The work of the surgery team at this point in the Mater's history was challenging and often groundbreaking as new possibilities in surgery opened up, and new ways to improve the life of cardiac patients. So it seemed entirely appropriate that the hospital should receive a visit from the first ever surgeon to perform cardiac transplant surgery, Professor Christiaan Barnard.[14]

Developments in Critical Care

Having received Professor Barnard in the Pillar Room, the surgeon was taken on a tour of the ICU. The intensive care unit had by then been in place for ten years, to offer specialist care for cardiac patients after surgery. The first ICU was originally a dormitory for resident medical students. When it was refurbished and equipped, it had a capacity for five beds and was named the Recovery Room. About a year later, a smaller room adjoining it was annexed as a two-bed acute coronary care unit.[15]

With specialist cardiac care developing apace, it was quickly understood that the nurses working in the ICU would need special training. In the early days, nurses had been assigned without any special training other than experience in a surgical ward. The then Matron, Sr Concepta Greene, felt that nurses should take post-registration education not just for critical care, but in other specialist areas, too. In 1969, a programme was drawn up and submitted to the Nursing Board (An Bord Altranais)

● *Christiaan Barnard sits with the nurses during his famous visit to the Mater.*

and to the Department of Health for their approval. It was the first time courses of this kind were made available in Ireland and they were enthusiastically received. In the meantime, Sr Attracta (Kavanagh), who had been given responsibility for the intensive care unit,[16] was sent to Birmingham's Queen Elizabeth Hospital to undertake their course in intensive nursing care. She subsequently went to Copenhagen in late 1970 to study the design and management of intensive care units and later to the Mayo Clinic, USA, to observe the day-to-day management of an ICU. At the Mayo Clinic, Sr Attracta got the opportunity to see the first use of computerised equipment, a development which was yet to happen in the Mater.

● *Sr Attracta Kavanagh, RSM, was in charge of the ICU from 1960 to 1979.*

biography

Professor Eoin O'Malley 1919–2007

Eoin O'Malley was born in 1919 in Galway into a well-known medical family. His father, Michael O'Malley, was professor of surgery in University College Galway and he played a major role in the development of medical services in the west of Ireland during his lifetime. Eoin O'Malley received his early education in Galway and later at the Jesuit College, Clongowes Wood, where he gained first place in Ireland in a number of Leaving Certificate subjects. He started his medical studies at Galway University and later University College Dublin. He qualified as a doctor in 1942, having attained first place in all his examinations and having won a gold medal in surgery. His career was brilliant throughout. After qualifying, he served as an intern in the Mater Hospital and continued his postgraduate studies for a further six years in

● *Eoin O'Malley*

Dublin, London and the United States. He obtained a Fellowship of the Royal College of Surgeons in Ireland (FRCSI) and the MCh degree from the National University of Ireland (NUI) in 1947. All the time his interest in cardiac surgery was growing.

In 1950, he was appointed assistant surgeon in the Mater and in 1952 a consultant surgeon. In 1953, he assisted surgeon John Corcoran in the first heart operation performed in the Mater. At this time interest was growing internationally in this complex speciality. Eoin O'Malley focused much of his spare time on developing not only his own skills, but the necessary skills of his surgical team to undertake further cardiac surgical procedures. He was appointed general and cardiac surgeon in the Mater in 1957. The following year he was appointed UCD Professor of Surgery, a position he held until his retirement in 1985. After his retirement he was awarded the title of Emeritus Professor of Surgery.

Eoin O'Malley was a man of few words. He was an excellent listener and whatever he had to say was borne out of a profound and considerable wisdom. He was a hard worker and was highly regarded by both his medical and nursing colleagues. It is generally accepted that his finest contribution to medical progress in Ireland was in the field of cardiac surgery, which ultimately led to the setting up in the Mater of the National Cardiac Surgery Unit in 1971, subsequently renamed the Eoin O'Malley National Cardiac Surgical Unit.

Eoin O'Malley took a keen interest in what was being taught to the nurses and by whom. He gained the co-operation of his colleagues in various specialities and disciplines, both from within the hospital and elsewhere, to contribute to the educational input of the programmes.[17] A lot of help, especially in the early days of the intensive care course, was given by one of his team, Maurice Neligan, then a junior member of the cardiac surgical team, but who would later become a leading surgeon both in Ireland and internationally. He was an excellent teacher and very enthusiastic about his work.

There is a vast difference between the skills and clinical competencies required today, compared with those in 1970, which has been driven by the nature and complexities of the surgery being undertaken, not to mention the high-powered equipment and new techniques now available.

In addition to the six-month programme, run in association with the School of Nursing, University College Dublin, as a Higher Diploma course in critical care nursing, a Graduate Diploma course in critical care nursing was set up some years ago. It is affiliated to University College Dublin, is a much longer and broader programme and requires nurses to have a primary degree in nursing and to undertake a number of clinical placements in intensive care units. In 2010, a special course for nurses, Cardiothoracic – Transplantation, commenced at the Mater, reflecting the rapid developments in transplant surgery which have taken place over the last twenty years, in which the Mater Hospital has lead the field.

A Time of 'Firsts'

● *Sr Gerard Egan.*

● *Ita Greene, who was theatre superintendent from 1987 to 1998.*

From the late 1960s to the present day, there have been a number of 'firsts' in surgery for the Mater. Sr Gerard Egan, then theatre superintendent, was witness to some of the most exciting developments in cardiac surgery. She was present at the first use of the 'pump', or heart–lung machine by Eoin O'Malley in 1961; she saw the first artificial heart valve (Starr-Edwards mitral valve to relieve mitral stenosis) inserted in March 1965, again by Professor O'Malley; she was part of the team when the first coronary artery bypass surgery to be carried out in Ireland was performed by Maurice Neligan on 1 April 1975, and when the first human heart transplant was carried out by Maurice Neligan, with fellow surgeon Freddie Wood, on 10 September 1985.[18] Sr Gerard was there for it all.

Sr Gerard would also witness the growth of the surgical team at the time. Professor O'Malley was the key surgeon and had performed most of the cardiac surgery at the Mater during these early years. Later, he was joined by Keith Shaw, who had been developing his skills at the Royal City of Dublin Hospital in Baggot Street, and in 1972 by Maurice Neligan, fresh from his studies at the Mayo Clinic. The number of cardiac surgeons gradually increased, along with developments in surgery, with Freddie Wood joining the Mater team in 1984 and David Luke a year or two later. By the time Neligan and Wood and a very dedicated surgical team carried out the first cardiac transplantation at the Mater in 1985, the cardio-thoracic surgery team had carried out 819 cases of open-heart surgery. But no matter how long or hard their hours of surgery, they couldn't keep pace with the growing waiting list for cardiac surgery. By the 1980s, by which time the department had become the National Cardiac Surgical Unit, over 1,000 adult open-heart cases were being performed annually. It was by then one of the biggest units in this part of the world.[19]

● *Prof. A.E. Wood.*

Sr Gerard retires in 1987 after twenty-seven years as theatre superintendent. Back row, from left: F.X. O'Connell, W. Hederman, Eoin O'Malley, P. McAuley, S. Heffernan, F. McManus, S. Smith, D. Moriarty. Front row, from left: Freddie Wood, Sr Gerard Egan, Maurice Neligan.

Critical Care at the Mater

The 1970s was a time of rapid expansion of the intensive care unit. As soon as the new cardiac theatres became available (in 1971), attention was turned to making more critical care space available. It always seemed to fall short of what was needed. As space and funding became available, extensions were built. The first major project was the

Susie Kehoe working in the intensive care unit.

reconfiguration of St Agatha's Ward (west wing). Shortly after, St Cecilia's Ward beside it was annexed on and the whole extension was then called St Cecilia's. This new development was officially opened in 1984 and it provided the much-needed intensive care beds – but not for long. As the amount of cardiac surgery continued to increase (1,124 cases in 1984), more ICU beds were needed.[20]

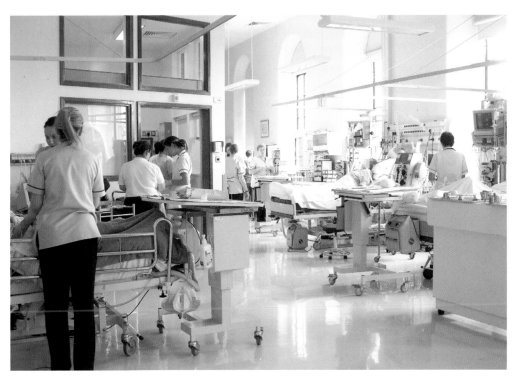

The intensive care unit.

In time, a 'step-down' facility, for patients who were doing well but still needed a degree of intensive care, was planned but remained on hold until after the opening of the new 353-bed ward block (phase 1A, 1989). When 1A opened, most of the patients on the top floor of the old building were moved to the new ward block, leaving an ideal area available for redevelopment. This included St Catherine's Ward beside the intensive care unit. In 1993, St Catherine's was turned into a nine-bed high dependency unit (HDU)[21] with the rest of this floor being turned into additional beds for pre- and post-operative cardiac surgical patients and renamed St Cecilia's 1, 2 and 3.[22] And, as heart and lung transplants became a reality, on 29 March 2004, a new heart–lung transplant unit was formally opened. It contains six high-dependency beds and two high-dependency isolation cubicles. This building stands on massive metal stilts (30m high) and is a prefab, as the facility will ultimately form part of the new Mater Hospital (Whitty Building).

Major changes were also made to enlarge the intensive care facilities along the west wing (also St Cecilia's). This involved placing a temporary ceiling over the ornate one of the first chapel built in 1886, and enlarging the available space by moving the corridor walls to allow for special (air-conditioned) cubicles for transplant patients. In addition, the whole place was designed to allow for special beds, monitoring equipment, treatment devices and space for the nurses and doctors to attend to very major cases.

When the Sisters of Mercy moved out of their old convent in 2005, a further extension to the ICU became possible using the adjoining top floor of the old convent.

● *The staff of the high dependency unit.*

Giving New Life

One of the most exciting developments in cardiac surgery in Ireland took place on 10 September 1985, when Maurice Neligan and Freddie Wood performed the first heart transplant. Their colleagues, F.X. O'Connell and Thomas Corrigan, had already performed the first liver transplant, which had proved to be hugely controversial. By the end of the year, four heart transplants had been performed; however, to the surgeons' frustration, the number of transplant cases had to be reduced because of the lack of financial resources. Nonetheless, by 1994, just nine years after the first heart transplant, one hundred cardiac transplants had been undertaken at the Mater with a very high success rate. An additional cardiac surgeon (John Hurley), with a special interest in transplantation, was appointed to the staff during that year.

Freddie Wood discusses a surgical case with members of his team.

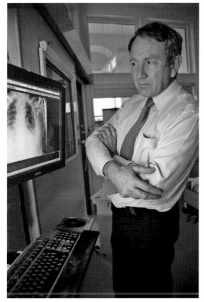

On 10 November 1994, to mark the completion of the refurbishment and the expansion of the unit, the then Minister for Health, Brendan Howlin, TD[23] and officials from the Department of Health visited the hospital for the official opening of the National Unit for Cardiac Surgery. In his speech, Howlin said: 'The new Intensive Care Unit can only be described as a "state-of-the-art" facility. It cost £3.5 million to develop and we calculate that the running costs will be in the region of £2 million annually. None of these facilities would function were it not for the dedication of the staff and the high standard of care... This Hospital has not earned its reputation by remaining static and today we have an example of that, which I would like to commend and to wish you every success with the work undertaken in it.'

Dr Dermot Phelan examines an X-ray.

The opening of the unit was a source of enormous satisfaction for Dr Dermot Phelan, who had been appointed Director of Intensive Care in 1986. It was an onerous job for a variety of reasons: pressure on ICU beds, the complexity of cases and new developments in cardiac surgery, to name but a few. In a quiet, dignified fashion, he has faced and continues to face his enormous responsibilities from day to day. On 8 May 2002, the whole unit – the National Cardio-Thoracic Surgical Unit – was formally dedicated to its legendary founder, Eoin O'Malley.

With heart transplants now a 'routine' operation, comparatively speaking, Freddie Wood and his colleague Jim McCarthy, together with Dr Jim Egan, respiratory physician, began to explore the possibility of lung transplantation, which had been performed outside Ireland since the late 1980s. The first single lung transplant was carried out in the Mater on 12 May 2005 on a 56-year-old Limerick mother of three, Veronica Doyle. She left 14 days later, walking unaided with her children. The transplant team included surgeons Freddie Wood, Jim McCarthy, Lars Nolke, Dr Deirdre O'Brien and

Mrs Veronica Doyle, the Mater's first single lung transplant recipient, presented this painting to the hospital to mark the occasion of her successful transplant in May 2005. With her are her family, Freddie Wood (surgeon) on the left and Jim Egan (physician) on the right.

The first lung transplant team gathers in the Pillar Room, 2005.

Professor Jim Egan.[24] According to Freddie Wood, this successful lung transplant really exemplified what modern hospital care is all about: Professor Egan commented: 'Organ transplantation in Ireland is very successful and we can be very proud of it. Veronica Doyle became the first person in Ireland to undergo a lung transplant operation in the Mater. The transplant team worked around the clock on what was an historic process.'

By the time the media had reported on this historic development, in September of that year, and a thanksgiving service had taken place in Christ Church Cathedral, a further three transplants had already taken place in the hospital. On 12 May 2005 another 'first' for Ireland took place: a device to assist a patient's failing heart[25] was implanted in a patient who was in urgent need of a transplant to keep him alive until a donor heart was available. At the end of the year a left ventricular assist device was inserted very successfully in a young patient by the cardiac transplant team.

On 14 January 2006 another 'first' for the Mater and the nation took place, that of a double lung transplant. A 58-year-old man from Co. Sligo underwent a five-hour operation to replace both his lungs with a transplant. He was suffering from chronic emphysema of the lungs. A team of 21 medical and nursing staff was involved, led by cardiac surgeons Freddie Wood[26] and Jim Egan. The patient survived it well.

Many transplants have taken place since and many lives have been saved. Of course, the sad reality is that for every donor organ made available, a valuable life has been extinguished somewhere and people are grieving their loss.

Mr Eddie Kelly, the Mater's first heart transplant patient, photographed with the nursing team. Back row, from left: Anna Sheehan, Mary O'Carroll, Pat O'Leary, Margot McDonagh, Jane Larkin, Sr Brigid Murnane, Mary Shanaghan, Mary Corcoran. Front row, from left: Avril Hederman, Aine O'Donovan, Eddie Kelly, Ursula Bullen

Some of the hospital's theatre nurses.

A Lifetime of Care

Many patients have lived with heart disease for many years, often since birth, and this small but unique group of people need extended specialist care. Many of them will have been coming to the Mater Hospital over a long period, and will know it almost as well as the medical staff. Some years ago, a clinic to provide a service for adults with congenital heart disease was opened at the Mater. It is currently in the care of cardiologists Dr Kevin Walsh and cardiothoracic surgeons Professor Mark Redmond and Mr Lars Nolke. Two very dedicated clinical nurse specialists are important members of the staff of this clinic: Rhona Savage CNS and Esther Doran CNS.

The National Pulmonary Hypertension Unit was established in 2001, to cater for the needs of people suffering from the disease. The director of this unit, now part of

President Mary McAleese opens the Pulmonary Hypertension Unit.

the Mater Centre for Lung Health on Eccles Street, is Professor Sean Gaine. The specially trained staff includes a designated pharmacist, for the benefit of the patients.

On 14 October 2011 the Maurice Neligan Congenital Heart Unit was opened by Dr James Reilly TD, Minister for Health. It is located at the cardiac ward and provides a special area where teenagers and young adults with congenital heart disease can drop in unannounced for a chat or advice with one of the specialist nurses. It is a fitting tribute to the late surgeon, who died in October 2010, and who made such a significant contribution to cardiac surgery in this country.

Prof. Sean Gaine.

The Minister for Health, Dr James Reilly, TD (second from left) and beside him, Dr Pat Neligan, along with the Neligan family and Mater staff at the opening of the Maurice Neligan Congenital Heart Unit, October 2011.

Fifty Years of Achievements – the Mater Cardio-Thoracic Team

1953: First mitral valvotomy performed by surgeon John Corcoran and team

1957: First open heart surgery performed by Eoin O'Malley: 17 December

1961: First operation using heart–lung machine: 9 March

1965: First mitral valve replacement procedure: 23 March

1965: First aortic valve replacement: 29 March

1975: First coronary artery bypass graft: Maurice Neligan and team: 1 April

1983: Mitral reconstruction/repair began in earnest

1983: Successful use of temporary left ventricle device

1984: Use of left internal mammary graft commenced

1985: First heart transplant: Maurice Neligan, Freddie Wood and team: 10 September

1990 The use of fresh homograft aortic valve began

1991 Video-assisted thoracic surgery introduced at the Mater

1993 National Homograft Heart Valve Bank set up between staff of the unit and the Blood Transfusion Board

1994 First Ross operation performed successfully

2002 Cox maze procedure introduced

2004 Lung transplantation

2005 Artificial heart programme

2005 First artificial heart implant in the country: 1 May

2005 First lung transplant in the country: 11 May

2005 Endovascular stenting of type 111 thoracic aortic aneurysms in association with the Mater Department of Interventional Radiology and Cardiology

2006 The use of the Novalung, percutaneous continuous lung membrane assist, in a patient awaiting a double lung transplantation. This system was used for 140 days (involving 17 device changes), the longest ever achieved worldwide and the patient went on to receive a successful double lung transplant in 2007

2006 First (double) lung transplant carried out – successfully

2007 Remote patient monitoring (Medronic) commenced

2009 Heartmate 11 programme – selected patients with end-stage heart failure discharged home with fully implantable devices awaiting transplantation

2012 Opening of the Maurice Neligan 'drop-in' clinic

The Growth of Specialisation in Surgery

With the rapid developments taking place in cardiac surgery during the second half of the 20th century, it is easy to overlook those in other areas of surgery, particularly in orthopaedic surgery.

Specialisation within surgery began, more or less, in the early 1960s. Each of the surgeons had his or her own particular interest. The frequent cases of gastrectomy, total or partial, for the relief of chronic gastric ulcers was replaced by the procedure of 'highly selective vagotomy' – in its turn largely replaced by very effective drugs. In the 1980s, new equipment allowed for the development of other surgical specialities, such as laparoscopic surgery, which shortened the length of time patients would have to spend in hospital and marked the disappearance of long ugly surgical scars. With the help of new scanning and X-ray techniques, 1987 was to see the introduction of the 'five-day' ward and the use of minimally invasive surgery in a wide variety of procedures, which led in turn to the growth of day-case surgery for short procedures such as on cataracts and some ENT problems. In 1991, a 15-bed ward was opened to accommodate day-case patients who, only a short few years before, would have needed longer stays for quite minor operations.

The Art of Orthopaedic Surgery

Problems concerning the musculoskeletal system of the body are as old as humankind itself. In Egypt, some ancient mummies have been found with rudimentary splints attached to their broken bones. In the early years of the Mater, apart from limb fractures, many patients presented with bone tuberculosis, including that of the spine, otherwise known as Pott's caries.[27] Many patients suffered from malnutrition, which meant that their bones had not grown properly, and many had rickets. At the time there were no X-rays, CT scans, MRI (magnetic resonance imaging) or PET (positron emission tomography) imaging, as we have today. The hospital report for 1928 mentions that a special 'fracture bed' was purchased by the hospital. It also mentions 'the use of electro-operative methods in bone surgery.'[28]

All the orthopaedic cases were classified at the time as surgical. It wasn't until World War I that the art of orthopaedics came into its own, until which time the only treatments available were bed rest, bandaging or amputation of a limb. Orthopaedics developed along with the growth of X-ray, and with the new knowledge that was disseminated worldwide by surgeons who had treated wounded soldiers, both at the front and in the various hospitals.

In 1930 Henry F. Mc Auley[29] was appointed assistant surgeon in the Mater and he set about developing orthopaedic surgery and a specialist orthopaedic clinic. His particular interest was in the treatment of bone disease and deformities due to tuberculosis, and in 1935 he was officially appointed the Mater's first orthopaedic surgeon. When the new outpatients department opened the following year, McAuley requested that orthopaedic patients receive special focus at the surgical outpatients clinic and also that all fracture cases seen in the casualty department should be referred to his new orthopaedic clinic. However, until 1993 there was no 'orthopaedic ward' as such; instead, a number of beds in the male and female surgical wards respectively were set aside for orthopaedic cases. This changed in September 1993 with the opening of a new orthopaedic unit, a section of which was reserved for patients with spinal injuries. Before the end of the year it was designated the National Spinal Injuries Unit[30] for the whole country. After the acute phase of their treatment, patients are transferred to the National Rehabilitation Hospital in Dun Laoghaire for rehabilitation.

During 2013 the orthopaedic patients will be moved to Level 5 (north block) of the new Whitty building and the spinal unit will be relocated to a well-equipped modern location on Level 5 (south block).

biography

Maurice Neligan

Maurice Neligan was born in Booterstown, Co. Dublin in 1937 and educated at Blackrock College and University College Dublin, where he graduated in medicine in 1962. He served as a resident intern and as a registrar in the Mater Hospital. During this time he became interested in cardio-thoracic surgery and decided to follow this specialty as a future career. After preliminary studies, he moved to the Queen Elizabeth Hospital in Birmingham to train as a cardio-thoracic surgeon. He returned to the Mater in 1969 and was appointed a senior surgical registrar. He was awarded a World Health Organisation fellowship which allowed him to travel to the Mayo Clinic, USA, to further his studies and skills in cardiac surgery. He returned to the National Cardiac Surgical Unit at the Mater in 1973 where he worked as part of the pioneering Eoin O'Malley/Keith Shaw cardio-thoracic surgical team.

● *Maurice Neligan (1937–2010).*

From the time he decided to follow a career in cardiac surgery, he mentally mapped out, not alone how he could advance his own career, but also how to turn the Mater into the premier centre for cardio-thoracic surgery in Ireland and beyond. His thinking as to how this could be achieved focused on four main areas: excellence as a surgeon; care and thoughtfulness where all patients are concerned; educational opportunities for all staff involved in cardiac surgery or patient care; and the need to keep the media informed of developments in this relatively new specialism in Ireland. All of this he managed to achieve over his 31 years as a cardiac surgeon in the Mater. During this time he became Ireland's best known cardiac surgeon. By 1974 he was undertaking very complex paediatric cardiac surgery in Our Lady's Children's Hospital, Crumlin in west Dublin.

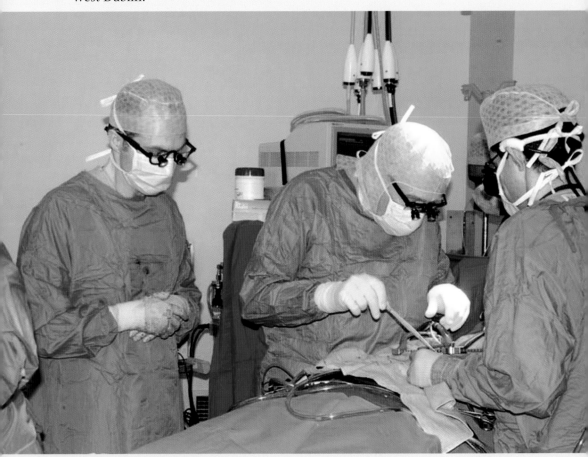

Maurice Neligan, cardiac surgeon, at work.

In 1975, he carried out the first coronary artery bypass graft in Ireland and thousands have been performed since. Frequently facing the problem of the 'failing heart', he undertook the first cardiac transplant in Ireland in 1985. It was a monumental undertaking, his skills being backed up by the exceptional skills of the team assisting him. In 1980, he was appointed Director of the National Cardiac Surgical Unit and remained in that post until his retirement in 2002. During this time the number of cardiac surgical procedures rose very significantly. New units began to open elsewhere, staffed by those who had trained under or worked with Neligan, who was by now ranked among the great international cardiac surgeons. He was known for his cardiac surgical skills and for his willingness to undertake surgery which others would refuse or have grave reservations about undertaking.

After he retired in 2002 he devoted his skills to writing a weekly article in *The Irish Times*. These articles largely reflected on the current healthcare situation in Ireland. He was always on the side of the disadvantaged patient, especially those delayed in hospital emergency departments or on waiting lists for admission. Now and again he would recall with humour his experiences as an intern doctor. In one of his articles he announced that he chose to go to the Mater because he could park his car outside the front door!

Sadly, Maurice Neligan departed this world in October 2010. His name and the extraordinary surgery he did lives on. In recent times a group called the Heart Children Ireland raised €50,000 to create and open a special clinic in the hospital – the Maurice Neligan Heart Clinic.[31] This clinic serves young adults who have undergone cardiac surgery at some stage of their young lives and who may want to consult with a Clinical Nurse Specialist. It was opened in 2011 by the Minister for Health, Dr James Reilly.

1   The surgeons were Andrew Ellis, Richard O'Reilly, Michael Henry Stapleton and Andrew McDonnell.
2   The first hospital report was written in 1866 and published in 1867.
3   Bristowe & Holmes, 'The Hospitals of the United Kingdom – Irish Hospitals – Mater Misericordiae Hospital. Dublin' (NLI) Parliamentary papers Vol. 28, 1864, p 712.
4   This statement is probably more for the benefit of Bristowe & Holmes, who commented in their report on the design of the hospital wards and the need for good ventilation. The need for patient privacy and the conservation of heat to make the wards comfortable was not a consideration.
5   See Chapter 4. This endoscope is now in a museum in the Royal College of Surgeons in Ireland.
6   Cruise, F.R. (1865), *The Endoscope as an aid to the diagnosis and treatment of disease*. BMJ (Archives), p 345.
7   The sterilisation of gowns and the wearing of masks was introduced circa 1885. It took some years for it to become an accepted standard in all hospitals.
8   Dowling, J. (1955), *An Irish Doctor Remembers*, Clonmore & Reynolds, p 40.
9   The very first anaesthetics were administered by the Hospital Pharmacist.
10 O'Malley, E. (1961), 'Surgical Progress', in Freeman, E.T., *Centenary of the Mater Misericordiae Hospital, 1861–1961*, p 47.
11 Atrial septal defects (ASDs) and ventricular septal defects (VSDs), otherwise known as 'hole in the heart' cases. A hole between either the two atria or the two ventricles of the heart needed to be closed. It was repaired using open-heart surgery.
12 The repair of a hole between the two ventricles of the heart – ventricular septal defects (VSDs) – was not undertaken until some time later.
13 *The Irish Times*, Friday, 19 February 1960, p 4.
14 Prof. Christiaan Barnard performed the first ever human heart transplant in South Africa on 3 December 1967.
15 According to E.T. Freeman, 'The coronary care unit (CCU) originally contained a bedroom occupied by the last of the non-trained women who originally assisted the Sisters of Mercy in nursing duties. An old lady had resided here for years. The small ward beyond it (current ICU) was a student's dormitory, and across the corridor the [1967] present ward kitchen [in 2011 a store for orthopaedic instruments and equipment] was the dormitory for three house surgeons', *The Mater Hospital before World War I* in *NUACHT*, Vol. 1, No. 5, March 1967, p 4.
16 Sr Josephine (Bourke) was the Operating Theatre Superintendent during these early days until 1960, when Sr Gerard (Egan) was appointed. Sr Attracta Kavanagh was the Sister in charge of St Peter's surgical ward during this period of change and she agreed to take on the responsibility for the intensive care unit as well as her ward duties. Eventually she became a full-time Unit Manager in charge of the ITU. It was an enormous responsibility, as it included the development of the facility as well as the day-to-day management and specialist education of a large nursing staff.

17 Professor O'Malley made an arrangement that all the lecturers should give their services free of charge, which they did very generously.

18 She was followed in 1987 by Sr Ita Greene, who was theatre superintendent until her retirement in 1998.

19 Luke, D. (2006), *Cardiac Surgery in the Republic of Ireland* in Heartwise. See: http:www.irishheart.ie/media/pub/heartwise/2006/surgery_in_republic.pdf.

20 *Mater Misericordiae Hospital, Annual Report 1984*, p 33.

21 This high dependency unit was opened to cater mainly for post-operative cardiac cases but also for any other surgical cases in need of HDU care. Eventually, on 29 March 2004 another HDU was opened on the same floor for post-operative cardiac surgical cases. It opens on to the east wing near St Cecilia's wards.

22 At the time these wards were called St Camillus' Ward, St Laurence's Ward and St Peter's Ward – the original names they were given when the hospital opened in 1861. St Catherine's and St Camillus' Wards were at the front of the hospital (south wing) and St Laurence's and St Peter's ward were along the east wing. The third ward along that wing was called St Brigid's Ward (currently called St Camillus' Ward).

23 Brendan Howlin TD (Labour Party) was Minister for Health from 12 January 1993 to 17 November 1994.

24 Halloran, C. (2005), 'Transplant unit named Best of Irish', *Irish Daily Star*, 3 November.

25 This implant cost €60,000 (12 May 2005).

26 Freddie Wood retired from the Mater Hospital in 2010. He had served as Director of the Cardio-Thoracic Team for many years.

27 Pott's disease/caries (tuberculosis of the spine) was not uncommon in the early days when treatment for TB was unavailable. Apart from severe pain in the back it often led to the so-called 'curvature' or kyphosis of the spine. This, in some, ultimately produced the skeletal deformity known as hunchback.

28 *Mater Misericordiae Hospital Dublin. Report for the Year 1928*, Dublin: Dollard, p 12.

29 Dr Henry McAuley was a brother of the well-known Dr Charles J. McAuley, who was by then a surgeon in the Mater. They came from Belfast and had very strong Republican 'leanings'. Charles McAuley served in the GPO during the 1916 Rising. He was a friend of J.M. Plunkett – one of the leaders who were executed. Plunkett was, at that time, suffering from TB glands in his neck and had been treated by 'Charlie' McAuley. During the Rising, McAuley set up a medical station in the GPO to treat the injured and of course to be there for his friend Plunkett, whose condition he was extremely concerned about. Charles McAuley worked as a surgeon in the Mater from 1916 to 1956. His brother Henry worked as a surgeon in the Mater from 1930 to 1958. They were tremendously dedicated professionals.

30 Unfortunately, appropriate and necessary funding for this national service was never put in place, making it very difficult to operate such an important specialism to the desired international standards .

31 Heart Children Ireland, through a partnership with Home Retail Group, raised €50k to create the Maurice Neligan Congenital Heart Clinic in the Mater Hospital. This clinic was formally opened by the Minister for Health on 14 October 2011. It is a drop-in clinic for young adults who have undergone cardiac surgery as infants or children and who wish to consult a cardiac nurse specialist at any stage.

CHAPTER 11

The Emergency Department

Perhaps no discipline has changed more rapidly or reflects more accurately the way in which society has developed than that of emergency medicine, and the Mater Hospital has been at the centre of that change. What is now the emergency department began very simply: when the hospital opened in 1861, it included both an 'accident room' and a 'dispensary', as they were called, both located beneath the main entrance on Eccles Street, on a long corridor which ran the length of the building, with wooden seats on either side for the patients. Generally, patients were few in the days when only poor people needed access to treatment for minor injuries and ailments.

The original medical staff put together a rota whereby one of them each day was scheduled to attend to the patients, starting at 9.30 a.m., assisted by the medical student assigned to him (in those days, doctors were almost exclusively male, and it was to be some years before the Mater admitted female medical students). The student was responsible for the care of any wounds and for applying splints and bandages when necessary. He was also expected to make notes on the patient's medical history. Each medical student was provided with a booklet[1] known as the 'pink book' on arrival at the hospital at the beginning of the academic year, which included all the medical information that was required to be documented when evaluating new patients. The medical staff used the time they spent in the dispensary to do a lot of student teaching. Until the 1960s, the number of patients attending this department remained relatively small. It's interesting to note that a report from 1888 states that the number of cases admitted to the hospital was 3,010 and the average length of stay was 27.9 days[2] and to compare these statistics with the current ones. The Annual Report for 2011 states that 215,000 patients attended the outpatients department and 50,000 attended the emergency department in that year. There were 16,696 admissions and 50,246 day cases.[3] The average length of stay was 11.16 days, a statistic which is somewhat distorted by an inordinate number of so-called 'delayed discharges'.[4]

It is not difficult to see that the workload changed substantially between 1888 and 2011. However, quite apart from the overall statistics, a particularly noticeable difference between the two reports is the spectrum of diseases treated. In 1888, the commonest disease dealt with in the hospital was tuberculosis in a variety of presentations and with many different names – the most frequent being pulmonary phthisis. The next most common disease was scarlet fever, frequently seen in children. Another condition, rarely seen now because of vaccination, but which was not uncommon in the early years, was that described as 'infantile paralysis', which we know better as poliomyelitis or polio.

The people who came to the hospital for emergency treatment in the early years either walked in themselves or were carried, or if they were lucky, transported in a horse-drawn cart. Children invariably arrived in the arms of an adult and were rolled up in a black woollen shawl or rug. Few of them had shoes and they generally wore ragged clothes. They were malnourished and dirty looking, due to lack of sanitary facilities in the tenements near the hospital. Few of them came with trivial complaints. In those days, even minor fractures and wounds were treated at home. If they went to the accident room it was because they were seriously injured, had major fractures, or had a wound or burn which was not responding to home remedies. For the first 30 years after the hospital was opened, children were admitted to a women's surgical ward, as there was no children's ward. Each ward had its share of cots – large enough to accommodate a six-year-old. Eventually, when increasing numbers of children were arriving with infectious diseases such as scarlet fever, a special children's ward was opened on the ground floor of the building near the accident room.

It was only during the 1960s, when the numbers of emergency cases began to increase, that a new department, the 'A&E' as it was known, was needed. In 1969, the new A&E seemed to be state of the art, with its own entrance for ambulances, two specially equipped cubicles for patients who had suffered a cardiac arrest and a number of other well-equipped examination cubicles. It had its own X-ray room and a small operating theatre. It was ideal for the time. Indeed, when US President Richard Nixon came to Ireland in 1970, officials from the American Embassy came to inspect the facilities available in the Mater's A&E department. They requested that the hospital make available a particular cardiac monitor in the resuscitation area, because Nixon was suffering from heart problems at the time. In the event of an emergency it was planned to airlift the president to the hospital, and a thorough check was made of landing possibilities. Aerial photos were taken of the campus to locate possible places to land, and an area to the east of the hospital was picked as a potential landing spot. In the event, the hospital facilities were not needed. However, within the next ten years, the A&E department would be tested by several large-scale tragedies in the city, and its inadequacies would be shown up.

The Dublin Bombings

The 1970s were grim years for the country as a whole and particularly for Northern Ireland, which had erupted in violence after the civil rights marches of the late 1960s. There was much concern that the violence would spill over to the Republic, and the country was gripped by fear and uncertainty. The Irish government planned to introduce emergency powers to deal with the paramilitary groups which were growing in strength on both sides of the border. Closer to home, in 1971 discussions took place in all the hospitals to prepare for an outbreak of violence in Dublin city. Contingency plans were drawn up, for both the city and the Mater hospital, on how to cope with a major disaster, and these plans were soon to be tested.

The bloodiest year of the Troubles was 1972, with the Bloody Sunday massacre, which resulted in the death of 14 people in Derry, a series of massive bombs in Belfast city centre, and the burning of the British Embassy in Dublin. The Mater received its first alert in December 1972, when two car bombs exploded in the city, killing a bus driver and conductor and injuring 127 people, who were caught in the blast of a second bomb, which exploded in Sackville Place, close to Dublin's busy O'Connell Street, shortly after the first.

A few weeks later, another bomb in the city killed one person and injured thirteen others, but the most devastating was yet to come. On 17 May 1974, three car bombs exploded in the city centre, in Talbot Street, South Leinster Street and Parnell Street, during the busy rush-hour period. Even worse, many people had been making their way on foot to Connolly Station, because of a bus strike. The Dublin bombs killed 25 people instantly and injured hundreds.

All the hospitals in the city were alerted, but particularly the Mater and Jervis Street, being the nearest to the first two bombs. The city's major disaster plan went into operation. At the Mater, many of the staff had heard the explosions and knew that something very serious had occurred. The emergency department made ready immediately to receive the injured. In a short length of time all the operating theatres were busy, as trolleys were pushed in that direction. The work of the surgical teams continued right through the night. The casualties were classified on arrival and colour-coded tags were attached to them as they arrived at the department, depending on the severity of their injuries. The designated wards, according to the plan, were cleared to receive the injured. The hospital restaurant was made available to receive the distressed relatives and friends, as was the Pillar Room, which was used by the press and other media.

The first to arrive at the hospital was a woman who came in a taxi, with blood streaming from her head and looking very dazed. Soon, the ambulances began to operate a kind of 'shuttle service' and the injured came covered with coats and blankets from Talbot Street. To assist the fire services, the Red Cross, St John's Ambulance Brigade, the Knights of Malta and the civil defence all joined in the rescue bid and helped to bring the injured to the hospitals in their ambulances.[5] Many of them also offered their services as volunteers to push trolleys as needed and to help control the crowd, which by now included not only the injured, but also routine visitors to the hospital. A number of gardaí stood outside the mortuary to help the many distressed people who arrived in search of relatives and friends. Others controlled the large crowds that quickly converged on the emergency department. Eventually these people were formed into a queue by a garda, to prevent mayhem. A team of reception staff who were kept supplied with whatever information was available, looked after those people waiting, trying to console them while offering them tea or coffee in the restaurant nearby.

According to a member of the staff:

We had just finished duty and were preparing to go home when a massive explosion occurred nearby. We looked at each other in wonderment. Almost immediately after the first, another explosion occurred. We ran outside on to Eccles Street and could see a huge plume of smoke rising into the sky from the city direction. While we were looking at it, the injured, covered with blood and some holding their injured faces, began to arrive at the hospital. Immediately we went back to work and met others doing the same. I was given a list of telephone numbers to ring and was directed to a phone which would not block incoming calls. The people I telephoned were mainly the senior medical and surgical staff and heads of departments who were on their way home after their day's work. Many were already on their way back because they had heard it on their car radios.

My colleagues were busy moving patients from a number of designated wards to make way for the injured and those who needed to be prepared for the operating theatre. There was light in all the theatres and trolleys and beds were moving along the top corridor with the injured – the unconscious, head and face injuries (some of them were woeful looking), fractured limbs, eye and ear injuries etc., which were dealt with all through the night. For many their ear-drums were perforated and for some, they'd remain deaf for the rest of their lives. A pal of mine told me she was in Jervis St Hospital on that famous night and when morning came and the day staff arrived, those who had worked all night sat down and had a bit of a party, to try and lift the spirits of the exhausted staff – senior consultants included.

One of the people who lent a hand in the Mater for the evening was a teenager who came in to his mother who was a telephonist in the hospital at the time. When he arrived she sent him down to the A&E to see if there was anything he could do to help. He soon found himself pushing a trolley, with one of the porters, to the theatre. I spoke to him later in the evening. He looked pale and tired. He admitted that at times he felt sick when he saw mangled bodies arriving to the hospital. The whole event was a night to remember and one I will certainly never forget. (P.N.)

Another member of staff remembers treating a patient whose leg was blown off almost to the thigh and who had a large amount of shrapnel embedded in his back. She says she will always remember this unfortunate man.

Gun Battle on the Corridor

The Troubles were also to come to the Mater in a slightly different guise. In late November 1972, Sean Mac Stíofáin, then Chief of Staff of the IRA, was admitted to a room in St Gabriel's Ward, suffering from the effects of a hunger strike while imprisoned in the Curragh. He was in a debilitated condition and the word had spread that he was near death. A plan was hatched by his supporters to rescue him from the hospital. On Sunday afternoon, 26 November, eight armed men made their way into the hospital, four of them dressed as hospital staff, two as priests and two as visitors. They made their way to the ward where four gardaí were guarding Mac Stíofáin. One of the gardaí was dubious about the appearance of the 'priests', but before he could

Sean Mac Stíofáin, the IRA leader in 1972, who was controversially 'sprung' from the Mater Hospital during a fierce gun battle. (© Alamy.)

A newspaper article on the botched Mac Stíofáin raid. (Courtesy of The Irish Times.)

react, guns were produced and shooting broke out on the corridor. At one stage, one of the gunmen grabbed the ward sister, Sr Dolours Murphy, and held her as a hostage with a gun to her back.

Bullets flew in every direction. Four men were injured by gunfire, two of whom were visitors. One of the gunmen was hit by a bullet in the stomach and was dragged by one of his colleagues down the corridor, before being abandoned. Nobody was seriously injured and those who were hit by bullets were quickly taken to the emergency department for treatment (the injured gunman was arrested following treatment). Two of the gunmen jumped into a lift nearby and were found in the operating theatre on the next floor. The rest just disappeared.

By this time, an angry mob had begun to gather outside the hospital and Mac Stíofáin's wife had to stand on the steps of the hospital and beg for calm. Eventually troops were called to protect the hospital and to disperse the crowds. They cordoned off the building and cleared the street of people. The protesters made their way to O'Connell Street, where they held a meeting outside the GPO. Mac Stíofáin was hastily taken away from the Mater to the Curragh military hospital for treatment.

The Stardust

● *The devastation the morning after the Stardust fire. (© Press Association.)*

Sadly, the Dublin bombings were not the only disaster to come to the Mater hospital. On the evening of 13 February 1981, the night staff arrived on duty expecting things to be much the same as at any busy weekend. However, shortly before 2 a.m., the hospital received an official alert from the city emergency services to say that the Stardust ballroom in Artane was on fire and that hundreds of young people were injured. The Mater was on emergency call and, in fact, was the nearest hospital to the disaster area.

No sooner had the call been received than cars began to arrive at the emergency department with the injured. As one of the staff recalled: 'In the space of a few minutes, we were surrounded by over a hundred young people, their faces blackened by acrid smoke and in a very distressed state.'

The first difficulty the security staff of the hospital had to deal with was trying to make way for the many ambulances to pull up outside the emergency department. Within the hospital the major disaster plan was in progress. Staff, including the Sisters from the convent, were alerted and they arrived to help. The restaurant (near the emergency department) was opened and distressed relatives and friends were taken there. According to one newspaper report:

> Anxious relatives, searching for news of the youngsters caught in the holocaust, had to make painful tours of city hospitals to try to trace injured relatives. For some, the effort was in vain. As nursing and religious staff at the Mater Hospital gently handled queries from worried parents, they won the admiration of friends and relatives, still numbed with shock. Whispered sighs of 'thank God' greeted each announced name of survivors as parents huddled together in the canteen where staff dispensed coffee and consolation. The Mater, nearest to the scene of the disaster, bore the brunt of the emergency effort.[6]

In spite of the major disaster plan, the staff were faced with unprecedented numbers of injured people, all young and very frightened. At times basic law and order was difficult to maintain. One of the nurses recalled assessing the injured and deciding on treatment, when suddenly someone turned on a tap and at the sound of the running water, the youngsters jumped up out of their trolleys and chairs and made their way to all the sinks in the department, where they ran cold water on their burnt limbs. Every tap in the place was turned on and nothing would encourage them away from the immediate relief. Eventually the water pressure in the hospital dropped. As fast as they could manage, the nurses filled syringes with more appropriate pain relief and coaxed the patients away from the sinks and back to the trolleys.

Another problem which arose was bewildered and injured young people wandering around the clinical area of the department. As one nurse recalls: 'While I was trying to put a dressing on the patient's arm as she lay on the trolley in one of the cubicles, I became aware that I had an audience watching me on the other side of her. I enquired if the patient was their friend and the answer was "no". This repeatedly happened during the night.'

Many of the injured were suffering from breathing difficulties and were quickly moved to the resuscitation area and on to the intensive care unit for respiratory support and treatment. Many simply never arrived to the emergency department, but were taken directly to the hospital mortuary. A total of 49 people died as a result of the fire that night.

Stresses and Strains

Apart from major disasters, emergency departments had yet to experience any significant overcrowding or difficulty. This was because up to the 1980s, most ill patients contacted their GP if they needed treatment, which would generally be given at home. Any accidents were taken to the 'casualty on-call'. At that time, there was a rota in operation, which meant that the Mater (and the other casualty departments in the city) only remained open overnight on every fourth night, a situation which would be unimaginable now. The pressure on A&E was manageable. During the 1980s, the nature and function of the emergency department began rapidly to change and overcrowding became a serious issue. One of the most difficult problems was that of bed availability within the hospital to respond to the needs of the emergency department. By 1994, admission delays were seriously impacting on all elective work and emergency patients were spending long hours on trolleys in the department awaiting admission. This problem was not unique to the Mater. It was common to most of the Dublin hospitals.

In 1995, the delays had grown and it wasn't uncommon for patients to have to wait on trolleys overnight. At one stage, the nursing staff in the emergency department became so frustrated at the situation that they decided to take industrial action. It had become impossible for them to move around the department and to attend to sick people according to professional standards. A lack of financial resources, and an increase in drug- and alcohol-related cases compounded the problem. Finally, in 1999, comprehensive discussions about the problems in the emergency department took place under the chairmanship of Professor John Crowe[7] and a committee was set up to look at the use of beds within the hospital, to see if the overcrowding problems could be resolved.

This committee examined the different routes to admission taken by the hospital's patients. They also looked at what was happening to discharged patients, identifying bottle-necks where efficiency and speed of patient throughput were being compromised. The committee eventually drew up what came to be known as the MED[8] (Medical Emergency Department) plan in 1999. The main focus of the MED plan was to make 'patient flow' through the hospital easier and its objectives were:

- To achieve a balance in clinical activity
- To eliminate admission delays for all emergencies
- To restore and improve the hospital's 'tertiary referral commitment'. (A tertiary hospital means one that has a full range of services for patients or offers care in a certain specialism, such as oncology.)

In effect, the MED plan centralised certain categories of beds for emergency admissions and made available a number of 'units', each devoted to the care of different categories of patient. These included an acute medical unit (AMU), which itself included a medical high-dependency special care unit, an acute medical unit for the older person, an acute stroke and rehabilitation unit, an acute cardiology unit and an acute surgical unit. The MED project was presented on 9 December 2001. Additional funding for it was provided by the Eastern Regional Health Authority.[9] The success of this new arrangement depended on the immediate discharge of all patients who had received medical care and were ready to go home. Unfortunately, suitable primary care support (in the community) was not available to any great extent, and so the MED project quickly found itself in difficulties. The necessary beds to keep the scheme progressing were simply not there because of delayed discharges and, unfortunately, the brief improvement in waiting times was to be short-lived.

Once more, lack of clinical space in the emergency department became a serious problem. In June 2005, work commenced on a 33-bed 'transit ward' for patients from the emergency department awaiting admission to the hospital, with the hope of reducing patient numbers in the department. This unit opened in December 2005 and was quickly filled with patients from the emergency department. Once again, patients could not move on because of the perennial problem of delayed discharges from the wards. In 2007, the unit was renamed St Michael's Ward and its remit redefined, and then further redefined in July 2010, this time to deal with elective surgery in order to reduce outpatient waiting lists.

During 2007, the Mater engaged the services of a UK company, Teamwork Management Services, to look at the problem of excessive patient waiting times in the emergency department and to develop an action plan for a system change towards acceptable integrated care.[10] The company looked at the problem in the Mater and in all of the north Dublin acute hospitals. They also, to some extent, studied the available primary care (PCCC)[11] services

● *The transit unit on stilts, beside the east wing of the hospital – it's clear why it was felt to move in the wind!*

available to those finding their way to emergency departments or who belonged to the 'delayed discharge' category in the hospitals. They recognised that the emergency department problem was widespread in north Dublin and that what was required were the resources to deal with the problem, to 'unblock' beds in the hospitals by providing the necessary options for care in the community. Without the right resources in place, the problem would be hard to solve.

Extending the Emergency Department

In the meantime, in order to keep pace with the rapid changes in emergency care, the emergency department urgently needed more clinical and treatment space. In 2007, it was decided to move 28 outpatient clinics from the existing outpatients department to a refurbished facility[12] in nearby Dorset Street. In 2009, the interim reorganisation in the emergency department was complete at a cost of about €2.5 million. This redevelopment project included the provision of a CT scanner within the department, rather than in the radiography department, all aimed at reducing patient waiting times. A number of other important changes were made in the hospital to enable a satisfactory patient flow[13] through the system. However, the most insoluble problem of all continued to be that of delayed-discharge patients, which reached the astounding figure of 120 patients during the summer months of 2009. In that year more than 35,000 bed days were lost due to this problem.[14]

It soon became obvious that the existing way in which hospitals cared for patients needed to be overhauled and a new system created. Individual or groups of hospitals tweaking their own systems was never going to achieve what was needed to meet the complex health needs of patients in the 21st century. Towards the end of 2009, the Health Service Executive set up a special task force under the joint clinical leadership of Professor Shane O'Neill and Professor Gary Courtney.[15] In 2010, they published the very innovative 'Acute Medicine Programme', a clinician-led initiative, which aims to standardise patient care nationally and to provide a better patient experience.

Some of the ideas put forward by O'Neill and Courtney have been adopted, particularly those which shorten the length of stay in the hospital.

In the Mater's case, the inadequacies of the 1936 emergency department, particularly around the patient's comfort and the space provided, continued, until, by the end of the 1990s, it was decided that the only solution was a modern, spacious, well-lit emergency department. It was decided that it should be located at level 0 (street level) of the new Whitty Building, with plenty of space for ambulances and with an entrance nearby to a 440-space car park. On 17 February 2013, the new emergency department opened its doors after the staff had held a short religious service in the department. The design of this new department is in keeping with international standards, making a lot of use of natural light, pastel colours, and comfort facilities for relatives in distress. The use of an elaborate communication system and colour-coded doors throughout is very impressive. The available space is enormous. It is reckoned that whereas a nurse on duty in the old A&E would walk, on average, six kilometres per day, in this new facility she/he will walk eight to nine kilometres per day. With a total of 28 rooms in the building, it would be easy to get lost in it!

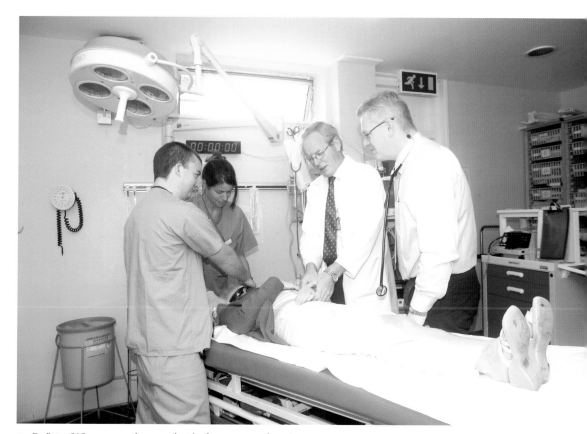

Dr Peter O'Connor examines a patient in the emergency department.

1   This booklet was compiled and produced by the hospital. It was reviewed annually by the medical staff and periodically updated.

2   *Report of the Mater Misericordiae Hospital for the year 1888*, Dublin: Browne and Nolan (1889), p 9.

3   Day cases arrive 'fasting' to the hospital at 7.30 a.m. They are admitted, prepared for surgery, have the procedure carried out under general or local anaesthetic and are returned to the day-case ward to recover. If they need pain relief they are given it. At a fixed time they are evaluated and allowed home – but only if someone collects them and can be responsible for them overnight. If this is not possible or if recovery is not evident, they are transferred to a ward and remain in hospital until they are fit for discharge.

4   Delayed discharge patients are those whose treatment is finished but who are awaiting support in the community, such as a place in a long-stay nursing home or home care. The number of patients in this category at any one time tends to fluctuate between 45 and 80 patients. This delays admissions from the emergency department, the OPD and those on waiting lists awaiting specific treatment.

5   This service was being co-ordinated by a centre at St James' Hospital

6   McMorrow, G. (1981), 'Tragic tour of hospitals', *Evening Press*, Saturday, 14 February, p 9.

7   Prof. J. Crowe, consultant gastroenterologist.

8   Crowe, J. (1999), *Short and Medium Term Medical Priorities for the Mater Hospital in the New Millennium.* Unpublished Thesis, Mater Misericordiae University Hospital.

9   The Eastern Regional Health Authority (ERHA) provided extra funds for the MED project through the Bed Capacity funds.

10 Teamwork Management Services UK (2007), *The Mater Misericordiae University Hospital Ltd, Managing the Problems of Excessive A&E Waits: Developing an Action Plan For The Whole System Change Towards Integrated Care.*

11 Primary community continuing care services (PCCC).

12 St Raphael's School was refurbished as a clinic. It was leased by the Mater for use as an OPD.

13 In 2009, a new patient flow process was put in place to replace bed management under the direction of the Director of Nursing and in association with the Director of the MED. The department deals with admission and discharge planning arrangements and with waiting list management.

14 Conlon, B. (2009), *Mater Misericordiae University Hospital: Annual Report 2009*, p 5.

15 Professors Shane O'Neill (Beaumont Hospital) and Gary Courtney (St Luke's Hospital, Kilkenny).

CHAPTER 12

The Mater Laboratory: Science in the Service of Patients

DR PEADAR MCGING FRCPATH, PRINCIPAL BIOCHEMIST

In modern times, practically every member of the population in western countries will have laboratory tests carried out at some time and hospital inpatients will have hundreds or sometimes even thousands of laboratory tests done. Despite this, few people know much about the clinical laboratory.

When the Mater Hospital opened in 1861 it did so without a laboratory. It was Edmund McWeeney, appointed as pathologist in 1888, who oversaw the establishment of the hospital's laboratory. Having studied bacteriology in Berlin under the direction of the great German scientist Robert Koch, generally regarded as one of the founders of the science of bacteriology and a Nobel Prize winner in 1905, McWeeney became the first person in Ireland to demonstrate the cause of tuberculosis (a bacillus) and to use a special test to identify the presence of the typhoid bacillus as a cause of a typhoid fever.

The original laboratory in the late 19th century.

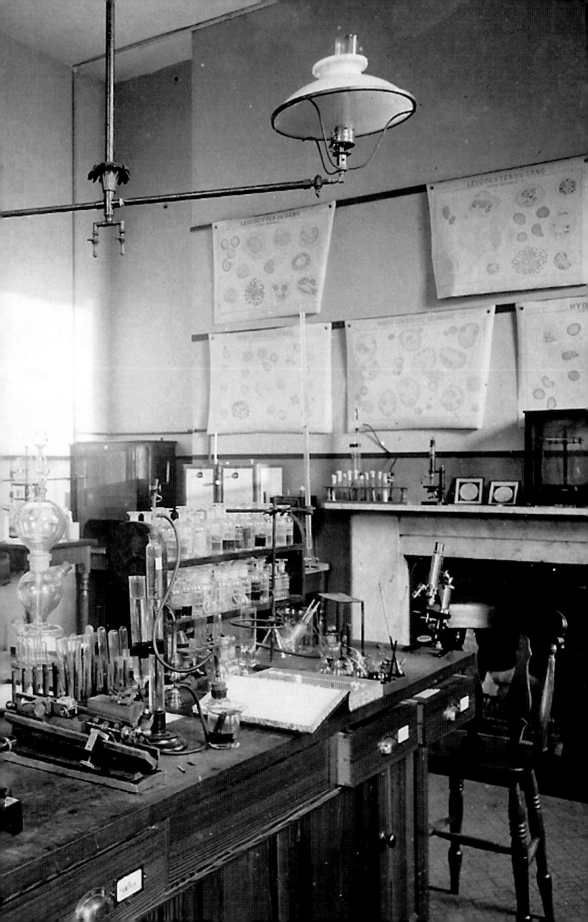

● *Archbishop Walsh, who opened the lab in 1890, is pictured here with Queen Mary on the occasion of her visit to Ireland with King George V in 1911. It was to be the last visit by a British monarch until that of Queen Elizabeth II a century later.*

Early Days of the Mater Laboratory

The Archbishop of Dublin, having provided funding for the laboratory, officially opened it on 23 May 1890. On Saturday 24 May, *The Irish Times* carried an extensive news report:

MATER MISERICORDIAE HOSPITAL

OPENING OF A NEW DEPARTMENT

The Most Rev. Dr. Walsh, Archbishop of Dublin, attended yesterday morning at the Mater Misericordiae Hospital, and officially opened a new department in connection with medical and surgical science – a Bacteriological Laboratory, the first of its kind in this country...

The Archbishop had a good grasp of one core difficulty in providing an excellent service – money – as is shown in his comment:
'Words, when they are of the right sort, are good enough in their own way, but as things frequently go in this 19th century, there is something at times more practically useful than words, and that is money.'[1]

For the first forty years of its existence, the laboratory was small and remained in its original location.[2] By modern standards it was quaint and quirky, with its rows of glass bottles of chemicals standing on a wooden work bench and some large charts hanging on the wall;[3] it was testimony to a time when each individual test carried out was laborious and time-consuming. Nonetheless, in the 1904 hospital annual report, Dr Christopher Nixon emphasised the contribution being made by the laboratory to medicine:

> In many cases not merely does the diagnosis of the existing morbid condition depend upon the report furnished from the laboratory – a report most frequently made as a result of some bacteriological or chemical investigation – but the line of treatment to be pursued is based upon the conditions which this investigation has determined.[4]

The annual report for 1913 outlines in some detail the workload of the department, with the chemical, haematological and bacteriological examination of urine making up the largest number of samples tested; there were also large numbers of sputum and tissue examinations (bacteriology and histology respectively). Twenty-five autopsies (post-mortem examinations) were performed in that year, including one sad case of a six-year-old girl 'knocked down by a bicycle, death 5 days later: meningeal haemorrhage and purulent meningitis' and also 'an unidentified female with cut throat (murder).'[5]

With the laboratory work continuing to increase, McWeeney felt he needed an assistant and in 1908, Dr William D. O'Kelly was appointed. He resigned in 1917. McWeeney continued the work of developing the department, installing new equipment and providing twice-weekly teaching sessions for the medical students. The founding father of the laboratory resigned in 1921 but continued his teaching role. When McWeeney died in 1925, Dr Andrew R. Dungan was appointed pathologist in September of that year. Unfortunately, his tenure was to be short, as he died in March 1929 (at the age of 27). Nonetheless, during his time at the Mater he had worked hard to advance the science of pathology. Dr William R. O'Farrell was appointed in 1929.

The annual report for 1928 indicates that in response to increasing numbers of tests, particularly chemical tests, 'the laboratories have been considerably enlarged, and several hundreds of pounds were spent on new apparatus.'[6] Dr William O'Farrell, who was now pathologist, guided the laboratory through a period of considerable change, including the move to a new purpose-built laboratory in 1936. The work of the pathologist grew in quantity and diversity, but by the early 1930s, the only additional staffing in the department was a semi-skilled assistant who helped Dr O'Farrell.[7] This was at a time when increasing demands were being made on the laboratory because of medical advances in the treatment of a number of metabolic conditions, such as the use of insulin in diabetes.[8]

The development of biochemistry at the Mater owes much to the work of Professor Henry Moore, who was appointed physician in 1918. Moore came to the Mater from the Rockefeller Institute, New York, where he had worked as a research assistant. In 1920, a new biochemistry department was opened under his direction.[9] According to E.T. Freeman, writing in 1954:

> His careful laboratory training in New York and the scientific approach to problems which he had witnessed and taken part in, equipped him to be a forerunner in the introduction of these methods to Irish medicine. In the Mater Misericordiae Hospital he was instrumental in setting up and equipping a biochemical laboratory long before such a department was operating in any medical school in Ireland. He was also at the very beginning of electrocardiography for cardiac cases, in the treatment of diabetes by insulin, and of the investigation of thyrotoxicosis by observation on the basal metabolic rate.[10]

A New Diversity

Professor Maurice Hickey[11] described how two new disciplines developed in the late 1920s and early 1930s.[12] This resulted in 'the division of the laboratory work into the four main sections we know today' – the two founding disciplines, bacteriology plus morbid anatomy and histology, together with two newer disciplines of chemical pathology, and haematology and serology. A significant factor in the history of the Mater laboratory was the collaboration between Henry Moore, Professor of Medicine, and William O'Farrell. The use of the expression 'clinical and biochemical' in the title of one of their papers is testimony to that.[13] Under Dr O'Farrell the amount of work undertaken by the department grew significantly both in quality (scientifically – especially under the influence of Professor Moore) and quantity, as medicine and surgery began to increase generally in the hospital. O'Farrell was an important person to have in place when the new, much larger, laboratory was being planned and ultimately opened in 1936.

A New Laboratory

The opening of the new laboratory was a major milestone. It was part of a large new building which faced the North Circular Road. As one newspaper reported, under a large headline, 'Imposing New Extension for Mater Hospital, Dublin':

> One of the most spacious hospital laboratories in Ireland has been incorporated in the addition to the Mater Hospital, Dublin. The new building also houses an extensive out-patients' department, and quarters for students and doctors. The main laboratory is an attractive room with up-to-date equipment.[14]

The laboratories still remain in that building to this day, albeit with a number of additions over the years, including a floor above it, the 1936 medical residence, and a further floor built later, initially as doctors' accommodation and eventually as additional laboratory space. According to an account of the opening in the *Irish Press* in 1936:

> Upstairs a pathological department has been installed and is divided into seven sections. At the entrance the museum and museum preparation room lie to either side. Beyond are the main laboratory, beside which the pathology and biochemical laboratory lie to the left, and the section theatre and media rooms to the right. Dr W.R. O'Farrell is in charge of this section.[15]

The report went on to describe individual sections of the laboratory:

> Mainly blood tests are carried out in the biochemical laboratory. One of the principal tests is titration for blood sugar. The blood of five different people may be tested at once.[16]

The need for sterile conditions in the bacteriology section was outlined thus:

> In the Preparation Room, through the two large sterilisers, the required wholly sterilised conditions are obtained … All tubes and containers are kept sealed with silver paper. Such extraordinary precautions are necessary because, for the growth of bugs which are to be examined successfully, it is necessary that the field of growth should be cleared of all other bugs and left free for the development and identification of the bacteria that is to be examined.[17]

The 1936 laboratory, viewed from the North Circular Road.

The First Scientist

Internationally, in the early 1930s, most pathologists practised all four branches of pathology, but soon, many began to recognise the need for scientific help with the new analytical techniques used for the increasingly complex tests requested by clinicians. In Ireland, the Mater led the way in this regard and soon after the laboratory moved to its new location, a young chemistry graduate, Isabella Carey, was appointed to the staff. She commenced work on 18 January 1937. In a letter written in 1979 to her god-daughter, she described how she started:

> When I first went to the Mater Hospital, there was no special niche for me. I had been selected from recent graduates in chemistry by the hospital board 'to give them a hand with chemical analyses'. Surprisingly there was a brand new laboratory recently built and equipped. It was bright, clean and spacious and complete with colorimeter, centrifuge, glassware, urea aeration apparatus, and Van Slyke manometric apparatus (for the measurement of gases such as oxygen and bicarbonate in the blood).[18] The laboratory staff then consisted of the pathologist, a trained nurse, and one laboratory attendant. It was agreed with the secretary of the board that my job description was 'biochemist' – the first clinical biochemist in an Irish hospital.

Things were distinctly different at that time, as she goes on to describe:

> Blood samples were taken by a nurse from all the wards in the hospital, which she then brought to the laboratory. She also assisted me with the blood tests. There was no phlebotomist, no porter service and no specimen-reception area. The maximum number of tests in any one day would be under 20 – about 8 blood sugars, 5 blood ureas, and 2 calciums and one or two others.

Each test undertaken in those days was done manually. It was time-consuming work that necessitated a very precise analytical technique. Isabella Carey remained only six years in the pathology department. According to her:

> Although my salary was marvellous for a lady at that time – 4 guineas per week, there was no salary scale, no career structure and no 'union'.[19]

In 1943, she left pathology to study medicine and returned to the Mater some years later to a post as clinical assistant in the new cardiac department.[20]

Service Expansion and the Modern Era

By the time William O'Farrell retired in 1946, the staff of the department had increased to six to meet the expanding workload. Three years earlier (1943) Maurice Hickey had joined the staff as assistant pathologist. He became pathologist when William O'Farrell retired and he remained in this position for almost four decades, combining his Mater work with a number of other appointments, including the newly established Professorship of Forensic Medicine in University College Dublin and that of State Pathologist.[21]

One of the most important developments in laboratory medicine at this time was the introduction of automation. The first Technicon Auto Analyser[22] was manufactured in 1957 and initial models were very expensive. The first Auto Analyser in the Mater was a basic single-channel Auto Analyser 1, purchased in 1965. It was supplemented by three more single-channel analysers in 1968.

Modernisation of the lab and its procedures was greatly helped by the appointment of Diarmuid UaConaill and Brendan Scully[23] who between them modernised working procedures as the laboratory entered the 1970s. Their work came at a time of great change in the laboratory, as modern processes changed the way in which lab work was done and presented new and exciting challenges. Key among these was the emergence of blood transfusion.

Like so many aspects of modern medicine, it is hard to imagine not having access to blood transfusions for patients suffering severe blood loss. It may seem surprising that the first human-to-human blood transfusion took place in 1818, but such procedures did not become commonplace until after World War II.

In the mid-1960s, blood serology was an emerging field, bolstered by the recognition of blood-group compatibility as an explanation for transfusion reactions in patients. The Mater's pathology laboratory set up a blood serology section in 1966.[24] Throughout the late 1960s and early 1970s, laboratory staff provided a blood transfusion service with specialist clinical support from St Vincent's Hospital. In 1978, Dr Brian Otridge was appointed to the Mater as consultant haematologist in charge of the newly established North Dublin Haematology Service.[25] Over the decades since, the Mater's blood transfusion

The inside of the pathology department.

department has continued to develop, including being the first hospital to establish a haemovigilance service. This service was set up to keep under observation patients who have received a blood transfusion and to report and record any adverse reactions.[26]

Another development in pathology, and one which was truly revolutionary, came in 1960, when Yalow and Berson published a seminal paper, 'Immunoassay of Endogenous Plasma Insulin in Man'.[27] Later, Rudolf Lequin would state, 'The impact of diagnostic immuno-assays (i.e., measuring specific proteins such as insulin in the human circulation with a high degree of sensitivity) on patients, clinicians, and the healthcare system in general is virtually unsurpassed.'[28] Today, nearly every section of the Mater pathology laboratories and the various research laboratories use immuno-assays[29] for tests such as hormones, therapeutic drugs, measurement of anaemia, detection of infection, cancer markers, and many other applications.

During the 1970s, further exciting developments would take place, including in endocrinology. In 1975, Dr David Powell was appointed to a new endocrinology post in the Mater. A graduate of UCD Medical School, David Powell had spent several years studying clinical and laboratory endocrinology at Harvard Medical School at Massachusetts General Hospital, experience which he brought to bear on his work

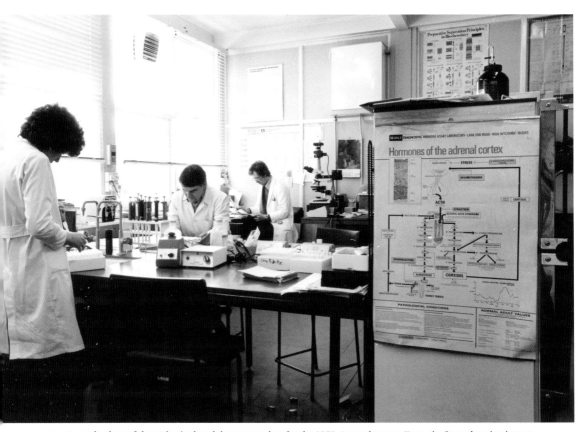

An early photo of the endocrinology laboratory, taken for the 1979 Annual report. From the front the scientists are Nuala Ward, Dr Seán Maguire, Dr Dermot Cannon.

at the Mater. In America, he had been involved in developing and refining radio-immunoassay for picomolar (really tiny) quantities of the calcium-controlling hormone PTH and fertility hormones. Together with Olwyn Lanigan, he led the expansion of the endocrinology service, through the introduction and development of new tests and new technologies. In time, the service from the endocrine laboratory covered all the main hormone assays and some specialised services, including seminal fluid analysis.[30]

The year 2010 saw endocrinology and biochemistry merge. This has led to many improvements in the endocrine service, including quicker turnaround times, new diagnostic protocols, and the development of even more sophisticated hormone assays on the new mass spectrometer.

One member of the endocrine department who made a substantial contribution to the endocrine laboratory is Dr Petr Skrabanek, who joined Powell in 1975 as senior research fellow. In 1968, as a 25-year-old medical student who had already gained a science degree and had been head of the toxicology department of Purkyně University in what is now the Czech Republic, he had made a second visit to Ireland to spend a month in a Dublin teaching hospital.[31] As part of the endocrine laboratory team in the Mater, Skrabanek was involved in producing many scientific publications, particularly on the neurotransmitter Substance P.[32] However, it was as a writer and communicator on wider medical matters that he achieved worldwide recognition. He spent nearly a decade in the Mater before joining the Department of Community Health in Trinity College in 1984. There he ultimately became associate professor before his untimely death, aged just 54.[33]

Modern Microbiology – an essential part of the diagnosis, treatment, and prevention of infectious disease

The appointment of Dr Rosemary Hone as consultant clinical microbiologist in 1975 saw the microbiology laboratory become an independent department within pathology, with Tony Murray appointed senior scientist in 1978.[34] The late 1970s saw the emergence of 'new' infectious agents and the microbiology department was the first Irish laboratory to offer a national diagnostics serology service for legionnaires' disease. In response to the international problem of hospital-acquired MRSA[35] infections, Ms Roma Ruddy was appointed in 1979 to the new post of infection control nurse.

● *Deirdre Mullis, medical scientist in microbiology, operating an automated antibiotic susceptibility analyser.*

Moira Davern, senior medical scientist in microbiology, operating the TB (tuberculosis) analyser in the special Category 3 laboratory.

In 1961, Professor Maurice Hickey described how 'the antibiotic era, commencing in the early 40s, has resulted in a vast increase in bacteriological work. In conditions due to bacterial infection it is necessary ... to test the effect of various antibiotics on its growth.'[36] In more recent times, measurement of an organism's susceptibility to antibiotics has moved from manual to automated technology, helping to meet the new diagnostic challenges of multiple resistant bacteria. Dr Niamh Corbally was appointed in 1994 as senior scientist in a new molecular microbiology laboratory. Detection of DNA from fastidious organisms[37] has hugely facilitated diagnosis and characterisation of infectious disease such as tuberculosis. A highly interactive clinical service is another important feature of the department's work.[38]

Immunology – Measuring the Patient's Immune System

The Mater laboratory has also been at the centre of developments in immunology since the service was first established in 1973. The origins of immunology go back much further: to the ancient knowledge that those who survived many diseases rarely contracted that disease again. When in July 1885, a nine-year old French boy was bitten by a dog with rabies, his family journeyed to Paris looking for a miracle cure for him. The revolutionary 'vaccine' produced and injected by Louis Pasteur achieved that miracle and a new area of medicine was born.

Charlotte Prior-Fuller, chief medical scientist in immunology, checking a specimen for anti-GAD ELISA. Anti-GAD is a test for auto-immune diabetes.

The immunology diagnostic service in the Mater Hospital was established by Dr James (Seamus) Kirrane. A histopathologist with a special interest in auto-allergic disease, he was persuaded to join the Mater pathology consultant staff in 1973. Bob Woods was the first chief medical scientist (1977–2006). The work of the modern immunology laboratory covers all aspects of a patient's immune response, both protective and harmful. It is most commonly used for diseases such as coeliac disease, auto-immune diseases and bone-marrow cancers such as multiple myeloma. In 2011, developments to help improve patient care included expanding the service for the T-cell marker CD4,[39] used to monitor therapy in HIV-infected patients.[40]

Clinical Biochemistry – using chemistry to diagnose disease and monitor treatment

In a report entitled 'Equipment for the New Biochemistry Lab', dated February 1971, Diarmuid UaConaill sought the purchase of a Technicon SMA 12/60 – a piece of equipment to improve the reproducibility and accuracy of a number of commonly performed biochemical procedures (and the only well-proved multi-channel analyser at present on the market) and a linked laboratory computer system. This new equipment was needed to cope with a workload which had increased from 25,000 tests in 1962 to 120,000 in 1971. The laboratory computer system did not arrive until 1988, but the 12/60 equipment arrived in 1974 and served the place well (with upgrades) until 1988, when three of the latest Abbott spectrum analysers were installed. These coordinate tests from miscellaneous instruments on to one platform. From then on automation of the core tests was standard. As well as laboratory analyses, the biochemistry department was able to provide point-of-care chemistry instruments in the critical high-intensity care wards. This enables immediate clinical management decisions to be made.[41] In parallel with automation, newer specialist technologies such as infrared spectroscopy[42] and mass spectrometry have been introduced.[43]

The Biochemistry Department in the mid-to-late 1970s, with, from the left, Frank Kyne, Senior Biochemist), John Ryan, Biochemist at the time and Edwin (Eddy) Wright, Chief Medical Scientist. Note the toolbox on the left: although we have progressed from manual techniques through semi-automated to fully automated systems the standard toolbox is as essential today as it was back then.

Laboratory Computers – a vital part of modern laboratory testing and patient care

● *The original Abbot spectrum analysers, with, from left to right, Frank Kyne (principal biochemist), Diarmuid Ua Conaill (consultant biochemist), Gerard Lavin (CEO, Abbott Diagnostics Ireland), Dr Peadar McGing (senior biochemist).*

In the late 1960s, laboratories internationally were generating a lot more patient results, thus creating difficulties for the service. The then relatively new idea of harnessing computer power looked like a possible solution. Shortly after Diarmuid Ua Conaill's appointment as senior biochemist, he visited two laboratories in the United Kingdom. On his return he made a case to the hospital for the installation of a computer system. It was all of 21 years before this was achieved! Meanwhile he acquired laboratory computers in various ways, as he explains:

> The first programmable calculator I got for the lab was a Casio, which could be loaded with programs of up to 30 instructions. It was expensive – about £600 [equivalent to €10,000 today]. I wrote programs for it and encouraged their use.
>
> Endocrinology got the first mini-computer in Pathology, a Wang PCS II (Personal Computer System) but in our submission it was a calculator, as the Department of Health was not keen to introduce computers. We called it ERIC, the Endocrinology Radio Immunoassay Calculator.[44]

Through the 1980s, the laboratory progressed its computerisation through Diarmuid UaConaill's programming skills, with generation of reports from two main biochemistry analysers saving time and reducing transcription errors. Through coordinated efforts from many individuals, computerisation was then developed in all the laboratories.[45] The pathology department in the Mater was one of the first to introduce an electronic requesting and reporting system. Today, the LIS (Laboratory Information System) links with the hospital's Patient Centre System to manage tests from the time the doctor orders them electronically, through to reporting. The TelePath laboratory system was substantially upgraded in 2011.[46]

Haematology – testing for diseases of the blood

In common with most pathology, haematology in the 1970s was a laboratory where all tests were performed manually, a process that was very labour intensive and time-consuming. However, as scientist Mary Doyle recalls, 'All of this changed in 1976 with the arrival of Consultant Haematologist, Dr Brian Otridge. Dr. O, as we fondly called him got us our first automated instrument, the Coulter S.'[47]

Today haematology is an interesting mix of standard automated tests – the department performs about 800 full blood counts and 500 blood coagulation (clotting) samples a day – with more exotic or manual tests such as thrombophilia screening, flow cytometry, and haemoglobin electrophoresis.[48] The clinical service begun by Brian Otridge – specialist in blood conditions – continues to expand under the leadership of Dr Peter O'Gorman.

Agnes McGonagle, senior medical scientist, checks the blood group of blood packs in the blood transfusion unit in the laboratory.

Stardust Disaster

The early morning of Valentine's Day 1981 will live in the memory of this country for a long time. Forty-eight dead and countless injured placed huge demands on the hospital system, a demand heroically met by a vast array of medical, nursing and support staff. Among those heroic support staff were the laboratory scientists. Bob Woods,[49] who was the scientist on call for haematology, blood transfusion and microbiology that night, remembers how at first the main demand was for blood products. With the assistance of his colleague Des McGoldrick, they were able to keep up a rapid response of preparing blood plasma for transfusion, ensuring that all the most urgent requests were met with minimum delay.

Many of the victims were suffering from smoke inhalation, which necessitated the measurement of arterial blood gases in the biochemistry laboratory. Des McGoldrick[50] still vividly remembers making countless trips up and down the stairs to the emergency department to deliver units of plasma the minute Bob had them ready. He also remembers the scene as he moved as quickly as he could through an area filled with burned young men and women being treated by countless doctors and nurses. As soon as he delivered the blood plasma it was straight back up to the laboratory to do more testing.

Histopathology – testing for changes in cells in tissues to diagnose cancer and other disease

The histology laboratory in the early 1980s.

From 1890 through to the early 1970s, histopathologists were the only medical consultants in the laboratory. Professor Maurice Hickey was head of the department for many years, working with fellow consultant histopathologist James (Jim) Dempsey. According to Collette McSweeney:

The laboratories in 1965 were very different but very efficient. They were small. Histology was the smallest lab. The bacteriology lab had a small partition behind which was the histology lab. Frank Leonard was in charge there, and his cigarette smoke was seen rising over the partition. Unlike today's society there were no disposables then, everything was washed, autoclaved, and reused.[51]

Peter Dervan (Professor of Pathology 1991–2008)[52] recalls how developments in the ensuing decade in radiology and surgery allowed smaller and more specific samples to be taken. This necessitated changes in histology procedures.[53] An example of this was providing cytology investigations on fine needle aspirates taken under ultrasound guidance.

Many developments have taken place in histology over the past few decades. One very important one is the new field of immuno-histochemistry. This technique uses antibodies linked to special stains in order to identify certain marker molecules within a tissue and within cells in that tissue, which is hugely important in the diagnosis of many diseases, particularly cancers. As we move further into the 21st century, histology finds itself in the realms of molecular diagnostics, with more and more tests based on genetic markers.

Heart Transplants – critically dependent on the laboratory

The success of modern transplant procedures owes a huge debt to the development of immunosuppressant drugs[54] capable of preventing otherwise fatal rejection and to laboratory testing to control blood levels. From development work for the first transplant in 1985 through to today's use of mass spectrometry, the Mater laboratory has been a leader[55] in this field.[56] Just as important as preventing rejection is detecting if it occurs, and doing so as early as possible. Back in 1985, standard histology took a few days to process, so the Mater histology laboratory set up a new procedure that involved processing tiny fragments of heart tissue with a result phoned to the surgical team within four hours. This information was crucial so that the team were able to assess within the first few days post-surgery whether the patient was rejecting the new heart and, if so, to adjust the anti-rejection medication.[57]

As well as these specific services all departments in the Mater laboratories provide standard, but vital, testing services for heart and lung transplants. Provision of blood products from the blood transfusion laboratory, prevention/diagnosis of infection by microbiology, and immunoglobulin measurement by immunology,[58] are but a small sample of laboratory contributions to this key service.

The Wider Team

The complexity of modern medicine is mirrored in the work of the pathology department, which commenced as one department and now comprises many individual laboratories, each divided into sub-specialities. Each of these is supported

● *The brand new phlebotomy department in the Whitty Building.*

by a dedicated laboratory office[59] and portering staff. A phlebotomy service[60] is supplied to the wards, to outpatients, and to GPs.[61] The mortuary, including the post-mortem service, is also under the jurisdiction of the Division of Pathology. Currently, a comprehensive diagnostic service is offered to the hospital, to GPs, and to users both regionally and nationally. Today, a total of 147 pathologists, scientists, laboratory assistants, clerical staff, phlebotomists, nurses, and porters deliver over 100,000 test results every week.

Some of the staff of the laboratory today.

1   *The Irish Times* (1890), 'Mater Misericordiae Hospital, Opening of a New Department', 24 May, p 6.
2   The laboratory was located on the ground floor/Eccles Street frontage beside the intersection with Berkeley Road.
3   *Mater Misericordiae Hospital, Annual Report 1904* (1905), Dublin: Dollard Printing House, p 47.
4   *Report of the Mater Misericordiae Hospital, Dublin, for the Year 1904* (1905), Dublin: Dollard Printing House, p 42.
5   *Mater Misericordiae Hospital, Annual Report 1913* (1914), Dublin: Dollard Printing House, pp 32–33.
6   *Mater Misericordiae Hospital, Annual Report 1928* (1929), Dublin: Dollard Printing House, p 48.
7   Hickey. M. (1961), *Centenary Mater Misericordiae Hospital, Dublin 1861–1961* (private publication), p 53.
8   Insulin was isolated in 1921. The Mater was the first hospital in Ireland to introduce the use of insulin for the treatment of diabetes. See *Mater Misericordiae Hospital, Annual Report 1928* (1929), Dublin: Dollard Printing House, p 12.
9   In 1927, Henry Moore was appointed Professor of Medicine in University College Dublin. He occupied the chair until his death in 1954.
10   *British Medical Journal* (1954), Obituary, H.F. Moore, MD.,DSc., F.R.C.P.,F.R.C.P.I. p 337.
11   Professor Maurice Hickey was appointed pathologist to the Mater in 1946.
12   Hickey, M. op. cit., p 53.
13   Moore, H. and O'Farrell, W.R. (1930), 'Note on a Case of Lipoid Nephrosis. Part I.—Clinical and Biochemical', *British Medical Journal*, 2(3632): 242–243.
14   *Irish Independent* (1936), 'Imposing New Extension for Mater Hospital', Dublin 8 May, p 9.
15   *Irish Press* (1936), 'Mater Misericordiae Hospital Extension', 14 May, p 7.
16   Ibid.
17   Ibid.
18   Van Slyke (USA) devised a simple method for measuring accurately the concentration of sodium bicarbonate in a millilitre of blood. For this assay he invented the Van Slyke volumetric gas apparatus, which was soon found to be so useful that it was found in virtually all clinical laboratories and many biochemistry laboratories as well. The culmination of his work on blood acid base balance was published between 1921 and 1924.
19   Letter from Isabella Carey to her godchild; reproduced in *Clinical Biochemistry News*, October 1996 (Vol. 2, no. 4), p 6.
20   Later Isabella worked as a biochemist in Professor Counihan's cardiology laboratory in the Mater and late in her career she returned to the main biochemistry laboratory, from where she retired in 1977.
21   The mid- to late 1970s saw increased specialisation in the pathology department and the appointment of a number of new consultants (as described elsewhere in this chapter). These additions to consultant staff necessitated change in the administration of the department. Dr Hickey became Director of Pathology, a role he retained until his retirement.
22   Originally invented in the early 1950s by Leonard Skeggs, the Auto Analyser was used mainly to reliably do routine repetitive medical lab analyses. It has since been replaced by more up-to-date equipment.
23   Diarmuid UaConaill was consultant clinical biochemist from 1971 to 2003; Brendan Scully was lab manager from 1968 to 1977, and he was followed by Tom Moloney, who was lab manager for thirty years until his retirement in 2007.
24   This new service was set up by John Brophy (1966–1967) and Brendan Scully (1967–1977), both of whom had previously worked in the 'Blood Bank'. The current chief medical scientist is Ita Lynham (appointed in 1992).
25   Dr Otridge was a full-time Mater consultant from 1988 until his retirement in 2003.
26   Mary Edgar was appointed as the first haemovigilance nurse in 1993. The job of a haemovigilance nurse is to check on patients who have had blood transfusions and to identify unexpected or undesirable effects of transfusion of blood components by ensuring they are reported and treated in a timely manner. In 1999 a National Haemovigilance service was set up by the National Blood Transfusion Service.
27   Yallow, R.S. & Berson, S.A. (1960), 'Immunoassay of Endogenous Plasma Insulin in Man', *Clin Invest* 39, 1157–75.
28   Lequin, R.M. (2005), 'Enzyme Immunoassay (EIA)/Enzyme-Linked Immunosorbent Assay (ELISA)', *Clinical Chemistry*, Vol. 51, 2415–18.
29   Immuno-assay is a technique for identifying and measuring minute concentration of a substance such as insulin, using its ability to bind to an antibody with amazing sensitivity.
30   The seminal fluid analytical service was established and run by Dr Dermot Cannon, principal biochemist.
31   While Petr Skrabanek and his wife were on a holiday in Ireland they learned of the Soviet invasion of their country. They decided to stay in Ireland, where Petr finished his medical degree in the RCSI and qualified in 1970.

32   A peptide (very small protein) that functions as a neurotransmitter, especially in the transmission of pain impulses from peripheral receptors (such as skin) to the central nervous system.

33   His obituary in the *Irish Medical Times* described Petr as a man who 'displayed courage in challenging dogma and rigour in exposing fallacy'.

34   Dr Rosemary Hone retired in 2002. Tony Murray was chief medical scientist 1981–2010.

35   MRSA infection is caused by methicillin-resistant *Staphylococcus aureus* bacteria. MRSA is known as a superbug, and its treatment can be very challenging.

36   Hickey, M., op. cit., p 55.

37   Fastidious microorganisms are those that will only grow if special nutrients are present in their culture medium.

38   Currently this clinical service is provided by consultant microbiologists Maureen Lynch and Margaret Hannon and junior medical staff; the chief medical scientist is Ursula Fox.

39   CD4 refers to the term *cluster of differentiation 4*, an abbreviation for the protocol necessary for identifying cell surface molecules.

40   Charlotte Prior-Fuller is the current chief medical scientist in immunology.

41   This area of service was developed over many years under chief medical scientist John Collier. It involves direct testing of the patients at ward level, which allows for immediate clinical management decisions to be made.

42   Infrared spectroscopy is a sophisticated and reliable technique widely used in research, medicine and industry. It can be used for detecting substances in the blood.

43   The biochemistry service is under the direction of consultant biochemist Dr Maria Fitzgibbon; the chief medical scientist is Helen Kavanagh.

44   Email to Dr Peadar McGing, January 2011.

45   Among the computerisation developments in the Mater Hospital was a greatly enhanced histology system built by Maurice Casey and Diarmuid Ua Conaill. Many changes developed in the Mater were subsequently incorporated by the supplier into their software updates.

46   In 2011 a new pathology information technology manager, Mags Scully, was appointed.

47   Martin Flaherty, chief medical scientist 1979–2011, oversaw the many developments which followed the initial semi-automated Coulter S analyser.

48   Some patients appear to have an increased tendency to thrombosis (blood clotting problems), which predisposes them to serious medical problems. It may be due to an inherited abnormality or the use of certain medical drugs.

49   Bob Woods retired as chief of immunology in 2006.

50   Des McGoldrick is currently a senior medical scientist but at the time of the Stardust disaster he was a young medical scientist.

51   Collette McSweeney joined the Mater lab as a young student in 1965. She gave 42 years of service as a scientist before retiring in 2007. Frank Leonard retired as chief medical scientist in 1985 and was followed by Brendan Tobin who was chief from 1986 to 2010.

52   Peter Dervan joined the histopathology consultant staff in 1978.

53   Histology is the study of cells microscopically.

54   Immunosuppressive drugs (anti-rejection drugs), are used to prevent the body automatically rejecting a transplanted organ.

55   The Mater was the pioneer in Ireland in this important field. The work of the Mater biochemistry laboratory in this regard was specially acknowledged by the cardiac surgeons at their 25th anniversary meeting.

56   Dr Seán Maguire learned the HPLC assay in London. Over the years that followed Seán, with fellow biochemist Frank Kyne, published many improvements to this assay in the prestigious *Annals of Clinical Biochemistry*.

57   Information provided by Brendan Tobin, who joined the Mater histopathology team in February 1985.

58   Immunology deals with the functioning of the immune system in states of both health and disease.

59   The laboratory office, under the direction of admin managers Maura Casey and Patricia Dowling, is responsible for much of pathology's interaction with users of our service.

60   The phlebotomy service consists of a small team of specially trained phlebotomists who visit the wards to take requested blood samples from the patients for testing in the laboratory.

61   Maureen Nolan, who joined the pathology staff as phlebotomist in 1968, was senior phlebotomist during a period of huge expansion in blood test numbers up to her retirement in 2008. The current senior phlebotomist, Siobhán Fitzpatrick, was responsible for significant upgrading of patient waiting and testing areas.

CHAPTER 13

Private Care in the Mater

I n the 1917 hospital annual report, numbers 33–38 Eccles Street are listed as 'The Private Nursing Home':

> The Houses are fully furnished and equipped as Nursing Homes for paying patients; there are three Operation Theatres, fitted out on the most approved aseptic principles, and every requisite of modern science is at hand for the treatment of disease.[1]

It is interesting to note that the author refers to the private nursing home in this way, using the term 'homes' throughout the report. The reason for this is because it was many years after the houses were purchased before they were connected internally to each other and, more important, to distinguish the 'nursing home', and the services it

The old Mater Private Hospital.

was providing, from the hospital nearby. At the time, attending a public hospital carried some stigma: one has only to consider the fact that once the hospital was built on Eccles Street, the residents in nearby houses began to move elsewhere, afraid of the spread of disease. One by one, the houses, particularly those adjacent to the Mater, were vacated and were quietly bought up by the Sisters. By 1919, the Mater had possession of all the houses from numbers 24 to 38 Eccles Street. Some were rented to accommodate the ever-increasing numbers of nurses employed by the hospital and others, numbers 33–38, were converted into an impressive new nursing home.

The Nursing Home Concept

Nursing homes came into their own in the early 20th century, when the middle classes, who would once have been cared for at home, began to attend hospital in increasing numbers. This in turn was due to the great advances taking place in medicine, with surgery becoming safer and more complex, the arrival of X-ray and the increasing use of anaesthesia, all of which meant that caring for the sick at home was becoming a thing of the past. Nonetheless, the wealthier classes expected to be cared for in some comfort and this led to the opening of private nursing homes throughout the city, some associated with hospitals, some independent of them, but used by medical specialists attached to the bigger hospitals. These nursing homes offered private, luxury accommodation, in single rooms in the style of the bedroom of an aristocrat. Patients were provided with a standard of care they would expect to receive in their own home during an illness.

In opening the Mater private nursing home, the Sisters of Mercy wanted to provide care for patients by specialists employed by the Mater, but they also hoped that the nursing home would be a source of much-needed revenue for the hospital, which suffered from persistent financial difficulties.[2] In the 1898 annual report, it is stated that 'the Private Hospital for Ladies, No. 37, has been a success and has been the means of bringing before the notice of the rich and influential friends the urgent needs of our poor patients.' The report goes on to say, 'the most recently established Home, No 36, for reverend and lay gentlemen will also, we trust, meet the purpose for which it has been established.'[3]

The need to build operating theatres became a pressing issue as surgery advanced and surgeons wished to carry out surgical procedures on their private patients in the nursing home itself. (Previously, surgeons would have operated on their patients in their own home on a makeshift operating table and assisted by a nurse from the hospital.) This highlighted a number of other related needs, the most important of which was the need for lifts and inter-house connecting corridors on all floors. Unfortunately, all of these needs had to wait until electricity was installed in the early 1900s. It was decided to locate three operating theatres on the second floor. The main theatre was built in number 38, complete with a lift and outside, a small concourse known as 'the rose garden'. Two rooms further along the corridor on the second floor were set aside for use as smaller theatres. Each surgeon brought his own surgical instruments with him to the theatre in a large leather bag. The instruments had to be sterilised before the procedure commenced, which in the early days meant using a boiling-water steriliser. All surgical drapes, after they were returned from the laundry, together with wound dressings, were packed, in a ritual fashion, into special metal drums and sent over to the main hospital to be sterilised in an autoclave. It was well into the mid-20th century before 'disposable' items, such as dressings, appeared. The metal drums and other equipment were transported by porters to and from the general hospital autoclave.

Apart from the clinical theatre areas, the private nursing home was beautifully decorated and furnished much like any Georgian domestic dwelling. The wall at the end of most of the corridors was covered with an enormous floor-to-ceiling mirror. This served to give the impression of space and that the corridor was, in fact, much longer. At number 36, the main entrance, two magnificent sitting rooms opened on either side of the entrance, with beautiful Georgian fireplaces in them, including brass fenders and decorative brass fire irons.

After they arrived for admission, patients were shown to one of these rooms to await a nurse who would accompany them to their room for formal admission. The largest rooms were on the first floor and, with their excellent views of the street, were usually used for VIPs, such as presidents, taoisigh, or Church dignitaries. Each room had large windows in it, with full-length net curtains and plush velvet drapes. A large bed with an ornate brass head- and footboard occupied the centre of the room. It was covered in beautiful white bed linen, edged with broderie-anglaise, pure woollen blankets, a white counterpane and an elegant quilt on top. The furniture was very comfortable and included some large armchairs, a chaise longue and footstools, and thick rugs were available for comfort and warmth. Prior to central heating being installed, all the rooms had fireplaces in them and coal fires were lit daily. All rooms were furnished with a mahogany dressing table on which stood a covered glass jug of drinking water and some dainty glasses on a silver tray, a fruit bowl with a beautiful silver fruit knife and fork with ivory handles and some small linen hand towels. The patient's tray for meals was also meticulously arranged.

The actual running costs of the nursing home were relatively low, in spite of the levels of luxury, and for many years it financially supported the hospital, the administration of which was combined with that of the nursing home. As we saw in Chapter 8, this became something of a bone of contention in 1923/24 when the inspector of taxes decided that it was a profit-making organisation, distinct from the main hospital.[4]

The Nursing Home Administration

For many years after the connecting corridors were put in place, the houses continued to operate as independent houses, with separate kitchens, staff and administrations. The Sisters of Mercy (all qualified nurses) were in charge, one per house, together with a Sister in each kitchen looking after the catering. There was a senior staff nurse in each house and the rest of the staff complement was made up of junior staff nurses and student nurses, who received much of their practical training looking after the patients. In a survey carried out in 1929, the bed capacity is noted as 92 and the staff listed as follows: nine members of the community, 48 lay nurses and 27 domestic staff. All of the staff, except the porters, were resident either in the home itself or in the nurses, home nearby. Each house had its own consultants, who negotiated the admission of their patients to that particular house with the Sister in charge. When the patient was admitted, the consultant arrived in due course with the patient's file in his briefcase and wrote details of the admission and the instructions to be followed by the nursing staff, after which the file, marked with the room number, was kept safely to hand. The Sister in charge was briefed by the consultant on the condition of the patient and his/her care requirements, and at the end of the patient's stay, the consultant collected the medical file and took it to his consulting rooms, to ensure seamless continuity of care. There were no junior medical doctors in the nursing homes: if need arose, the consultant was contacted and he made any necessary arrangements. The system would appear to have worked well. According to Sr Marie of Mercy, who worked in number 30,

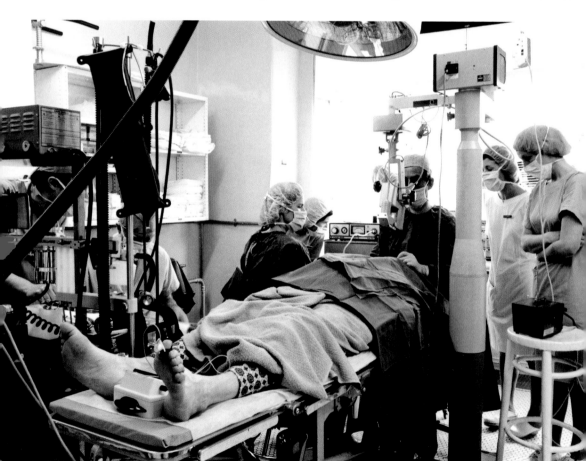

Eye surgery in the private hospital 1970.

'We were a very happy family and we knew everyone personally.' Sr Marie of Mercy was well known for her kindness and the attention she gave to her patients.[5]

By early 1970, however, the place had slipped into debt. It was no longer serving the primary purpose for which it had originally been opened, i.e. to serve as a financial support to the main hospital. The reasons for this were many, the chief being poor financial administration. From the outset, some patients were never charged for their stay; usually heads of state or members of their family, clergy, relations of medical staff, or sometimes simply because they pleaded inability to pay. Some chose to ignore the need to pay the bill at all! The nuns did not have any system in place for pursuing such people. Another problem was the tradition of keeping patients who should have been transferred to secondary long-term care or to a convalescent home in the place sometimes for years with negligible payment, or no payment at all. This might have been acceptable in the early days, when the nursing home was little more than that, but by 1970, the cost of patient care was rising rapidly and the complexity of patient treatment required a quicker turnover and shorter lengths of stay.

The Mater Private

In 1972, it was decided to change the name from Mater Nursing Home to Mater Private Hospital and to run it as an independent business entity. Sr Gemma Byrne was in charge and it became obvious that she had a long-term plan in mind for the place. Her first intention was to turn it into a profit-making business. By 1974, there were no long-stay patients, no non-pay cases and the bed occupancy rate was improving. Sr Gemma's next move was to eliminate the need for services to be provided by the main hospital to the nursing home, but here she was less successful. A fully self-contained private hospital was still some years away, and would depend on developments associated with cardiac surgery to take on a life of its own.

Towards the Future

As time passed, the building began to show its age, hardly surprising when we consider that these houses were probably built in the 1790s, and it became clear that a brand new private hospital would be needed.[6] However, the location posed something of a problem. Many of the houses on Eccles Street, particularly on the hospital side of the street (but not owned by the Sisters of Mercy), were in an advanced state of deterioration by 1980. Most of them were falling down and in many, only the front wall to just above the entrance survived. Weeds were growing out of the shells of the buildings, giving an unsightly appearance to the street. In spite of the fact that this terrace included the famous 'Number 7', the mythical home of James Joyce's Leopold and Molly Bloom in *Ulysses*, there was no preservation order in place. Eventually, these houses and the old Dominican Convent and school, together with the derelict Bertrand Russell school, all on the north side of Eccles Street, were purchased by the Sisters of Mercy for hospital purposes.

The nurses' station at the Mater Private.

Meanwhile, at the October 1976 meeting of the hospital board of management, Sr Josephine Bourke, Superior General, asked the board for its opinion on three central questions: first, what they considered to be the future prospects of the Mater Private Hospital; second, whether it would be advisable to continue to maintain a private hospital in close association with the main hospital; and third, given the financial state of the hospital at the time and early discussions then in train for the main hospital (Phase 1A) building developments, was it even advisable to build a private hospital and if so, where?

After much discussion, it was decided that a new private hospital on a new site (on Eccles Street) should be built and that, in order to thrive and to attract private patients, it should be a state-of-the-art hospital with the latest facilities and equipment. In 1978, a project team was assembled to decide on the bed complement and cost implications of this project. In their report they considered that there was a very definite future for private hospitals in Ireland; that the existing place should continue on the Mater site, for the time being; and that a new private hospital should be built with approximately 120 beds. They estimated that the capital cost would amount to approximately £4 million, a gross underestimation as it transpired.

In August 1980, Sr Josephine Bourke completed her term of office as Superior General of the Sisters of Mercy (Dublin) and Sr Cora Ferriter was appointed her successor. The final decision about a new private hospital ultimately fell to her and her team at Carysfort Park. Over the next few years, they sought advice and listened to all the pros and cons of this expensive development over the next few years, including contributions from the Archbishop of Dublin, Dr Dermot Ryan, then Chairman of the hospital's board of management. Indeed, the discussions went all the way to Rome, as authorisation was

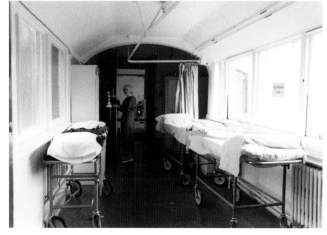

The trolley bay.

sought to build. There were many in Dublin and beyond who were against such large expenditure on what was essentially a private facility. Many felt that it was contrary to the Mercy founding tradition to serve the poor, which had been the cornerstone of the hospital's foundation. Nonetheless, eventually it was decided to proceed with it.

A New Private Hospital

Construction commenced on the Mater Private in early March 1985 and the hospital was opened for patients in May 1986. The new hospital was magnificent, to say the least. The architectural priorities had obviously been focused on patient comfort, energy conservation and to create a building in harmony with the existing architecture in the area. The CEO when it opened was Sr Gemma Byrne, who had masterminded the project from the beginning. Director of Nursing was Sr Therese Martin Crowley, who had been matron in the old private hospital. She became responsible for the enormous task of transferring the patients to the new MPH. She remained as Matron until 1987, when she was succeeded by Sr Mary of the Incarnation Doyle.[7]

When the MPH, as it became known, opened it had a complement of 148 beds. What turned out to be one of the busiest departments in the place was the imaging/radiology department, which had an MRI scanning unit and a CT scanner. The Mater was the first Irish hospital to install an MRI system, in 1986. A PET/CT scanner was installed in the main hospital, in a purpose-built unit built in 2005. This was a major capital development, jointly owned by Mater and MPH and developed as a public/private scheme. The success of the new MPH was instant and within only a few years, it became clear that the hospital would need to be expanded and new operating theatres built.

Unfortunately, some years after the opening of the new Mater Private, the debt the Sisters of Mercy had incurred in building the hospital was preventing them moving forward with other building projects. These difficulties triggered long-standing discussions within the congregation about the conflict between running a private hospital and the order's ethos of caring for the poor. So in 2000, when a request for further funding for a large and very expensive extension reached her office, Sr Helena O'Donoghue, the order's Provincial Leader, took the time to think about and discuss the matter in some detail. One must remember that in addition to the original debt, by the year 2000 two further extensions had already been added on at a combined cost of €23 million. Sister Helena decided that the situation was unsustainable, especially as the financial returns to the congregation from the MPH were virtually negligible. The numbers of Mercy Sisters working in it were gradually diminishing and there was no way of knowing what the future would hold.

On 2 October 2000, Sr Helena announced that it had been decided that, all things considered, the Order would disengage from the MPH. It was not intended to sell it: instead it had been decided to arrange for a seamless bowing-out, where ownership would be transferred to all staff members with at least seven years' service. To enable this to happen and to look after the legal implications of the move, a special board was put in place to deal with it.

After the sisters withdrew from the private hospital, it went on to become a thriving business. In 2005 the print media were reporting on the hospital's substantial pre-tax profits:

> Under the terms of the 2000 deal, the takeover group assumed the hospital's debts of €13.96 million and agreed to pay the nuns €27.93 million over twenty years. The group was backed by the Allied Irish Bank... The company had €13.76 million in cash at year-end, up from €7.32 million.[8]

In 2007, a company by the name of Capvest bought the Mater Private Hospital for €350 million. According to *The Irish Times:*

> AIB has emerged as financial backer to UK private equity firm Capvest in its €350-million buyout of the Mater Private Hospital in central Dublin...[9]

And so the history of the new Mater Private Hospital goes on, but without the Sisters of Mercy. There is still a great relationship between the Mater Private Hospital and the Mater Misericordiae University Hospital. Just as they did in the early 20th century, many of the Mater's consultants look after patients in MPH as well as in the public hospital.

Finding a Future for the Old Mater Private

After the patients and staff moved to the new private hospital in 1986, the future of the old building was uncertain. Shortly after number 38 was vacated in 1986, the existing operating theatre was turned into a (temporary) theatre for eye surgery. The lower ground floor was used to house the CT scanning department (imaging/radiology). Some of the rooms were turned into offices. All of these facilities would, it was expected, be relocated eventually to the new hospital development on completion of the Phase 1A (bed block) then being built. Unfortunately, the unexpected happened. A fire in the upper part of number 38 did an enormous amount of damage and so the ophthalmic theatre had to be relocated elsewhere in the old hospital.

After the hospital development plan for Phase 1B, and Phase 2, was abandoned in 1994 due to lack of finance, the hospital turned its attention to the growing pressure for space for a long list of developing services. The old Mater private hospital, now empty, seemed an obvious choice for the location of some of the services. When the building closed a preliminary survey of it was carried out with a view to making it structurally safe.[10] In 1994 thoughts turned to fully restoring these houses when funds became available.[11]

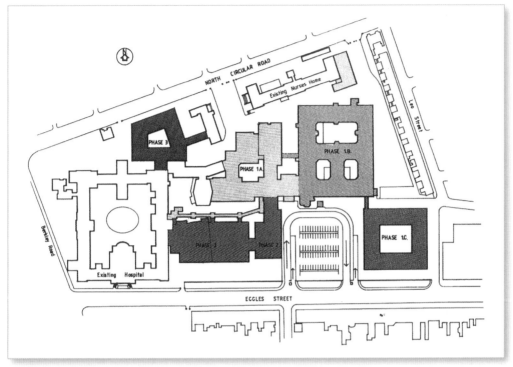

● *The site of the planned Phases 1B and 2 of the Mater development, which ultimately did not go ahead. Part of this plan was to demolish the old Mater Private building, located to the right of the 'Existing Hospital' and facing Eccles Street.*

A New Role for the Nursing Home

In 1988, Professor Joseph Ennis, consultant radiologist, had become increasingly concerned about the incidence of breast cancer among Irish women, and the significant mortality rate. At this time, Ireland was known to have breast cancer rates higher than other EU countries and Professor Ennis wanted to understand more about why this should be.[12] He set about developing a breast screening

● *The Breast Check Clinic.*

project, using mammography, with funding he received from the European Community, supplemented by the Mater Foundation (a sum of £800,000), Femscan, Quinnsworth and the Sisters of Mercy. With this funding in place Professor Ennis was able to go ahead almost immediately to set up the first of two pilot programmes. In June 1989, Dr

Mary Codd, whose expertise in epidemiology and biostatistics (UCD) was considered invaluable, was appointed project co-ordinator and on 24 October that year, the Eccles Street Breast Screening Programme, the first of the pilot programmes, was launched by Dr Rory O'Hanlon, Minister for Health at 46 Eccles Street.

The overall objective of the programme was to evaluate a target age group as recommended by the European Commission: women born between 1 January 1925 and 31 December 1940. In February 1992, the first letters to women in this target group, inviting them to attend for a mammogram, were sent out and each woman offered an appointment date. The response was good and within a month of her appointment, each attendee received a personal mammography report (the hospital had arranged for the possibility of positive or 'doubtful' results). The project was a great success, and because of the high volume of responses, in 1997 a decision was taken to turn a large section of the old Mater private hospital into a breast screening unit to enable further expansion of this service. In 1998, the Eccles Street breast cancer screening programme finally evolved into a national screening programme and a sum of £1.3 million was allocated to the Mater to restore this section of the old hospital and turn it into the programme headquarters. In addition, substantial capital grants were made available to enable the place to acquire state-of-the-art mammography equipment together with equipment needed for new biopsy techniques and ultrasound.[13] In March 1999, the national breast screening programme commenced as BreastCheck – Eccles Unit. It was officially opened on 25 April 2000. Since then, women aged 50–64 from all over Ireland have been offered free mammograms on a rolling basis in regional clinics as part of the BreastCheck programme.

Breast Healthcare Unit – 38 Eccles Street

The then Minister for Health, Mary Harney, at the official opening of BreastHealth, 38 Eccles Street.

Once the breast screening service was established at number 36, the need for a breast treatment service for those diagnosed with symptomatic breast problems became obvious. Furthermore, it would be a bonus to have a treatment service nearby to allow for some sharing of staff and services as the need arose. It was decided to use number 38 for this purpose and to locate a specially equipped breast unit there. The facilities and the staffing of the Symptomatic Breast Health Unit, as it was then called, were developed with the aid of funding received from the Eastern Regional Health Authority and the Mater Foundation.[14] In 2005, BreastHealth Mater was officially opened by the Minister for Health. It 'provides a comprehensive diagnostic and therapeutic service for women presenting with breast symptoms'.[15] This clinic was refurbished and redeveloped in 2010 and now serves more than 12,000 women each year.[16]

Diabetic Day Centre

● *Dr Ivo Drury, who shaped care for diabetics at the Mater Hospital.*

In 1978, the old day centre at 48 Eccles Street had been opened for the outpatient management of people with diabetes mellitus. Deirdre Creegan, a very able nurse manager with a special interest in diabetes, organised the unit as best she could with very limited financial resources, and it was under her management and leadership that the care of diabetic patients in the unit flourished. Creegan, whose special interest (apart from the care of diabetic patients) was in ongoing education for nurses, was pivotal in establishing the higher diploma in diabetes nursing in conjunction with University College Dublin in 1996. She was a founder member of the Federation of European Nurses in Diabetes.

When the unit moved from its cramped location across the street to number 30 Eccles Street, the new location enabled staff and students to undertake research or further studies on the subject of diabetes, as well as caring for patients in a more spacious clinic.

The diabetes unit is dedicated to the physician who devoted most of his working life at the Mater to the study of diabetes and caring for those who had it, Professor Ivo Drury. Drury is still remembered for his contribution to endocrinology as a whole, but most of all for his work for diabetics. He was an inspiration to many who worked with him or studied under him. According to Stephen O'Rahilly, who was a UCD medical student and is now Professor of Metabolic Medicine at Cambridge University: 'Professor Ivo Drury was an incredibly generous man, utterly admirable. His great lament was that he hadn't been able to do more for science.'[17]

● *The Diabetic Day Centre.*

Professor Drury was appointed to the staff of the Mater as a medical physician in charge of endocrine disorders in 1947. In his early years, he had the good fortune to work under one of the most famous and distinguished professors of medicine in the Mater and indeed in Ireland, Professor Henry Moore.[18] Professor Moore had studied endocrine diseases, particularly diabetes, in Berlin and later at the Rockefeller Institute, New York as a research assistant. Moore returned to the Mater in 1925 with the intention of setting up a modern laboratory approach to the investigation and control of disease, particularly in relation to the treatment of diabetes mellitus with insulin, which had recently been discovered. He set up and equipped a biochemical laboratory, which he located in 38 Eccles Street. Professor Moore stimulated a special interest in diabetes in his young student and so Ivo Drury was to walk in the steps of a great teacher, just as many have walked in his inspirational footsteps since. The diabetes day centre at the Mater now caters for large numbers of patients and offers a full and comprehensive diabetes support programme, including insulin education, dietary advice, retinopathy screening and specialist pre-pregnancy and adolescent clinics, among other services for diabetic patients.

Other departments located in number 38 include a day-care unit for patients suffering from chronic renal (kidney) disease. This unit is located on the second floor. It was formally opened by the Minister for Health on 1 July 2005. The hospital's department of clinical photography has its headquarters in this building too.

● *The staff of the diabetes day centre. Deirdre Creegan, who set the unit up, is second from the right at the front. Prof. Firth, on the extreme left of the photo, is the medical officer in charge of the department.*

1   Mater Misericordiae Hospital Dublin (1918), *A Report for the year 1917*, Dublin: Dollard Printing House, p 16.
2   The name Mater Nursing Home was in use until about 1975, by which time it was considered outmoded.
3   Mater Misericordiae Hospital Dublin (1899), *A Report for the year 1898*, Dublin: Dollard Printing House, p 6.
4   [1932] T.I.T.R. 388.
5   Sr Marie of Mercy O'Connor (1918–2011) in an interview in 2005 after she had moved to the new Mater Private Hospital. She retired from active nursing in December 1997.
6   According to Maurice Craig in his book, *Dublin 1660–1860: The Shaping of a City* (Liberties Press), Archdall bought the Eccles Estate in 1748. He commenced building the streets in this area,then part of the Gardiner Estate. See page 230 (footnote) in Craig's book.
7   Sr Mary Incarnation Doyle was Director of Nursing in the MPH from 1987 to 1992. She was succeeded by Sr Maura Irwin, who had been her assistant.
8   *Business News* (2005), 'Mater Hospital Pretax Profits Rise to €13.56m', *The Irish Times*, 27 August.
9   Beesley, A. (2007), 'Capvest buyout of Mater Private backed by AIB', *The Irish Times*, 3 July 2007.
10   April 1987.
11   The refurbishment of 30–38 Eccles Street was done in three phases at an overall cost of over £3 million.
12   Browne, M. (1993), 'Breast Cancer Rate High in Irish Women', *Irish Medical Times*, Vol. 7, No. 39, September 24, p 1.
13   Mater Misericordiae University Hospital, *Annual Report 1998*, p 20.
14   The Mater Foundation was established in 1985 as the official fundraising body of the Mater Misericordiae University Hospital.
15   www.breasthealthmater.ie/about-the-unit.
16   The total number of patients seen in 2010 was 12,062 (Mater Hospital, Unit Performance Review. courtesy of Catherine Clarke, corporate planner).
17   See: http://condor.depaul.edu/mfiddler/hyphen/Fat%20Genes.htm.
18   Professor Henry Moore was from Cappoquin, Waterford. He graduated from University College Dublin in 1912 with a first class honours degree and a travelling studentship. He was elected a Fellow of the RCPI in 1931 and a Fellow of the RCP, London in 1939. He was appointed to the staff of the Mater in 1917. He died at home after a short illness in 1954 aged 66.

The doorway to the old (1923)
nurses' home.

CHAPTER 14

Nursing at the Mater

It would be difficult to overstate the importance of the role of Florence Nightingale in nurse training. It was she who initiated the idea that all nurses should be trained, after her own experiences in the 1853–6 Crimean War. So influential were her ideas that, towards the end of the 19th century, hospitals in both England and Ireland were opening training schools for nurses. Nightingale insisted that trainee nurses (*probationers* as they were called then) should be resident during their training in what was called a 'nurses' home' and that life in this home would enhance another aspect of nurse education which Nightingale saw as essential – an appreciation of the arts and of the finer things in life. A 'home sister' would be appointed to attend to the needs of the 'lady nurses'. The word 'sister' and the probationers' uniform reflected to the role nuns played in nursing at this time.

Nightingale's plans were certainly ambitious and were helped greatly by the fact that she had the financial means to do all of this; few hospitals were ever able to include such comprehensive nurse training in their prospectus. However, Nightingale sought to radically move away from the Dickensian model of the 'pauper nurse' of the 18th and 19th centuries and she achieved it, albeit slowly. 'Pauper nurses' were untrained and largely unpaid women who worked mostly, but not exclusively, in the workhouse wards caring for the sick. They were elderly women and had often been patients in the workhouse themselves. Where they were unpaid, they received extra privileges such as food, liquor or one-off cash payments – depending on what they were being asked to do. These nurses were considered by the authorities at the time to be 'the blackest spot in the Poor Law administration'.[1] Although pauper nurses were not a feature of the Mater, nursing there was provided by the Sisters until 1891, when the Sisters took the decision to go ahead and open a training school. It was a big undertaking, but somehow the time was right: the building of the hospital was as complete as they could manage financially for the time being and they felt that they might be leaving themselves open to grave criticism if they did not train and educate their nurses.

Sr Berchmans Barry was most likely the person behind the proposal to develop the school and she began by acquiring number 32 Eccles Street for that purpose. Next, Sr Berchmans employed Mary McGivney as matron, with responsibility for the

Miss Mary McGivney, Matron of the hospital in 1891.

management and education of the 'nurse probationers' and the two women drew up a programme of training and studies based on the existing Edinburgh three-year system.[2]

Sr Berchmans and McGivney interviewed prospective candidates in the autumn of 1891, and the school was opened on 23 November of that year. They chose to follow a system which originated at the big London hospitals in which two 'classes' of nurses were trained: those intending to make a career of nursing; and those who were 'ladies of means', who paid a fee to learn the art of nursing in order to help the sick as a humanitarian activity. These latter would have been a lot older than the average probationer and they were not bound by the same rules:

Paying probationers will also be received; fee £40.[3] No distinction is made between ordinary and paying probationers, but the latter are not obliged to remain for the three years unless they choose to do so.[4]

Matron Mary McGivney and her first class of trained nurses in 1895.

Apart from the paying probationers, the average student paid a fee of £10. This sum increased over the years and was payable in two instalments during the first year of training. (The payment of fees was a feature of the hospital-based nurse training programme which came to an end in the 1990s and which was replaced by the first diploma in nursing course, and later, the degree course at University College Dublin. The fees were a useful source of revenue for the hospital.)

Sr Berchmans selected the first intake of student nurses in 1891 very carefully. A lengthy list of regulations was laid out prior to their arrival, as this selection shows:

1. The Sisters of Mercy receive Probationers for training as Hospital, District or Private Nurses. Candidates' applications should be forwarded to the Lady Superior at the Hospital, subject to whose selection they will be received as Probationers.
2. The age considered desirable for Probationers is about twenty-three to thirty-five, single or widows.
3. Testimonials of good character indispensable.
4. Candidates must attend, at their own cost, at the Hospital for approval when required.
5. The term of training is three years. The first year is spent entirely in the Hospital, until after the candidate has passed the examinations of the Hospital; during the second and third years she may be sent on such private or special duty as she may be considered suitable for. Probationers will only be received on the distinct understanding that they will remain for three months on trial... At the end of three months the candidate, if found efficient, will be engaged as Probationer.
6. Candidates are required to provide the indoor uniform according to hospital regulations. Outdoor uniform is provided by the Hospital at the end of the first year of training.[5]

On 23 November 1891, the nurse training programme commenced. The first class of students comprised sixteen young women, but only five arrived on the first day and the rest came in ones and twos over the next six weeks. Records do not explain why this was, but it had possibly to do with the fact that the probationers would be replacing the existing ward assistants and financially the hospital could not afford an overlap. Of the first intake of students, ten completed the course, and the remaining six left for reasons given in the school register as 'general unsuitability', 'insubordination' or 'ill health'. All who finished the training took up their positions as qualified nurses. Because of the ready supply of nuns and the expense of employing the graduate nurses, not many were taken on by the Mater, instead going on to nurse elsewhere.

The following year a class of 32 girls were accepted for training followed by 28 the year after. This put pressure on the available accommodation and so in 1893, number 35 Eccles Street was acquired and later number 36 was added, to become the nurses' home. However, space still had to be found for the staff nurses employed by the hospital – often selected from the women they had trained – and who all expected to live in. In 1920, a space was selected on which to build a dedicated nurses' home, at the rear of numbers 30–37 Eccles Street on a site originally occupied by stables. It wasn't long, however, before this building became inadequate and an extension had to be added, consisting mainly of cubicles for the more senior nurses. By now the place could accommodate 170 nurses. The nurses' home (which would be called Rosary House in 1954), had a sizable lecture theatre, two dining rooms and two sitting rooms in it, but from all accounts the accommodation continued to be inadequate.

A Nurse Education Programme

When nurse training schools opened in London, the teaching programme, which focused on theory as well as practice, was controversial. There was no state registration in Ireland (or England) until 1919, and so the standard and content of nurse education programmes was set by the hospitals themselves and records of results were kept by them. Few medics agreed with Nightingale that nurses needed any theory at all as part of their training. As far as many were concerned, all that was needed was a pair of hands. Sr Berchmans and Miss McGivney ignored the view of the medics and arranged lectures as well as practical experience, with the medical board's support. It was decided to send all first-year students to the wards from the beginning to teach them the art of practical nursing.[6] In their second and third years, they received lectures from the medical staff. However, most of the teaching was carried out by the matron and she was assisted by Margaret Harrold, the first Assistant Matron, who was appointed in 1925.

The hospital-based system of setting standards in nursing was not without its opponents. In late 1893, before the first class of student nurses at the Mater had completed their programme, a letter was received by the hospital from the famous Margaret Huxley,[7] Lady Superintendent of Sir Patrick Dun's Hospital. Huxley had trained as a nurse at St Bartholomew's Hospital, London, and was now concerned with the standard of nurse education in Dublin. Her approach was to set up a central school in Dublin where students from all the training schools could attend lectures. According to her:

> Each hospital was a law unto itself as regards the education of its nurses, and their education was almost entirely dependent on the generosity and good will of the medical staff and the matron, who after their busy day's work, more or less regularly, gave the nurses a lecture.[8]

On 16 December 1893, Huxley held a meeting to which she invited all the matrons and some medical representatives, including Mary McGivney and Sir Joseph Redmond (physician) from the Mater. Huxley presented her proposals for a central school, including a standardised examination for all nursing students and a central register of trained nurses. There is no record as to why the Mater decided not to avail of this opportunity, but it may well have had to do with finance, as the participating hospitals had to bear the cost of the scheme. It is also entirely possible that the hospital wasn't ready to cede power in such a valuable resources as nurses to an outside body. Margaret Huxley went ahead with her plans and in 1894 she opened the Dublin Metropolitan Technical School for Nurses. In January 1894, she wrote to the Mater offering them a system of 'conjoint teaching and examination of nurses' at the school. It was discussed at a meeting of the medical board on 18 January 1894 and the following reply was drafted:

> The Board of this Hospital, having carefully considered the proposals of the Committee in reference to the education and examination of nurses, do not at present see their way to alter their system of teaching and therefore regret that they cannot co-operate in the proposed scheme.[9]

Miss Huxley went on to become a key member of the movement for state registration of nurses in Ireland. When the Nurses' Registration Acts[10] were passed in 1919, she was appointed by the government as a member of the first Nursing Council of Ireland. Sir Arthur Chance, from the Mater, Chairman of the Irish Nursing Board,[11] was also invited to become a member of the council.[12]

Florence Nightingale was against the idea of registration from the beginning and so it was left to the next most powerful nurse in Britain, Ethel Bedford-Fenwick, to fight a battle for nurse registration which had lasted over thirty years until 1919, and to break the monopoly of the hospitals on deciding who should be given the title of 'qualified nurse'. Gerard Fealy, in his book on the apprenticeship training of nurses in Ireland very ably sums it up:[13, 14]

> In pursuing state registration, Bedford-Fenwick was also attempting to break the monopoly that voluntary hospitals exercised in recruiting and training nurses and in this way she was promoting the professional and economic independence of nurses. For this reason the voluntary hospitals were opposed to state registration. With any change to the status quo, the voluntary hospitals could lose their influence as the principle employer and supplier of nurses and they would be obliged to employ nurses on terms set by a state regulatory authority.

He goes on to elaborate further:

> The Nightingale system of probationership training was providing the voluntary hospitals with a relatively cheap, disciplined and compliant worker whose conditions of employment and methods of training they also controlled.[15]

In spite of the political turbulence, what tended to happen in practice at this time was that qualified nurses were judged by the reputation of the hospital at which they had trained. The Mater had an excellent reputation and the certificates it issued to nurses were considered to be very valuable.[16]

The nurses' home in 1923.

The lecture room in the nurses' home – the black belts denote that these are senior nurses.

After the nurses qualified, they remained at the hospital and worked a further year as what came to be called a 'badge nurse', somewhere between a staff nurse and a student nurse. These nurses were given their hospital badge, but would not be awarded a hospital certificate for one further year, which was financially advantageous to the hospital, as it could benefit from the skills of qualified nurses at a lower rate of pay. This arrangement was not unique to the Mater. It operated in most if not all of the hospitals with training schools, some of which sought to keep the qualified nurses for as much as two years and some for as little as six months as 'badge' nurses. Another source of revenue was 'home care', where hospitals advertised the availability of nurses for the care of the sick in their own homes and people would pay the hospital direct for the service, as this advertisement from 1898 shows:

TRAINED NURSES

A Training School and Home for Trained Nurses has been for some years attached to the Hospital. Thoroughly trained and experienced Nurses (who have passed a qualifying examination in nursing) will be sent immediately to any part of Ireland on receipt of a letter or telegram addressed to the Lady Superior of the Hospital. Telephone 445.

TERMS

Medical Cases … … … … … … … … … … … …	£1. 1. 0 per week
Surgical Cases … … … … … … … … … … …	£1. 1. 0 per week
Mental Cases … … … … … … … … … … …	£2. 2. 0 per week
Massage Cases … … … … … … … … … … …	£2. 2. 0 per week
Massage Cases … … … … … … … … … …	£0. 5. 0 each attendance

Travelling expenses and washing are charged for in addition.

If the Nurse be required for a day, or part of a day only, the charge is 10s. 6d. An extra charge of 10s. 6d a week will be made if the Nurse returns to the Home for any of her meals or for sleeping.[17]

In the 1898 hospital annual report, under the heading: 'Private Wards and Nurses' Fees', the income generated by this arrangement amounted to £1,244. 0. 6, a not-inconsiderable sum.[18]

The Matrons of the Mater

biography

Mary McGivney

Mary McGivney, from Collon, Co. Louth, was appointed the first Matron at the Mater in 1891. She was only 26 years of age when she took up the post. How she came to be chosen is not on record, but it is entirely possible that she was recommended by her local parish priest in Louth. She was certainly qualified for the job: she had trained at the Royal London Hospital, where the matron, Miss Eva Lückes, was an ardent follower of the Nightingale principles. McGivney had a very difficult time during her training at the London Hospital. While she was there, the business her father owned in Collon was burned to the ground, maliciously it was thought. It became the subject of much local and legal controversy. This upset her intensely, but apparently she did not share the problem with those around her, instead becoming quiet and withdrawn. Lückes grew to dislike her and by all accounts made her life very difficult.

Eventually, on the advice of one of the surgeons, Mary McGivney returned home to Ireland. The surgeon who had advised her, Frederick Treves, was famous for his care of Joseph Merrick, the 'Elephant Man', his patient in the London Hospital and who afterwards Treves took to his own home to be cared for.

Given that there had been a serious misunderstanding between Mary McGivney and Lückes at the Royal London, Sr Berchmans was clearly taking something of a risk employing her, but McGivney turned out to be the right person for the job and an asset to the school of nursing at the Mater.[19] She was enthusiastic and anxious to make a success of the appointment. McGivney was much respected by the medical staff on whom she depended for help with lectures for the nurses. They spoke very highly of her and her polite and courteous approach around the wards. In 1961, Dr. E.T. Freeman paid tribute to her on the occasion of the hospital's centenary:

> Miss McGivney retired in 1920 after 28 years of devoted service, during which she established on a firm basis the training school at the Mater. I can recall her clearly – a slim brisk elderly lady in a grey silk dress moving around St. John's corridor.[20]

McGivney became a member of the first board of the Irish College of Nursing in 1917 and a member of the Irish Matrons' Association. By 1920, her health was failing and so she decided to retire to her home in Collon. Due to a prolonged illness she did not enjoy much of a retirement. She died on 20 December 1932.

Mary McGivney was succeeded by Sr Madeline Sophie McCormack, who had trained under her at the Mater, and who joined the Sisters of Mercy in 1909. Popular with her colleagues, Sr Madeline Sophie appointed Margaret Harrold as assistant matron, and together they prepared the first class of student nurses for state examinations under the new General Nursing Council of Ireland. They also had responsibility for those already qualified to enable them to register under the new 1919 Registration Act.

Miss Harrold, affectionately known by the students as 'Madge', worked for a total of 41 years as assistant matron, during which time she contributed enormously to the training school but also to nursing as a profession. In 1933, 1938 and again in 1943 she was elected to the General Nursing Council (Ireland).

Born in 1890 in Newcastle West, Co. Limerick, Margaret was devoted to the caring professions. Initially, she took up teaching and only later selected nursing as a vocation. Before she came to the Mater she had an exciting life as an active member of Cumann na mBan, Sinn Féin and the Gaelic League. In 1918, after some discussion with the Bishop of Limerick, she set out for Dublin and the Mater

Margaret 'Madge' Harrold, one of the most influential of all the Mater matrons, on her retirement in 1960.

Hospital, where she commenced nurse training under Miss McGivney. At the end of her training in 1920 she was awarded a silver medal.

Margaret Harrold had great leadership qualities and any nurses who studied under her benefited from a quintessentially 19th-century brand of nursing discipline. She continued to work at the Mater until 1923 when she went to London for postgraduate training and experience and was appointed assistant matron on her return, to teach practical nursing. She retired in 1960 and returned to her home in Limerick. Shortly after her death, in 1970, it was decided that an award, the Margaret Harrold Memorial Prize, would be made annually in her honour to a member of the nursing staff for 'courtesy, loyalty and devotion to duty'. A bronze plaque was placed on the wall in the foyer of the School of Nursing, recalling what she had contributed to the Mater.[21]

The Development of Nurse Education at the Mater

In 1944, Sr Concepta Greene from Co. Wexford was appointed Matron. She took over responsibility for all nursing and patient care. At this point, her superior was Sr Ann Magdalen Fane, who was keen to address the perennial problem of nurses' accommodation. Previously, the expansion of the nurses' accommodation had been ad hoc, with extensions added here and there as need dictated, but Sr Ann Magdalen determined to do better, sending Sr Concepta and some colleagues to the USA to look at large medical centres and the types of nurses' accommodation they offered. When the team returned, plans were drawn up for a large six-floor building on the North Circular Road. Because of objections by the local residents, the number of floors was reduced to five.

Sr Concepta Greene, Matron 1943–1972.

The estimated cost of the development was a worry to Sr Ann Magdalen. She sought a grant from the government, but she was ignored. But Sr Ann Magdalen was not to be defeated. As a personal friend of Phyllis O'Kelly, wife of Sean T. O'Kelly, then President of Ireland, Sr Ann Magdalen persuaded her to invite the Minister for Health, Dr Noel Browne, to lunch at Áras an Uachtaráin. After their lunch, Mrs O'Kelly would invite him to drive to the Mater to see the awful nurses' accommodation for himself. This was in 1951, shortly before his resignation as Minister for Health following the storm over the 'Mother and Child Scheme', in which Dr Browne's plans to provide free healthcare for mothers and young children were opposed by the Church and by members of the medical profession. Even though Dr Browne agreed that a new place was needed, as time passed the necessary grant failed to materialise. When word reached her of his resignation, Sr Ann Magdalen contacted him and reminded him of his promise and was duly rewarded for her persistence when he signed the agreement for a grant (£195,000) for a new nurses' home, to be paid from Hospitals Trust funds.

Nurses write in the spacious living room of the nurses' home in 1961.

Nurses wait in the rain at the opening of the College of Nursing, 1954.

On 24 September 1951, the feast of Our Lady of Mercy, the site for the new nurses' residence was blessed by Reverend John Moroney, hospital chaplain. The first sod was turned to the sound of cheering nurses. It was ready for use in 1954 and was formally opened on 14 July of that year by President Sean T. O'Kelly and blessed by Archbishop John Charles McQuaid. Among the invited guests were Éamon de Valera, T.F. O'Higgins and other members of the government, together with the president of University College Dublin and the dean of the medical faculty.

● *The opening of the College of Nursing was attended by numerous dignitaries, including Sr Concepta Greene, Archbishop John Charles McQuaid, President Sean T. O'Kelly, E.T. Freeman, Tom O'Higgins, Éamon De Valera and Phyllis O'Kelly. The nurses are Angela Mulcahy and Nellie O'Brien.*

The Mater School of Nursing was situated on the lower ground floor of the nurses' home building. For the first twelve years of its existence, nursing education was fairly traditional, except that the teaching was undertaken by Sr de Lourdes Cooney and Sr Lucia Therese, who had trained as nurse tutors in Scotland.

The 'block system' was introduced in 1966 and was immediately popular. The system consisted of 1–2 month lecture 'blocks' in the nursing school, where the student nurses were totally free of ward/patient responsibility. During this time they received their salary as usual and at the end of the 'block' would return to work on the wards.

When Ireland joined the EEC in 1973, the way in which nurses were being educated was discussed in Europe. According to Simone Veil, French Minister for Health, 'the training offered to nursing students should enable the trainees to integrate as far as possible into the various health systems of the Community.'[22] She emphasised that all training should include more experience outside the hospital; however, this wasn't always possible in reality. At the time, nursing students in EEC member states were

● *Sr de Lourdes Cooney, Principal of the School of Nursing 1955–1988.*

Sr Lucia Therese Cassidy, Nurse Tutor 1955–1970.

classified as 'students' by some countries and as 'employees' by others, including Ireland and England, so outside training would have enormous implications where Irish students were concerned, mainly in the event of staff shortages, but also for nurses undertaking the post-registration course studies at the Mater in the 1970s.[23]

In 1977, the (Nursing) EEC Directives came into force. They impacted on nurse training schools in a number of ways: the number of hours of theory in the school was to be not less than 4,600 hours during the lifetime of the course; each clinical teaching session was to last for at least an hour and clinical experience and knowledge were to be widened over 1–2-month periods depending on the type of experience being gained, e.g. community care, psychiatric, paediatric, obstetric and care of the elderly.

This had many implications for the Mater School of Nursing. The hospital needed to increase the student nurse intake and to negotiate with specialist hospitals and, as nurse education became increasingly academic, the consequences for the Mater, which had employed student nurses for many years, were significant – and expensive. It would appear that the student nurses were going to disappear from the workforce. An interim arrangement came into effect when the diploma in nursing programme was introduced in 1997. Finally, a degree programme in nursing began in 2002 and from then on, student nurses have been full-time students on a four-year programme at UCD. The student nurses are seconded to the hospital for practical ward experience, initially coming for short periods and, towards the end of their studies, they spend an entire year working on the wards. During the time they are in the hospital they become the responsibility of the Nurse Practice Development staff and the CPCs (clinical practice co-ordinators) in the Centre for Nurse Education, Nelson Street.

A Vision of the Future

In 1969, Sr Concepta Greene, when she was Matron, had seen an important need for increasing specialisation in nursing to meet the complex needs of patients. Sr Concepta duly got permission from the Department of Health and An Bord Altranais to set up a number of post-registration courses for nurses in intensive and coronary care, operating theatre technique and emergency nursing.

The courses, which commenced in 1970, would last six months and a nurse tutor was assigned to draw up the necessary programmes and to assume responsibility for each of the courses. In 1997, specialist post-registration courses were awarded higher diplomas and links to UCD began. By late 2011, the Mater successfully received accreditation from UCD for a series of clinical professional development courses.

- *Patrice O'Sullivan, Principal of the School of Nursing 1988–2004.*

- *Anne Carrigy, Director of Nursing 1998–2008.*

- *Sr Incarnation Doyle, Director of Nursing 1992–1998.*

- *Student nurses in 1997, with some of the teaching staff of the School of Nursing.*

The Centre for Nurse Education

The old nurses' home is demolished to make way for a brand new Centre of Nurse Education, with Anne Carrigy and Sr Eugene standing on the rubble in 2007. (© Fennell Photography.)

In 2003, plans for a new adult hospital were afoot and the 1954 nurses' home was to be demolished. Before building could start, a new location for the nursing school was needed, and it was duly built on Nelson Street nearby. The Centre for Nurse Education, as it was now called, was formally opened by An Taoiseach Bertie Ahern on 31 July 2006.

The opening of the centre marked the culmination of decades of rapid development in nursing in Ireland. Change has been driven by many elements, chief of which are the rapid medical developments within hospitals and worldwide, developments in education, both professional and in general, changes in consumer demand, in healthcare delivery and, of course, the changes taking place in technology. The structure of nursing itself and the nature of 'caring' within hospitals has changed dramatically over the past decade and, for professional and economic reasons, is likely to continue to change in the future.

If the nurses from the Nightingale era were to visit the Mater today, they would be amazed at the structure of the profession and the knowledge base of the nurses there, and at their ability to deal with the seriously ill or injured. The patients who arrive at the hospital today are quickly categorised by nurses and moved to an appropriate clinical area for initial treatment. If needed, they are then prepared for more definitive or specific treatment, either by specialist nurses or by the medical staff. New equipment has made it possible to determine a patient's illness or injury with far more speed and accuracy than heretofore. The use of computers to the extent that we find in the Mater would be hard to explain to our 19th-century colleagues. It is tempting to wonder what they might think of a patient with a spinal injury being X-rayed in the west of Ireland, the film being transmitted by NIMIS (National Integrated Medical Imaging System) to the Mater emergency department for evaluation and treatment advice, and/ or arrangements being made to transport the patient by helicopter direct to the Mater for treatment in the spinal injuries unit – all in an afternoon.

1   *British Medical Journal*, 1897.

2   At this time, Edinburgh (and St Thomas's in London, where Nightingale set up her school of nursing) would seem to have been ahead of most of the other British hospitals. They had a good name, probably due to being run by a so-called 'Nightingale-trained nurse', and this became a mark of distinction.

3   The lady probationers were obliged to pay for their upkeep during training. They did not receive any stipend from the hospital for work they may have done. There are no records to indicate how many of them enrolled, or for how many years this arrangement lasted.

4   *Report of the Mater Misericordiae Hospital Dublin, Under the Care of the Sisters of Mercy, for the year 1898* (1899), Dublin: Dollard Printing House, p 31.

5   Ibid. This document is very long and outlines the regulations in great detail.

6   This approach became very controversial, but it was considered to be the best one at the time.

7   Margaret Huxley (1856–1940) was a niece of Prof. T.H. Huxley, the scientist. She trained as a nurse at St Bartholomew's Hospital, London, when Mrs Ethel Bedford Fenwick was Matron there. Huxley was Matron in Sir Patrick Dun's Hospital Dublin, 1883–1902. She opposed Nightingale's approach to nurse registration and played an important role in achieving nurse registration in Ireland.

8   Falkiner, N.M. (1920), *The Nurse and the State* (online) available at http://www.tara.tcd.ie/bitstream/2262/4317/1/jssissiVolx1v29_60_pdf.

9   Medical Board Minutes, January 1894, pp 321–322.

10 The Nurses' Registration (Ireland) Act became law on 23 December 1919. The Nurses' Registration Act in Britain became law earlier in the same year.

11 'The General Nursing Council, Ireland – An Incorrect Statement' (1920), *British Journal of Nursing*, 28 February, p 129.

12 Sir Arthur Chance served as a member of the first General Nursing Council for Ireland from 1919 to 1924.

13 Fealy, G. (2006), *A History of the Apprenticeship Nurse Training in Ireland*, Routledge, p 84.

14 Rafferty (1966, p 66), Dingwall, Rafferty, and Webster (1988, p 81), referenced in Fealy, op. cit.

15 Fealy, G., op. cit., p 84.

16 The Medical Board designed a very detailed certificate in 1915 for the nurses who passed their examination.

17 *Mater Misericordiae Hospital, Dublin. Thirty-Seventh Session, 1898–99*, p 13.

18 *Report of the Mater Misericordiae Hospital, Dublin, under the care of the Sisters of Mercy, for the year 1898*, Dublin: Dollard Printing House, 1899, p 8.

19 See Nolan, Sr Eugene, *School of Nursing Centenary 1891–1991*, pp 7–8.

20 Freeman, E. (1961), *Centenary Mater Misericordiae Hospital 1861–1961*, p 32.

21 This plaque is now in the entrance hall of the Centre for Nurse Education on Nelson Street.

22 Commission of the European Community (1989), 'Health Care and Nursing Education in the 21st Century'. Address by Mme Simone Veil, Brussels, EUR 12040.

23 Staff Nurses who undertook post registration courses in 1970 were classified by the Dept. of Health as first-year staff nurses for the purpose of salary calculation; irrespective of the number of years of service they had given.

Archbishop John Charles McQuaid blessing the opening of the medical library.

CHAPTER 15

Medical Education at the Mater

When the Mater Hospital opened in 1861, it had two primary objectives: the care of the sick and medical education. However, in the early days, there was some conflict as to how this education would be offered. The subject of 'resident pupils' – all medical students at the time were given a room in the medical residence or 'the Res', hence the term 'resident pupil' – was raised at the first meeting between the medical officers at the hospital and the Reverend Mother, and it was decided to interview candidates with 'the necessary qualifications' to be residents at the hospital. It was agreed:

> That no candidate be deemed eligible to the office of resident pupil in the Mater Misericordiae Hospital, who has not attended at least two years of medical lectures and hospital practice.[1]

However, the Reverend Mother expressed her dissatisfaction that:

> ... there was an air of informality in the selection of resident pupils held on the 11th inst. as the names had not been submitted to her for objection or approval. The Reverend Mother further requested Mr Cruise to summon the Medical Board for 11 o'clock on the next day [14 November 1861] for a meeting with her.[2]

Something of a diplomatic tussle ensued, after which it was agreed 'that for the first year, qualified surgeons only should be deemed eligible as resident pupils'. In December, further interviews were held and two applicants 'with the necessary testimonials' were selected, having first been presented to the Reverend Mother for her approval. However, once again, there was dissent, this time from the physicians, who objected to the surgeon-only policy. Finally, it was decided to advertise in the newspapers, and the right candidates emerged. After the thorny issue had been resolved, a prospectus was drawn up for the students attending for lectures and 'clinics'. This became an annual publication.

Teaching students was considered by the hospital medics to be an important duty and was carried out every morning, starting with a lecture at 9.30 a.m. Each student paid a fee at the beginning of term, which was held in a special 'Medical Board Fund'. Its uses were many and interesting. In 1862, it was used to purchase 'instruments required for the use of the Hospital – Cupping Apparatus, Tooth Instruments, Stomach pump, some Catheters, apparatus for testing urine and a Post Mortem Case.'[3] The fund would also be used to pay the salary of the hospital's first pathologist, Dr Edmund McWeeney.

The two main areas where the teaching of students took place in the early days were the dispensary and the main operating theatre (the risk of infection was little understood at this time). When student numbers increased, the wards were used more often as teaching venues. Each morning the students assembled in the ward, the doors were closed, a blackboard and chalk was pulled into the middle of the floor, and silence prevailed as the physician or surgeon held his teaching clinic. This was usually followed by 'rounds' as they moved from bed to bed for a brief discussion on each patient's condition. This went on for many years, although it was clear that a proper lecture theatre was needed. When the new laboratory was built in the early 1930s, it included a lecture theatre which held 36 people. This soon proved too small, but it had been useful in the early days. According to E.T. Freeman in 1967:

> We thought this was a magnificent piece of work (the new residency, laboratory with its lecture theatre, and outpatients dept. block) with individual bedrooms for 26 people. The past thirty years have shown it to be altogether too small.[4]

He goes on to explain why:

> The 'intern year' squeezed out the resident students and the greater number of interns and registrars overcrowded the living space to an intolerable degree. The laboratory became too small in its turn and the lecture theatre which we thought so wonderful when it was the first of its kind in Dublin, was soon unable to accommodate anything greater than a single clinical class.[5]

This displacement of resident medical students and the overall lack of educational facilities in the hospital would appear to have rankled with Freeman for many years. He watched the beautiful nurses' residence and school of nursing being built and opened in 1954.[6] As the debt on that building was eventually paid off (with the aid of Mater Hospital Pools funds) Freeman began to think about the possibility of responding to the educational needs of medical students and the overall needs of staff. During the Centenary celebrations in 1961 he produced something of a 'wish list', his dream for the future of the Mater, which included: more laboratory space, enlarging and re-equipping the X-ray department, a central sterilising unit, day rooms for patients, replacing the out-of-date central heating, re-roofing the hospital and providing a new convent for the sisters. It was a long and comprehensive list and perhaps the most interesting item on it was his plan for a large staff restaurant, a lecture theatre, student lecture rooms, a medical library and recreational facilities for the junior medical staff. It may have seemed at the time that Freeman's dream was just that, a remote possibility, but within a decade a new building project was under way, a three-storey block to the east of the hospital.

> The large main building will be used exclusively for teaching and recreational purposes. It is of three floors and consists of two wings meeting at a very obtuse angle...The auditorium projects towards Eccles Street... On the ground floor there will be a large students' common room and beyond that cloak rooms for men and women. Behind the high back wall of the auditorium, a modern and fully furnished squash court with showers and changing rooms is provided.
>
> On the second floor are the students' library and three classrooms whilst in the further wing there will be three professors' rooms and a room for the Hospital's Dean ... Finally, on the top floor will be a canteen to seat up to 200.[7]

It seemed that Freeman's dream was about to come true, but at enormous cost. A grant for the staff canteen was provided by the Department of Health and the rest was paid for largely out of funds from the Mater Hospital Pools.

● *The hospital library.*

Edward T. Freeman

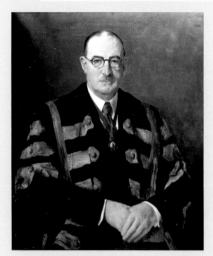

A portrait of E.T. Freeman

Edward T. Freeman (1891–1974) is probably the Mater's best-known physician. He was born and educated in Dublin, studying medicine at UCD, qualifying in 1914. He served as a house doctor at the Mater, after which he went to India for seven years. He had an interesting journey back to Ireland, undertaking postgraduate studies in Paris and London on the way. In 1922, he took up a post at the Mater as a pathologist and assistant physician. He developed an enormous practice, mostly as a general physician, but he also followed an interest in tropical diseases, probably as a result of his time in India. In 1930, he was appointed Senior Physician to the hospital and shortly after was appointed Fellow of the Royal College of Physicians of Ireland. In 1949, he was elected President of the Royal Academy of Medicine in Ireland.

Apart from his excellence as a physician, Freeman co-ordinated and controlled the medical activities in the Mater. This broadened out into offering advice to all the Reverend Mothers during his 34 years as a senior physician and as chairman of the medical board. This was always appreciated. Freeman was tireless in his ideas: as he walked the length and breadth of the hospital his brain was always pondering on things such as reorganisation, fundraising, building developments – anything that might improve the hospital or alleviate the structural difficulties which were a feature of the hospital during his time there. In the years before he retired, he managed to achieve many of his ambitions for the Mater. He oversaw the building of a large staff block which provided many of the facilities he saw as essential for the staff, particularly the junior medics. This block offered a large staff restaurant, an auditorium which today bears his name, lecture rooms, a medical library and a large area with sitting rooms and other recreational facilities for the resident medical staff. It was opened in 1970. In spite of his considerable achievements, E.T. Freeman was a gentle man and was much missed when he retired in 1971.

Changes in Medical Education

At the end of the 19th century, E.T. Freeman's vision for medical education was still some way away, but significant changes were taking place all the same, as an outstanding American educator by the name of Abraham Flexner led the way. He set out to study the American medical school educational system and the changes he suggested would be adopted all over the world. A graduate of Johns Hopkins University,

Flexner undertook graduate studies at Harvard and at the University of Berlin and his big project was a detailed examination of the academic structure of medical education in the United States. Eventually, he put forward a complete reform system in 1910. Following the Flexner Report, medical education in the States began to change, as new standards were introduced and colleges began to follow scientific protocol more closely. Word of changes to the academic medical curriculum quickly reached Europe and Flexner was soon on his way to review medical education there.

While Flexner was in Europe, the British had already begun the process of reflecting on their system of medical education, which was little short of chaotic at the time. Most of the education was being undertaken by small (non-university) medical schools and only 7% by the universities. Unfortunately, any progress towards changing the system was interrupted by the outbreak of World War I. After the war, an interdepartmental committee on medical schools was set up, under the chairmanship of Sir William Goodenough, who produced a landmark report in 1944.

The process of reform had begun in Britain, but little was happening in Ireland, until a committee was set up in the Royal College of Physicians, under the chairmanship of E.T. Freeman,[8] to study the findings and suggestions of the Goodenough Report. Interestingly, Freeman was not terribly impressed with the report, in particular the suggestion that a compulsory intern year be introduced after qualification. 'This intern year killed our resident student system. There was no longer room for them.' The naïveté of Freeman's view would be revealed just a couple of years later.

Irish Medical Graduates Rejected

In 1951, the American licensing bodies drew up a list of the nations from which they would consider applicants for a licence to practice medicine in the States. To the shock of the Irish medical profession, this list did not include the Irish Republic.[9] Deciding that it was a possible omission rather than a decision, the Irish Medical Association and Dr Michael Tierney, President of University College Dublin, decided to invite representatives from the American Medical Association (AMA) to Ireland to evaluate the standards of medical education for themselves. Four delegates from the AMA arrived in Dublin in 1953 and visited all the medical schools and the associated teaching hospitals in the country. They were interested in the selection of students and their supervision throughout the medical programme, the educational content of each year and the ability of the universities to provide the necessary scientific element to an acceptable standard. They also looked at the teaching hospitals, their relationship with the university and the clinical teaching, as well as the bedside teaching they provided. They were not impressed with what they found. In due course they sent a report to the Irish Medical Association (with a copy to the General Medical Council in London).

Undoubtedly those responsible for medical education here were disappointed by the report's findings. When asked by the media about this report, Dr Michael Tierney responded:

None of us is surprised at the main criticism that our medical departments are ill-housed and under-staffed. The governing body is well aware of the efforts which are being made to improve both, and of the necessity for a greatly increased endowment to make comparisons with English – not to speak of American – schools tolerable. It must be regretfully recognised that a properly equipped medical school is, in these days, very expensive.[10]

As far as the Mater was concerned, the delegates were reasonably impressed with what they observed when they visited it:

Mater Misericordiae Hospital, Dublin has a fine building and is in the process of constructing a new nurses' home. It has well-developed and well-staffed and equipped departments of pathology, biochemistry, radiology and physical therapy, as well as three resident medical officers. All tissues removed at surgery are sent to the pathology laboratory. About 120 autopsies are done yearly. This hospital makes a very favourable impression with its facilities, staff and equipment, but the records made by the students themselves are brief and incomplete.[11]

Reporting collectively on the hospitals associated with University College Dublin, the report says:

Some of the hospital's junior medical staff and chaplain, 1961.

The relationship between the School and St Vincent's and Mater Hospitals are particularly close and well developed for teaching purposes. The bedside teaching in these hospitals appears to be of a high order, but apparently little emphasis is placed on the resident student making complete histories, physical examinations, laboratory work-ups and progress notes on their assigned patients.

By American standards, the students are not carefully selected; they are, however, required to take a pre-medical year; five medical years and one intern year of training. The clinical training is quite loosely organised and left to a considerable extent in the hands of a large group of hospitals with a minimum of control by the school.[12]

Attention was drawn in the report to a number of other unacceptable features of medical education in the Republic, such as the number of teaching bodies (five in all) dealing with medical education and the ten independent general teaching hospitals in Dublin associated with the various medical schools. It also drew attention to the understaffed and poorly equipped departments in the medical schools.

However, perhaps their biggest concern was the loose affiliation between the NUI and the hospitals and the complete lack of co-ordination between the hospitals themselves when it came to teaching.[13, 14]

In considering medical schools for inclusion in its list, the Council places great emphasis on the importance of the school's having full control and supervision of all phases of a medical student's education. The Council understands that much of the instruction in clinical subjects at the National University of Ireland is given at hospitals that are not under the control of the medical schools and by teachers who are not in the faculty at the medical school and who are not responsible directly to the faculty of the medical school.

Following the American delegation's visit to Ireland, the British then came to see for themselves. They were somewhat disenchanted but careful about what they said, probably because they were in need of Irish doctors for the newly launched National Health Service (1946). By this point, 1953, Irish graduates had lost their entitlement to practise in most of the states of the USA and this was causing immense concern in Dublin.

Of the problems needing to be addressed, the loose affiliation between the hospitals and the medical school had to be the first, followed by the appointment by the NUI of professors of medicine and surgery to the Mater and St Vincent's Hospitals, neither of which were straightforward procedures.[15] Lengthy negotiations ensued, as Dr Tierney outlined to the Reverend Mother at the Mater the arrangements which the college was going to have to put in place to make it possible for its medical graduates to register abroad. He went on to explain the implications for the hospital and its staff of being categorised as a 'teaching hospital', which would mean putting in place more complex structures than before, and making 'joint appointments by the hospitals and the governing body' (of the NUI). It would also necessitate the appointment by University College Dublin of full-time professors with a right to a minimum of twelve beds (a professorial unit) in each hospital. It was from these appointments that the title of 'consultant' evolved. When professors visited other hospitals on a consultancy basis, they were referred to as 'consultants'. From this, the position of 'medical (or surgical) consultant' emerged and ultimately became a grade in its own right. Up to then no such appointment existed in either the Mater or St Vincent's.

Consultations and discussions between UCD's legal advisers and the hospitals became both complex and protracted. It was about 1959 before the final agreement was eventually signed. Part of the reason for this foot-dragging was probably the latent fear at the Mater that, if power could be removed from the place that easily and changes enforced which perhaps they did not altogether agree with, what might be next? A rumour existed that with the building of the hospital at Elm Park and the proposed new university campus at Belfield (on the south side of the city), the Mater might, in time, find itself sidelined, not least because of the distance between the college and the hospital. The fear was not unfounded: in January 1960, the Sisters of Mercy offered a site to UCD on the Mater campus on which to build a medical school. This was turned down because by then the governing body of UCD had decided to go ahead and start building the campus at Belfield – including the medical school. In the event, the medical school remained in the city for many years, being one of the last departments to move from Earlsfort Terrace to Belfield.

By 1961 there were nine (UCD) professors on the staff of the Mater:
- Thomas Murphy – Social and Preventive Medicine – later became President of University College Dublin
- Timothy Counihan – Medicine
- Eoin O'Malley – Surgery
- John A. Geraghty – Radiology
- Edward O'Doherty – Otolaryngology
- Maurice Hickey – Forensic Medicine
- Eamon de Valera – Midwifery & Gynaecology
- Paul Cannon – Pharmacology
- Frank Durkin – Dental Surgery

The Catherine McAuley Education and Research Centre

During the decades that followed this shift in medical education, great advances took place in cardiac surgery and in child and family therapy. In 1996, Professor Hugh Brady[16] was appointed Professor of Medicine and Therapeutics at University College Dublin, with an appointment to the Mater. He was instrumental, along with Professor John Fitzpatrick, in setting up a feasibility committee to look at the educational needs of the hospital.[17] Professor Brady was very anxious to improve the education facilities at the Mater and, if possible, to bring them up to world class standards, i.e. with top-class research facilities, as well as facilities for holding international symposia and conferences in well-appointed lecture rooms and catering facilities, which were independent of the hospital from a budgetary point of view. Within ten years, his vision would have been realised in the Catherine McAuley Education and Research Centre.

The committee was set up mainly because the university had agreed to

● *The Catherine McAuley Centre.*

make a financial investment in the two main teaching hospitals (the Mater and St Vincent's), to develop student facilities and academic units. This committee drew up a list of requirements for medical education at the hospital, which was presented by Professor Brady to the hospital executive for consideration on 12 August 1997. It came with a suggestion that with further funding, they might consider the redevelopment of numbers 41–46 Eccles Street, with a view to turning them into a modern medical education centre. The University College Dublin Dean of the Faculty of Medicine committed £1.5 million towards the development of educational facilities at the Mater.

By January 2000, the overall plan for a large modern academic development had been committed to paper. The development of the Catherine McAuley Education and Research Centre was on its way for certain, with Hugh Brady as project leader. The architects were TP Kennedy & Partners and the plan included a new auditorium, a very impressive concourse area and a proposed pedestrian tunnel under Eccles Street to the main hospital.[18] On 7 January 2000, a meeting was held in the CEO's office, at which oncologist Desmond Carney and surgeon Ronan O'Connell proposed that number 48

Eccles Street[19] should form part not only of the new centre, but also of an oncology academic unit for which they had managed to procure substantial funding. In February 2001, all agreements and leases were signed for the £4.5 million building. Funding came from a number of sources, including the Mater College of Postgraduate Education and Research, the Higher Education Authority

● *The Freeman auditorium, named after the great E.T. Freeman, who pioneered so much medical education at the hospital.*

and the Department of Education as well as Atlantic Philanthropies. When finished, the entire centre would consist of: a state-of-the-art undergraduate education centre (41–46 Eccles Street); a postgraduate education centre (48 Eccles Street); and a modern research centre (49–51 Eccles Street), which, in time, would become a component of the Dublin Molecular Medicine Centre (DMMC). The ultimate plan was for the three related components of the centre to be linked internally and also by a covered walkway behind the buildings. Access to the centre would be located in Nelson Street.[20]

From the left, Prof. Muiris Fitzgerald, Sr Margherita Rock and the current President of UCD, Hugh Brady, at the opening of the Catherine McAuley Centre.

At the end of 2001, building commenced and in the latter half of 2004 the first phase of the development was complete and ready for use. It was formally opened on 4 October by An Taoiseach, Bertie Ahern. There was great rejoicing at such a splendid educational resource with such excellent use of space. As far as the reconstruction of the houses was concerned, numbers 43, 44 and 45 Eccles Street were completely rebuilt and numbers 41, 42 and 46 were renovated.

The Gunne Lecture Theatre in the Catherine McAuley Centre.

At 48 Eccles Street, the Institute for Cancer Research became part of the Postgraduate Medical Centre, largely due to the work of oncologists Professor Desmond Carney and Dr John McCaffrey, who had been fundraising for many years. Donations came from cancer patients, their families and friends, from the Mater College, from consultants, especially Desmond Carney himself, as well as from the pharmaceutical industry. The wife and family of the late Fintan Gunne were particularly enthusiastic fundraisers and a lecture theatre was named after Gunne in September 2004.

Genetic research also took a great leap forward during this time. On 22 September 2004, work commenced on the Genome Research Unit located at numbers 49, 50 and 51 Eccles Street. It was funded through an award from the Dublin Molecular Medicine Centre[21] and from the Higher Education Authority's Programme for Research in Third-level Institutions.[22] It was completed in 2006 and the Tánaiste and Minister for Health, Mary Harney, officially opened it on 3 April. Dr Peter Doran was appointed Director.

Ireland's First Academic Medical Centre

The establishment of the Catherine McAuley Centre was a milestone in medical education, but in the later 2000s, another step forward would be taken by Professor William (Bill) Powderly, Head of the School of Medicine and Medical Sciences at University College Dublin, when he was appointed to the Mater. His 'dream' for the hospital was that it would form part of an academic medical centre involving the Mater, St Vincent's and UCD. An academic medical centre is not a physical entity, but rather a futuristic approach to medical treatment and patient care, uniting academic, administrative and legal structures, which takes medicine truly into the 21st century and which can carry enormous benefits for patients. On 27 September 2005, Professor Powderly outlined to the Mater board of directors a new structure for the proposal, which would establish a new relationship between the two hospitals and University College Dublin. The following year a working party was set up to discuss the development of the academic centre. On 10 September 2007, the formal launch of the Dublin Academic Health Care (DAHC) project took place in Newman House, St Stephen's Green, Dublin. The DAHC appointed Bill Powderly as Chief Academic Officer to oversee the first phase of its development – to develop a suitable governance and operational structure for the combined hospitals and UCD Medical School.

At a meeting in 2011, the DAMC Chairman, Thomas Lynch, said, 'we cannot stand still – we will be changed whether we like it or not'. John Morgan, Chairman of the Mater Board, insisted that the original motivation behind the development of the DAMC wouldn't be affected by the economic downturn. He assured all present that while it may make things difficult for the hospitals for some time, with the dedication and commitment of all, it would undoubtedly be the way forward in the future.

1   Mater Misericordiae Hospital (1861), *Minutes of Meetings of the Medical Board, 1861–1899*, p 8.
2   Ibid., p 12.
3   Ibid., p 44.
4   Freeman, E.T. (1967), 'The New Buildings', *NUACHT*, Vol. 1, No. 7, December, Mater Misericordiae Hospital.
5   The reason for this was due to the recommendations of the Goodenough Committee's report on the reorganisation of medical education in the UK in 1944, mentioned by Dr Freeman later in his article: see http//www.ncbi.nlm.nih.gov/pmc/articles/PMC2285893.
6   The nurses' residence was demolished in 2007 to make way for the new adult hospital.
7   Freeman, E.T., op. cit., pp 21–22.
8   Freeman was President of the Royal College of Physicians in Dublin between 1952 and 1955.
9   Conway, E. & Fitzgerald, P. (1954), 'Background to the American Report on Irish Medical Schools', *Irish University Review*, Vol. 1, No. 1 (Summer) p 5.
10 'The Main Criticism is Not a Surprise' (*Irish Independent*, 2 December 1953), p 8.
11 Ibid.
12 Ibid.
13 Mulcahy, R. (1955), 'U.C.D.'s Liaison with Teaching Hospitals Examined', *The Irish Times*, 3 December, p 8.
14 Breathnach, C.S. (2000), 'The Medical Sciences in Twentieth-Century Ireland', *I.J.MS*. Vol. 169, No. 3, p 224 available at http://www.ijms.ie/Portals/_IJMS/Documents/16.
15 The appointment of full-time professors is regulated by the Irish Universities Act 1908.
16 Professor Hugh Brady is the current President of University College Dublin.
17 Professor John Fitzpatrick, University College Dublin Professor of Surgery and Consultant Urologist, was appointed to the Mater in 1986. He held the post of Associate Dean for Postgraduate Studies (Faculty of Medicine) from 1995. He retired from the Mater in 2011.
18 This proposed underpass was never built.
19 This house was still occupied by the Diabetic Day Centre at the time.
20 Based on a communication from Professor Hugh Brady UCD to Sr Margherita Rock RSM, Chairperson, Mater Hospital Executive/Council, 21 November 2001.
21 The Dublin Molecular Medicine Centre is a research collaboration between UCD, TCD & the RCSI.
22 UCD–Mater GRU *Annual Report 2007*, p 12.

CHAPTER 16

Running the Mater

The history of governance at the Mater closely reflects the history of the hospital itself, in that in the 152 years since it opened, it has gone from a large but relatively straightforward haven for the sick poor, to the complex and busy place it is today. It has also gone from being run in a simple manner by a group of dedicated nuns to the current board of directors, reflecting a range of interests and responsibilities at the hospital.

Initially, the hospital was run, like all the Mercy convents, from Baggot Street, where the Reverend Mother (Mother Mercy Norris) and her assistant (Sr Rose Burke) resided at the time. There it was decided which Sisters would be assigned to the Mater, what experience was needed and what their responsibilities would be. One Sister was given overall responsibility for the day-to-day management of the place and the standard of patient care. She was known as the Local Superior (or Superioress) and when the hospital opened in 1861, Sr M. Patrick Kickham was appointed to this position. However, the main management of the hospital was largely the responsibility of Sr Rose Burke. She dealt with the medical staff, signed any necessary documents, ensured that the rules and regulations were observed and sanctioned the purchase of equipment or special services.

It was clear from the early days that the Mercy Sisters were very much in charge of the place. This was evident when at a meeting with the medical board of the hospital on 15 September 1861, Mother Mary of Mercy Norris, according to the minutes of the meeting, 'read out for them the rules by which they were to be guided'.[1] The medical officers present were then invited to sign their names at the bottom of these rules,[2] which they did.

In the beginning the Sisters made it clear that the hospital was essentially a service mainly for the sick poor of Dublin. The Reverend Mother reluctantly agreed to tuition fees for medical students, but made it clear that no patient, regardless of means, was to be charged a fee. The nuns were giving all of their services free and would live themselves 'at no charge to the hospital',[3] and the same was expected of the medics.

At times, the Sisters' insistence on making all staff appointments led to serious conflict, especially around the hiring of medical staff. Usually the appointments or important decisions were made in consultation with the medical board,[4] but every now and then, depending on the relationship between the Baggot Street administration and the chairman of the medical board, differences of opinion arose and then the Archbishop would be drafted in to keep the peace and to ease negotiations.[5] It is interesting to note that during the thirty years that Sr M. Berchmans Barry was Superioress at the hospital (1882–1912) there were no such recorded difficulties. She was an extremely popular leader and the hospital progressed significantly under her management.[6]

By today's standards it might all sound like a fairly straightforward institutional arrangement, but the nuns' remit was very wide and included a lot of tasks which today would be provided by companies and outside agencies. For instance, all the laundry was done in the hospital laundry; the cleaning of the place was done without the aid of the equipment available today, rather with sweeping brushes, mops, cloths and feather dusters! In addition, each ward had two open fires and these had to be set every morning and buckets of coal brought to the wards for use during the day. The farm, which included some animals, had to be attended to by a small farming staff (this continued up to the late 1950s when car parks, staff tennis courts and more building sites began to be needed). Farm produce was an important source of revenue for the hospital for many years.

Local Governance Introduced

When Catherine McAuley founded the Sisters of Mercy, her very simple monastic structure suited the times and was used to run the Mater for many years after it opened.[7] However, as the hospital moved into a new century, the complexity and sheer volume of hospital activity began to expand exponentially and it became obvious that this administrative structure, particularly the process of decision-making at a distance from the hospital, i.e. from Baggot Street, was inappropriate and unsustainable.

Things began to change markedly in the decade before World War II. Most of the changes were brought about by the detailed financial accountability being demanded of the Mater because it was availing of Hospitals Trust Funds as the main source of revenue. This source of revenue proved something of a mixed blessing, as we saw in Chapter 7, and in 1936 the hospital was in serious financial difficulties. The then local superior, Mother Brigid Brennan, applied for funding, but the application lacked key information which any financial expert would have been able to provide. Consequently considerable delays arose, with funding not being released for almost a year and then only when pressure was brought to bear on the Minister for Health. It was clear that the old system no longer worked.

In the 1940s, the Archbishop of Dublin, John Charles McQuaid, became aware of some of the shortcomings of the existing governance system. After much research and consideration, permission had to be sought from Rome to change the system to a more suitable governance structure. When permission was granted in 1954, a change to the Mercy Constitution was made and was agreed to by the Dublin Sisters of Mercy at a special meeting held at Carysfort Park. While this change made it easier for the local superior to manage the hospital, year by year further administrative difficulties were becoming apparent in areas such as finance and the mushrooming area of hospital administration, not to mention the ever-increasing complexity of medicine and surgery being undertaken in the hospital.

Where finance was concerned, the need for funds kept rising. After 1954, the superior took over the onerous task of trying to manage the entire hospital, its staff, the private nursing home and the convent with very little assistance. Her main source of administrative assistance was Sr Claude Meegan, who worked as hospital secretary and accountant. While Sr Claude did an incredible job and was a significant help to the superior, in time it became obvious that no one person could do this difficult and complex job. According to the Gearoid MacGabhann, the first CEO of the Mater and Chairman of the Executive Council:

> She [Sr Claude] was a person of great ability, outstanding integrity, hardworking, loyal and sincerely devoted to the interests of the hospital. During her long term of office many changes occurred in hospital administration. In the early days, administration was relatively simple and straightforward, but with the passing of years, many more complex structures in the health services developed – not the least of these changes being the introduction of the I.S.A. and P.A.Y.E.[8] systems. Sr Claude adapted to all these changes in her quiet unassuming fashion without further help. During the traumatic experience of the World War, when commodities were subject to severe rationing, Sr Claude somehow managed to overcome all difficulties unobtrusively. In later years she again experienced the difficulties occasioned by two bank strikes which could have had a paralysing result on the finance of the hospital, but her expertise in overcoming difficulties was again demonstrated...[9]

It was clear that, from 1954 onwards, there was a great need for a well-organised administrative system with a highly trained staff, and most importantly, a high degree of financial expertise. Interestingly, as the size and volume of work in the hospital grew from the 1950s, so also did the number of nuns working there. The number of Sisters in the place peaked at 70–80 in or around 1970, then remained somewhat static, between 1970 and 1980, before beginning to fall. As their numbers fell, the cost of patient care began to rise gradually above the calculated 'cost of living index'. This occurred for a number of reasons but particularly because the Sisters' unpaid service now had to be replaced by paid and superannuated employees. Secondly, the Sisters' economic way of running wards and the hospital as a whole gave way to a more expensive means of achieving the same end.

The Consultative Council on the General Hospital Services

E.T. Freeman and Archbishop McQuaid at the Centenary celebrations in 1961, flanked by a guard of honour of nurses.

By mid-1960, it was time for change and this reflected the wider changes taking place in hospital services at the time. In 1967, the government had set up a consultative council to examine all the general hospital services, their location, the changing pattern of public demand for health services and the fast-developing element of medical specialisation. The purpose of the council was to make proposals as to how the services might be rationalised within the existing financial situation of all the hospitals: most of the hospitals in the state were operating with sizable deficits, including the Mater. The membership of this expert committee was largely made up of physicians and surgeons from the big university teaching hospitals and the university medical schools, including Bryan Alton and Eoin O'Malley from the Mater. It was chaired by Professor Patrick Fitzgerald, Professor of Surgery, University College Dublin.

This committee issued its report in 1968. It became known as the Fitzgerald Report.[10] In the report, it was suggested that the hospital system should be reorganised into three regions, Dublin, Cork and Galway, and that there should be two types of hospital: regional hospitals (two in Dublin – one of which would be the Mater) and general hospitals. The report focused extensively on the subject of healthcare administration in the state and in the individual

Mother Gabriel, Dr Eamon De Valera and President Éamon De Valera at the Centenary celebrations.

hospitals, which would have been the subject of some in-depth discussion between committee members and the religious orders. The Fitzgerald Report marked the beginning of a shift in governance of hospitals in Ireland, because it was the first significant attempt to rationalise the size and location as well as the services being provided by the hospitals in the main cities and rural areas and to promote medical education on a par with international standards. As things have worked out, there have been many more surveys carried out and reports written since.

● *A meal in the Gresham Hotel to celebrate the hospital's centenary in 1961. Note the painting of the Mater in the background.*

Time for Change

On foot of the Fitzgerald Report, and the Health Act 1970, which created the health boards which would run the system until the late 1990s, it was clear that change was needed at the Mater and in February 1970, Mother Gabriel O'Leary, then Superior General of the Sisters of Mercy, made a significant announcement to the community.

She and her advisers had drawn up a constitution for the hospital which allowed for the setting up of a board of management to take over the administration of the hospital. Mother Gabriel emphasised that the chief reason for the change lay not in the professional work of the hospital itself, but in the burden administration was placing upon the community, who had to run the hospital and provide all the nursing services as well.[11] While all the nuns present at that meeting assured her of their loyal support and cooperation, there was a sense of fear among those present, largely fear of the unknown. The sisters wondered what role they would have in this new organisation, and how their work might change. The members of the hospital's medical board, which had been in place since the foundation of the hospital, were also concerned, as Mother Gabriel outlined her plans to them, which included a change of title from 'board' to 'council' (which title would eventually revert to 'board', due to possible confusion with the Medical Council).

On 13 March 1970, the first meeting of the new hospital board took place. The Chairman, Archbishop John Charles McQuaid, gave a short opening address. He was very clear about why a new administrative system was necessary and what it was hoped it would achieve: that is, to improve the way the hospital was run. The Archbishop paid tribute to the work of all the staff at the hospital and to Professor Edmond Sheehy for agreeing to act as his deputy. The sisters were well represented on the new board, reflecting their continuing role in the running of the hospital. The members of this first board were:

- Archbishop John Charles McQuaid (Chairman)
- Professor Edmond J. Sheehy (Deputy Chairman)
- Reverend Mother Teresa Joseph Moylan, Superioress
- Reverend Mother Mary Walburga, Superioress, Convent of Mercy, Coolock
- Elizabeth Lovatt-Dolan
- Margaret McMahon
- Dermot J. O'Flynn (Secretary)
- Joseph P. O'Hanlon
- John F. O'Mahony
- William Sandys
- Dr Brendan Senior

Following the first meeting of the board seven additional members were invited to sit on the board: Sister John Berchmans Connolly (Matron), nurse Therese Monaghan, Dr Bryan Alton, Dr Ivo Drury, Professor Eoin O'Malley, James J. Nolan (Department of Health), William Finlay (Senior Counsel).

The first working meeting of the new board of management was held on 24 March 1970 at 4.30 p.m. in the Pillar Room. Professor Sheehy took the chair.[12] This meeting was probably the most important ever held since the foundation of the hospital. It was not an overly long meeting, but it was carefully planned and dealt with a number of important issues: ownership of the hospital; the accounting arrangements and overall financial situation; and the focus of power and channels of communication within the hospital. Professor Sheehy made it clear that the Sisters of Mercy remained the sole owners of the Mater Hospital and that they continued to hold the 'right to determine not only how the hospital is to be conducted, but also any other questions of policy concerning the destiny of the hospital in the future medical structure of this city and of this country.'[13] He then went on to talk about the overall objectives of the new board and the principles by which it would be guided in its work.

The first duty of this new board was to select and appoint a secretary/manager to the hospital (a role that would later evolve into that of CEO). They decided that until one was appointed, the board and auditors would help the sisters with the administration of the hospital. It was also necessary to keep the various departments and hospital personnel informed of impending changes to the existing hospital administration. Critically, much of the focus of the board members during the following few months was on the existing dire financial situation. There was simply no money: no money to pay the various hospital suppliers, no money to repay an overdraft in the bank, and no funds for the many requirements of an increasingly busy hospital. Mr Sandys and Mr O'Flynn, both board members, helped Sr Claude to reorganise the financial system whilst looking for a new accountant for the hospital. Professor Sheehy then proceeded to advise the main staff groups within the hospital of the changes about to take place. New administrative appointments began to appear in January 1971. The first was Sr Lucia Therese Cassidy, who was appointed in January as an administrator. On 18 February Gerard Smith (Gearoid MacGabhann, as he was later known as to distinguish him from an existing consultant surgeon of the same name) commenced as secretary/manager and in May of that year, Edward McGrath joined as hospital accountant. The task MacGabhann and McGrath faced can only be described as formidable, particularly from a financial point of view.

'New Look' Nursing

From 1960 onwards, the complexity of both medicine and surgery, particularly cardiac surgery, began to make new and very different demands on the nursing staff. It became clear that more nurses were needed. Unfortunately at this time, the nursing administration responded to requests, mainly from the wards, for more staff simply by increasing the intake of student nurses.[14] As nurses qualified, they were duly appointed to the wards as staff nurses, the numbers gradually increasing all the time, at a time when there was a great shortage of qualified nurses and midwives in Ireland and England.[15]

Rarely was consideration given to the costs involved, and the hospital quickly began to run into a serious deficit. In 1963, the Hospitals Commission, unhappy at the number and structure of the nursing staff at the hospital, responded simply by withholding altogether the nursing salaries grant. The Commission examined closely the situation at the Mater and reported on it in 1971: one of the main recommendations

Sr John Berchmans (Matron), Gearoid MacGabhannn (Secretary-Manager), Sr Rose Philippine (Superioress) and Dr Joe Ennis (Radiologist).

233

was the need for more qualified nursing staff in the wards, fewer student nurses and an increase in ward ancillary staff, such as ward clerks and household staff.[16]

Arguments rumbled on and still the nursing salaries grant, which by this time had been withheld for six years, was not reinstated. Negotiations were lengthy and focused on the hospital achieving an acceptable number of nurses overall, including an acceptable staff/student ratio and an overall nursing staff structure throughout the hospital. Much of the negotiations with the Commission were undertaken by Gearoid MacGabhann, on behalf of the hospital. Agreements on both sides were worked out and this included approval for a substantial grant (not the withheld nurses' salaries grant, which would not be paid for eight years after it fell due) to buy much-needed new equipment for the wards, which, up to this time, the hospital could not afford to purchase. Sr Concepta Greene, Matron, resigned in 1972[17] and a new Matron, Sr John Berchmans Connolly, was appointed in her place. It fell to Sister John to put in place these staff agreements.

The Sisters of Mercy and Sisters of Charity Joint Healthcare Venture

The Mater's Sr Sebastian Cashen (left) and Sr Francis Ignatius Fahy of the Sisters of Charity at the announcement of the Mercy/Charity venture.

In February 1973, the Chairman of the Board of Management of St Vincent's Hospital, Elm Park, Dublin, requested a joint meeting with the Mater board of management to consider the possibility of a closer association between the two hospitals. One further meeting was held on 9 April and that seems to be as far as it went. However, the initiative would appear to have planted a seed of interest among the Superiors of each of the Congregations, who began to see some possibilities for establishing a closer relationship. At the time, the hospitals owned and run by the two Congregations were:

- Mater Misericordiae Hospital, Eccles Street
- St Michael's Hospital, Dun Laoghaire
- National Rehabilitation Hospital, Dun Laoghaire

Sisters of Mercy Hospitals

- St Vincent's Hospital, Elm Park
- St Mary's Orthopaedic Hospital, Cappagh
- Children's Hospital, Temple Street

Sisters of Charity Hospitals

In 1987, Sr Francis Ignatius Fahy, Superior General of the Sisters of Charity, and Sr Sebastian Cashen, Superior General of the Sisters of Mercy, began to discuss the benefits which they perceived would accrue from a coming together of the six hospitals in Dublin, Their main reasoning was a desire to continue the tradition and ethos of caring and medical excellence developed by both Congregations over 150 years. They felt that if the hospitals could work in closer collaboration, more could be achieved, including securing the future for Catholic voluntary hospitals. Having discussed the idea with the Archbishop, the Minister for Health, the legal advisers to the religious congregations and others, they put in place a 'co-ordinating committee of the six voluntary hospitals with a selected core-committee to develop the initiative'.[18] On 25 June 1991, the Charity/Mercy initiative was launched as a new company, the Charity/Mercy Healthcare Company Ltd. A board of directors was put in place in 1992 and a group chief executive was appointed the following year. In the interim, the two Superiors were at pains to reassure everyone that it was a joint venture and not a merger or a rationalisation of the hospitals.

Desmond Connell, Archbishop of Dublin, Minister for Health Dr Rory O'Hanlon and Sr Sebastian Cashin at the launch of the Mercy/Charity joint venture.

In September 1992, a communication outlining the board's organisation structure, which announced that the board would eventually assume full responsibility for the management of all six hospitals, was sent out. There was consternation in the hospitals, particularly among the respective boards of management and senior staff. They requested a meeting with the two Superiors General, together with the chairman and members of the group board. In the meantime, the chairpersons of the individual boards and the medical consultants met to discuss the plans, about which they felt distinctly negative. The Mater consultants boycotted the meeting with the group board. It was clear that this was not a popular initiative.

The Charity/Mercy Healthcare Company Ltd never really achieved what it set out to do. In 1993, the staff of the six hospitals rejected the idea of a single controlling body at a distance from the hospitals. The company continued for some months and in time it became dormant. In 1995, it went into liquidation.[19]

The Future of Temple Street Children's Hospital

During this time and throughout the Mercy/Charity discussions, particularly in the late 1980s, the future of the Children's Hospital, Temple Street, was being discussed.[20] As the building of the bed block (Phase 1A) at the Mater was nearing completion and attention was turning towards the next phase of the Mater development plan, the Minister for Health made a suggestion to the two congregations to consider that perhaps the Children's Hospital be relocated to the Mater site. Nothing immediately happened. Further development of the adult hospital (Phase 1B) was put on hold and eventually shelved altogether. Discussion around hospital developments between the Sisters of Mercy and the Sisters of Charity continued. They set about rationalising the ownership of the hospitals to secure the future of four of them. It is interesting to note that, in the discussions, no money was ever mentioned! On 29 April 1999, the following communication was circulated within each of the hospitals involved:

The Sisters of Charity and Mercy exchange hospitals to secure strong future for the Voluntary Hospital Sector in Dublin

The Religious Sisters of Charity, Trustees of St Vincent's University Hospital, Elm Park and the Children's Hospital, Temple Street and the Sisters of Mercy, Trustees of the Mater University Hospital, Eccles Street and St Michael's Public Hospital, Dun Laoghaire announced today (29 April 1999) that they are to exchange Trusteeship in two of their hospitals. The Sisters of Mercy will become Trustees of the new Children's Hospital, Temple Street, which is to be built on the site of the Mater. The Sisters of Charity will become Trustees for St Michael's Public Hospital, Dun Laoghaire. When implemented, at a date not yet determined, the two voluntary acute hospitals on the north side will be under the Trusteeship of the Sisters of Mercy, with the two on the south side coming under the Trusteeship of the Sisters of Charity. The initiative is to secure the future of all four acute voluntary hospitals in Dublin into the next Millennium...[21]

A New Children's Hospital

In 1999, the Mater and Children's Hospital Development Ltd (MCHD) was established as a joint initiative of the two congregations, to oversee the development of the Mater and Children's Hospital Campus at Eccles Street. It was to be funded under the National Development Plan, and at the time the estimated cost of the building was €340 million. The children's hospital was to be a 205-bed hospital. However, in 2005, the then Minister for Health (Mary Harney TD) announced that a children's hospital (to replace Temple Street Children's Hospital) would not be going ahead because the Health Services Executive (HSE) had decided to build a National Children's Hospital which would include all three children's hospitals in Dublin:

- Crumlin Sick Children's Hospital
- Temple Street Children's Hospital
- Harcourt Street/Tallaght Children's Hospital.

This required further tendering because the size required was now considerably larger. The Mater submitted a new design and the proposal was accepted above a large number of others who had submitted proposals too. However, when the plan reached An Bord Pleanála, it was rejected on the grounds that its height, bulk, scale and mass would have a 'profound negative impact on the Dublin skyline'. In 2011, there was a change of national government. The new administration initiated a further review of the proposed locations. This time the new government rejected the Mater site in favour of the site at St James's Hospital. By this time it had cost the Mater in excess of €50 million.

New Millennium – New Changes

At the last Board of Management meeting of the 20th century[22] Sr Helena O'Donoghue, Sisters of Mercy Provincial Leader, announced that the new millennium would see a new governance structure put in place for the Mater Hospital. On 3 October 2000, it was announced that the Mater would be incorporated into a company limited by guarantee, in which the Sisters of Mercy would continue to be the majority owners of the hospital. The following Press statement was released:

Announcement by Sisters of Mercy

– Mater Misericordiae Hospital to be incorporated as a Limited Company

The Sisters of Mercy today announced several major decisions in regard to their contribution to health services in Dublin. The main decisions are as follows:
- Mater Misericordiae Hospital to be incorporated into a limited company.[23]
- Withdrawal from and transfer of ownership of the Mater Private Hospital.
- Exchange of ownership of two Dublin hospitals, Temple Street and St Michael's Dun Laoghaire with the Sisters of Charity.

Sr Helena O'Donoghue, Provincial Leader, South Central Province, said today, 'It is time to consider the changing role of our Congregation in Irish society. We are taking measures to ensure the most appropriate structures for effective delivery of our health care services in the years ahead. The Congregation of the Sisters of Mercy is fully committed to the continuance of our caring ministries in so far as this is possible. We want to ask for the support of everyone involved in ensuring the decisions announced today are effectively implemented in the interests of care and compassion for those who are sick, into the future.'

Mater Misericordiae Hospital to be a Limited Company
The Mater Misericordiae Hospital, a large acute voluntary Catholic hospital with over 2,000 employees, will be incorporated into a company limited by guarantee, in which the Sisters of Mercy shall continue to be owners. The governance and management will devolve to a Board of Governors and an Executive Board of Management. The new structures will enable the hospital to respond to the fast growing developments in healthcare. Having guided the hospital since 1861, the Sisters of Mercy are confident that their lay successors have the determination and expertise to ensure the continued success of the hospital in the years ahead.

The Sisters of Mercy will be the members of the new company, together with a nominee of the Archbishop of Dublin and two representatives of Catholic lay organisations [the Catholic Nurses Guild of Ireland and the Society of St Vincent de Paul]. Their task is to effect the wish of the Sisters of Mercy that the Mater Misericordiae Hospital should continue to be a Catholic, voluntary hospital into the future...[24]

Thus, in January 2002, the Sisters of Mercy established a company structure incorporating the Mater Misericordiae University Hospital (MMUH) and Children's University Hospital, Temple Street (CUH) and later Cappagh National Orthopaedic Hospital. With charitable status the newly formed parent company (MMCUH) became the owner of all the properties involved and the protector of the voluntary Catholic identity of the constituent hospitals. The Sisters of Mercy remain the majority shareholder.

Today the Mater Misericordiae University Hospital is classified as a charitable voluntary hospital.[25] It holds a unique place in the delivery of healthcare not only to the local community in north Dublin, but also to the rest of the country with its important tertiary referral services. It forms part of a group of companies operated by MMCUH comprising:

- Mater Misericordiae University Hospital
- Children's Hospital, Temple Street
- Cappagh National Orthopaedic Hospital

The core objective of the Mater has always been to deliver high-quality services. This is mediated today through the various specialties, the most important of which are as follows:

- National specialties:[26]
  - National Cardiothoracic Centre, including heart and lung transplantation
  - National Spinal Injuries Unit
  - National Pulmonary Hypertension Unit
  - National Service for Extra Corporeal Life Support (ECLS)
  - National Adult Isolation Centre for Infectious Diseases
  - National Bone Anchored Hearing Aid service

- Tertiary referral centre for:
  - Ophthalmology
  - Pain Medicine
  - Oncology/Haematology
  - Stroke
  - Plastic Surgery
  - Dermatology
  - Ear, Nose and Throat (ENT)
  - Neurology
  - Gynaecology

- Other specialties, including regional services:
  - Gastroenterology
  - Respiratory Medicine
  - Endocrinology
  - Medicine for the Elderly
  - Nephrology
  - Orthopaedics
  - Infectious Diseases
  - General & Vascular Surgery
  - Urology
  - Child Psychiatry
  - Adult Psychiatry
  - Rheumatology
  - Dental Surgery
  - Emergency Medicine

- The Mater Hospital is one of eight National Cancer Centres for:
  - Breast
  - Lung
  - Gynaecology
  - Prostate
  - Spinal
  - Rectal Cancer

The hospital currently serves a catchment population of 235,000. Of this population, 14% are over 65 years of age and 28% are living alone. In addition to the age profile, a large number of patients belong to the lower socio-economic group. This presents problems for the hospital largely in terms of secondary and long-term care for those unable to return home after their inpatient treatment has finished. For the hospital as a whole, it presents an enormous challenge. The following are some recent (2011) statistics:

Activity (annual):
- Inpatient discharges   16,300
- Day cases   40,305
- Emergency department attendances   47,000
- Outpatient department attendances   215,000

The hospital budget for 2011 was €196m (€250m in 2009).[27] The necessary financial constraints have led to a very challenging economic environment for the hospital over the past few years. In addition, because of the rising cost of patient treatment and the ever-increasing numbers seeking admission to the hospital, a new philosophy and management system of patient care is currently being developed. Unlike the approach

BOARD OF GOVERNORS
- From left (sitting): Mary Day, Desmond Lamont, Mary Finlay-Geoghegan, Sr Margherita Rock, Donal Walsh (Chairman) Sr Helena O'Donoghue, John Morgan, Thomas Lynch, Siobhán Brady. From left (standing): Mona Baker, Rosemary Ryan, Gordon Dunne, Tony Kilduff, Martin Walsh, Dr Brendan Kinsley, Patrick Mahony, Suzanne Dempsey. Missing: Eve Linders, Sean Sheehan, Eamon Clarke, Fr Kevin Doran, Prof. Conor O'Keane.

BOARD OF DIRECTORS
- From left (sitting): Dr Nuala Healy, Sr Eugene Nolan, Mary Day, John Morgan (Chairman), Kevin Finnan, Sr Margherita Rock, Martin Cowley. From left (standing): Eamon Clarke, Thomas Lynch. Missing: Don Mahony, Dr Mary Carmel Burke, Prof. Conor O'Keane, Dr Brendan Kinsley, Fr Kevin Doran, Eddie Shaw.

to patient management when the hospital opened in 1861, when patients remained in the hospital until they were strong and well enough to return to their homes, today this is usually not possible, because of the urgent need for beds to be made available, to admit either the seriously ill or injured from the emergency department or patients awaiting treatment who have been seen in the outpatients department.

The first meeting of the board of directors of the Mater Misericordiae Hospital took place on 6 February 2002. The chairman was Mr John Morgan. Since then there have been many changes of membership, but many members of the original board are still in place.

BOARD OF DIRECTORS
January 2013

John Morgan (Chairperson)
Don Mahony
Sr Margherita Rock
Eamon Clarke
Dr Nuala Healy
Dr Mary Carmel Burke
Sr Eugene Nolan
Martin Cowley
Tom Lynch
Eddie Shaw
Fr Kevin Doran

Mary Day	Chief Executive (acting)
Professor Brendan Kinsley	Chairman, Medical Board
Professor Conor O'Keane	Clinical Director
Caroline Piggott	Director of Finance
Mairead Curran	Director of Nursing (acting)
Patrick Mahony	Company Secretary

Since the foundations of the hospital, its organisation and governance have been an ebb and flow between the Sisters of Mercy and the medical and lay community, but as medicine has advanced and the running of the hospital continues to become ever more complex, a different structure has been needed to keep this busy ship afloat. The changes which have taken place over the last century and a half are encapsulated in this statement from Sr Helena O'Donoghue, now Mercy Healthcare Resource Coordinator, in September 2011:

Today, the presence of the Sisters of Mercy has diminished after 150 years and their presence within the hospital has almost disappeared. In this context, their capacity to fulfil the onerous governance responsibilities is limited. With this in mind the Sisters will in, due course, be considering various options which would ensure the future of the Mater Misericordiae University Hospital as a publicly-funded, tertiary-referral, high standard hospital in the Catholic tradition. Such a future will inevitably involve a greater presence of lay people in the governance structures; people committed to the values and ethos of the Mater, working in collaboration with the State to provide quality healing and care for the vulnerable sick people in our society.

The preservation of the voluntary sector is vital in a democracy, whether faith-based or not. In the healthcare area, this is widely present in places like Australia and the USA.[28] The Mater Hospital, yesterday and today, stands alongside the best hospitals at home and abroad in providing top-class medical care in a fully responsible and responsive manner, providing diversity and alternative choice under the overriding values of compassion and dignity for all.

This has proved to be very satisfactory to date. The question which arises now is what of the future? With few Sisters of Mercy in existence and an age profile which will see the passing of their presence in the hospital and on the various boards in the not-so-distant future it is obvious that a different kind of planning is necessary as the hospital moves further into the new century.

1   Mater Misericordiae Hospital (1861), *Minutes of Meetings of the Medical Board*, 15 September, p 1.
2   Ibid.
3   *Report of the Mater Misericordiae Hospital (Under The Care of the Sisters of Mercy) for the Year 1888*: Dublin: Browne & Nolan, p 6.
4   No indication exists as to how communication was maintained between the Mater and the Convent of Mercy, Baggot Street. Some letters are extant and it is obvious that the Assistant Rev. Mother (M. Rose Barry) was a frequent visitor to the hospital, especially during the early days.
5   It is interesting to note that none of the Archbishops ever took the side of the staff (or, on occasions, aggrieved students) against decisions taken by the nuns. In the case of one appointment, the Archbishop did seek some information from the Rev. Mother as to why they had appointed a particular physician to whom the medical staff were objecting, but that was as far as it went.
6   Sr Berchmans Barry employed the first Matron (Mary McGivney) and set up the School of Nursing at the Mater in 1891. With Miss McGivney, she selected the first student nurses. She was a cousin of Mother Vincent Whitty, who built the hospital.
7   A monastic structure is a relatively simple form of governance which relies strongly on the motivation of the members and internal control mechanisms. Technically there is one person in charge (the superior general) who sets out individual or small group responsibilities. It depends on a specific (religious) relationship between the superior and the members of the community. It necessitates a lot of informal structures, mutual trust, knowledge of personal responsibilities among the membership and a certain degree of autonomy over decision making. It works well in small groups of religious with an identifiable purpose. It only worked in the Mater in the very early years.
8   I.S.A. – social insurance payment for patients. P.A.Y.E – tax scheme for staff salaries (Pay As You Earn).
9   MacGabhann, G. (1979), *Mater Misericordiae Hospital, Annual Report 1979*, Dublin, p 6.

10   *Outline of the Future Hospital System – Report of the Consultative Council on the General Hospital Services* (1968), Government Publications.

11   At this time, all the ward and departmental Sisters in the hospital were nuns.

12   Board of Management minutes of 24 March 1970, Mater Hospital Archives.

13   Sheehy, E. (1970), 'Address by the Deputy Chairman at a Meeting of the Board 24th March 1970', p 1 (unpublished report).

14   In the 1960s, nursing as a career became very popular and consequently the 'waiting list' for the Mater School of Nursing grew bit by bit until eventually, by 1982, it exceeded 8,000.

15   During these years there was a serious shortage in both Ireland and the UK of registered nurses and midwives.

16   Registered general nurses were in short supply at this time in both Ireland and England.

17   Sr Concepta Greene was a gentle, kind person, much loved by both staff and student nurses. By 1970, she was in poor health. In 1972 she was appointed to the National Rehabilitation Hospital as the Mother Superior.

18   Mater Misericordiae Hospital, *Annual Report 1989*, 'Address given by the Executive Chairman of the Board of Management', p 17.

19   It went into liquidation on 20 January 1995.

20   Temple Street is in close proximity to the Mater, only some metres further down the street.

21   *Mater News* (1999), 'Sisters of Charity and Mercy exchange Hospitals in innovative move to secure strong future for Voluntary Hospital Sector in Dublin'. Special News Edn, April, Vol. 2, No. 4.

22   The last meeting was held in September 1999.

23   It was incorporated as Mater Misericordiae Hospital Limited on 18 December 2001. The company changed its name on 23 January 2002 to Mater Misericordiae University Hospital. It was permitted to omit the word 'Limited' from the company title. The company is limited by guarantee and does not have share capital.

24   *Heart of the Mater* (2000), copy of the press statement released on 3 October 2000 regarding the Sisters of Mercy, December, Vol. 3, No. 17, p 9.

25   Charitable voluntary hospitals were defined in Victorian times as independent charities established for the benefit of the poor who, according to Victorian values, were respectable working-class people who had fallen on hard times because of sickness.

26   Courtesy of Mr Brian Conlan, Chief Executive Officer, Mater Misericordiae University Hospital, 20 April 2012.

27   The current recession (since 2007) has gradually seen a reduction in the annual allocation of funds to the hospital from the Health Service Executive.

28   There are many healthcare institutions in Australia and the USA owned or in the care of the Sisters of Mercy.

CHAPTER 17

Building the Future

T he rapid medical developments which took place during the 1970s made it clear to those running the hospital that the original 19th-century building would need to be refurbished. An ageing Victorian building simply could not meet the increasingly complex needs of its patients. Furthermore, the attempts to 'modernise' the wards over the previous twenty years had resulted in a reduced bed capacity, which became problematic when the rate of admissions via the emergency department began to grow. The emergency department itself and the outpatients departments were also too small for the increasing demands being made on them. So, in 1971, architects William Byrne & Son were charged with planning a major new addition to the hospital. This extension would provide not alone more bed space, but also new emergency and outpatients

● *The building of phase 1A of the new development.*

The physiotherapy department in the new block.

departments, operating theatres, a physiotherapy department, radiology and a host of other much-needed services. The brief for the architects was that existing patient services would have to be maintained without interruption during construction and that the new building would have to be built in phases over a number of years.

It was decided to build on land to the east of the existing hospital, which had originally been purchased by the Sisters of Mercy in 1879 with plans to build a fever hospital on it, for which there was enormous need at the time, but which was never built.[1] The 1981 development would be built in three phases: Phase 1A would contain mostly bed space and some support departments and would be connected by a long corridor (the link corridor) to the original hospital. Phase 1B would accommodate a large outpatients department, emergency department, operating theatres, catering, and other supply departments. Phase 2 would include some bed accommodation and other clinical services; and Phase 3 a new laboratory block (to be built near the existing laboratory) and new hospital teaching facilities.

The entire development was approved by the Department of Health in 1977, under the governance of the then Minister, Charles Haughey. To facilitate the development, most of the existing buildings on the north side of Eccles Street had to be demolished. They included a small hotel, the Dominican convent and school, the Bertrand Russell school and a number of houses in an advanced state of dereliction.

John Sisk & Sons were contracted to build the new development and work on Phase 1A, the large ward block, began on 1 September 1981. Unfortunately, this ambitious building project coincided with the deep recession of the 1980s, and during 1984–85, funding for the development was reduced by the government. This meant that Phase 1B, which was to be completed at the same time as Phase 1A, had to be deferred. In fact, after Phase 1A was completed, no further building took place.

The building of Phase 1A finished in 1986, but once again, lack of funds meant that it couldn't be fitted out or opened, with the exception of one or two service areas which were urgently needed, such as the telephone exchange and the pharmacy, both of which had been servicing the entire hospital from cramped locations,[2] one beside the Pillar Room[3] and the other in a small room in the outpatients department.[4] It would be a further three years until the entire ward block was opened, on 15 February 1989.

First the rheumatology department was moved to its new location and then, on 1 September 1989, the formidable task of moving the patients from the medical wards

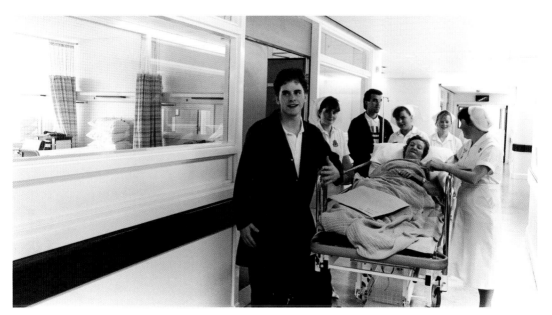

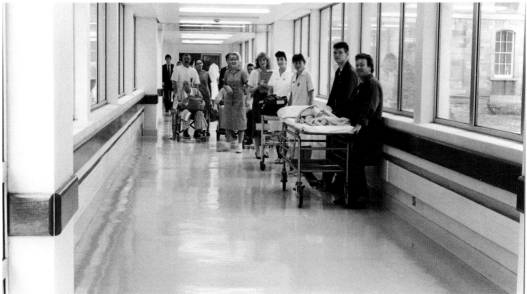

● *Moving patients to the new ward block in 1986.*

of the old hospital to the beautiful new wards and rooms of Phase 1A commenced, a move which at times resembled the the biblical move to the Promised Land.

The actual transfer of patients presented an enormous challenge: some patients were too ill to consider moving at all and other arrangements had to be made for them. For the remaining patients, the hospital went off 'emergency call' and was helped out by Beaumont and Connolly Hospitals during this time. It took some time to settle all the patients into the new wards and for the staff to get used to the changes, but after the years of waiting for these new facilities, there was great staff enthusiasm, which led to enormous co-operation at every level.

247

Phase 1A is a seven-storey, L-shaped block with a total of eleven standard ward units in it. When the place opened, each unit consisted of 31 beds – four six-bed wards, one two-bed ward, two single high-dependency rooms, two isolation rooms and one single room.[5] Located on Level 7 was a 12-bed intensive coronary care unit, with up-to-date cardiac monitoring equipment and beside it a 31-bed ward for cardiac patients. On Level 0, the ground level, of the new building a small (temporary) theatre suite was built. Many other patient and staff facilities were included in this building, some permanent and some to await a more suitable location in Phase 1B.

The Minister for Health, Rory O'Hanlon, opens Phase 1A in 1989.

The formal opening of the building took place on 10 November 1989. Those who were invited to the ceremony assembled in the spacious entrance concourse. Sr Margherita Rock (then Executive Chairperson of the Board of Management) opened

The blessing of Phase 1A.

the proceedings by welcoming all present. The Archbishop of Dublin, Desmond Connell, was invited to bless the building and all within it. This ceremony included a short prayer service with beautiful singing by the Mater Hospital folk choir, led by Pat Feehan, who had composed some special music for the occasion. The Minister for Health, Dr Rory O'Hanlon, performed the official opening ceremony and Sr Sebastian Cashen, Superior General of the Dublin Sisters of Mercy, presented the hospital with a large bronze statue of Our Lady of Mercy sculpted by Imogen Stuart to mark the event and to remember the largest and most significant development at the Mater since its opening in 1861.

Esther Freeman sits at the nurses' station in the new Phase 1A.

The spacious concourse in Phase 1A on the day of opening.

New Developments in the Old Hospital

After the new ward block was opened, a large part of the general hospital activity shifted to the new building. When it became evident that the next phase of the hospital building plan was unlikely to go ahead, discussions began on how the existing space in the old building might be used. A number of hospital facilities needed urgent upgrading. In 1990, three sections of the old cardiac ward in the east wing (ground floor) were turned into a new medical records department, the old one having completely outgrown all available space.[6] This department, with its new extended library facilities, and a capacity for 220,000 files, opened in 1993.

● *The medical records department in 1993.*

The next department to come into being was the hospital inpatient enquiry service or HIPE, which was set up in 1993. It is located close to the medical records department, because its focus is to distil accurate data on the clinical work undertaken at the hospital for submission to the Department of Health. Initially, this consisted of checking the discharge summary in each patient's medical record and assigning an international code (for statistical purposes) to it, but the process has since become more sophisticated. When this new department opened it was under the direction and management of epidemiologist Dr Mary Codd, assisted by Eibhlin Loughman, who was employed in 1993 as HIPE/Casemix coordinator. With the assistance of the computer IT department, a new discharge summary system was designed and implemented in September 1994 to provide more information on clinical work. This department has grown beyond anything anticipated when it was originally opened. HIPE data continues to be a fundamental management tool not only for the hospital itself, but also nationally: data is gathered from all hospitals for the HSE and the Department of Health and Children to enable planning and health budgeting at national level.

A New Life for the Pathology Department

As we saw in Chapter 12, the volume of work being undertaken by the pathology department at this time grew rapidly, in some areas by as much as 26%. It called not alone for more space but also for up-to-date equipment as the discipline became more sophisticated. Construction work commenced almost immediately on the new pathology department, which was opened in June 1993 by the Minister for Health, Brendan Howlin. Also in 1993, the more complex business of developing a modern orthopaedic and spinal injuries unit began to be considered. Adapting an ageing building to the needs of this fast-growing and demanding speciality tested the ingenuity of the architects and the project team. St Agnes' Ward, which had for a number of years been the home for orthopaedic patients, closed for renovations during 1993. Part of this refurbishment would consist of configuring the space to accommodate spinal injuries cases, which were increasingly being sent to the Mater. In 1990, Comhairle na nOspidéal had made a recommendation, subsequently confirmed by the Department of Health in 1994, that all acute spinal injuries should be treated at the Mater in the National Centre for Spinal Injuries.[7] In 1993, long-term rehabilitation arrangements for patients with spinal injury were made with the National Rehabilitation Hospital.[8] Since then the number of spinal injury cases admitted to the Mater has progressively increased year by year. During 2013, St Agnes' Ward will be transferred to level 5 of the Whitty Building. A purpose-built orthopaedic ward is located in the north block and the spinal unit in the south block of the new building.

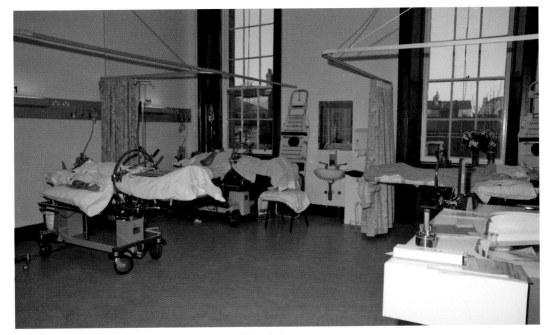

The spinal injuries unit in St Agnes' Ward in the old hospital.

President Mary McAleese with the staff of St Agnes' orthopaedic ward, including John Morgan on the left and Brian Conlan on the right.

Also part of the original redevelopment plan, which had had to be shelved after Phase 1A was the restructuring of St Aloysius psychiatric ward. Plans for the ward had, in fact, been developed in 1990. However, it became clear that because of the growth of psychiatric need and the academic requirements of a teaching hospital, essential developments to the ward simply couldn't be delayed.

At the time of the renovations, psychiatric services for Dublin North Central Area 7 were being rearranged to provide a joint service between the Mater Hospital, St Vincent's Hospital, Fairview and the Eastern Health Board (HSE). This service model is still in place: it is a community-based model which provides a comprehensive psychiatric service mainly for people in Dublin 7. The department of psychiatry also provides a service for patients elsewhere within the hospital, as the need arises, and is a national tertiary referral service. The refurbished unit opened in 1994 and is currently under the stewardship of Professor Patricia Casey, senior consultant psychiatrist.

The National Infectious Diseases Unit – St Bernard's Ward

The work of the National Infectious Diseases Unit has grown over the years and it provides an all-important national service in the care and management of infectious disease. One of the 'newer' types of infectious disease being treated here is HIV/AIDS. In 1992, discussions took place between the hospital and the Department of Health regarding the setting up of a much-needed AIDS/HIV service. It was commissioned in July 1992 and a grant of £400,000 was made available to equip the unit. Dr Gerard

Sheehan was appointed to the hospital as consultant in infectious diseases in 1993, and one of his first tasks was to set up an outpatients clinic,[9] which continues to treat increasing numbers of patients from year to year.

When the ward unit, now named St Bernard's, was ready for use in January 1994, those in need of inpatient treatment could be admitted and five additional beds were added to the unit in 1996 to cater for the increasing demands on the service. Later in 1994, a special infectious diseases laboratory was commissioned to serve specialist requirements and to enable the research to be undertaken that is so important in the fight against infectious disease.

In 2005, Professor Bill Powderly (Professor of Medicine and Therapeutics, UCD and consultant in infectious diseases) joined the staff. Professor Powderly is a world-renowned expert in infectious diseases and an international authority on HIV infection and fungal infections. In October 2005, he was joined by Dr John (Jack) Lambert, consultant/senior lecturer in infectious diseases.[10] During 2007/8 the unit underwent major restructuring and upgrading to meet some of the unique needs of this service. It became Ireland's first national isolation unit and was opened on 19 December 2008 by Minister for Health Mary Harney.[11] Two of the isolation rooms have particularly high specifications and are separate from the rest of the unit, with different air-handling systems. The unit cares for patients referred from all over Ireland who are diagnosed with hazardous and highly infectious diseases. The unit is also equipped to provide essential care for potential victims of bio-terrorism.[12]

Minister Brendan Howlin at the opening of the Intensive Care Unit.

The Growing Needs of Cardiac Surgery

One very significant redevelopment project, which began in 1994, was restructuring and updating the intensive therapy unit (ITU) and the development of a much-needed high-dependency unit adjacent to it.[13] As the amount of cardiac surgery was gradually increasing, the existing facilities for acute and specialist care associated with post-operative management of major surgery were a growing concern. At the same time, the incidence of major trauma and other cases in need of intensive- and critical-care management was rapidly increasing. By 1992, the existing unit was admitting over 1,200 patients per annum.[14] Located on the top floor (Level 3) of the west wing, it was in vital need of enlargement and refurbishment to bring it up to the required standard of a national cardiac surgery unit. Eventually, in 1993, the Department of Health provided £1 million to enable the work to begin.[15] The entire top floor of the original hospital was refurbished to include the necessary intensive care unit (ICU) restructuring; high-dependency beds and additional beds for cardiac surgery patients. A small five-day ward for surgical cases located at the end of the east wing and within easy reach of the emergency department was also included as part of this project.

The ICU was absolutely stripped to the bare outside walls and roof during the refurbishment, and when the ceiling[16] was taken down it brought into view the original highly ornamented chapel roof, built in 1886. Some discussion took place at the time as to whether this should be restored; unfortunately the funds were simply not available, but it seems appropriate that this marvel should lie intact above the false ceiling and the busy ward below.

The refurbishment of the National Cardiac Surgical Unit was a great achievement and the facilities in it were at last equal to the excellence of the surgical, clinical and nursing care at the Mater. On 10 November 1994, the new unit was officially opened, consisting of:

- 18 intensive care beds
- 9 high-dependency beds
- 43 cardiac surgery maintenance beds
- 17 five-day general surgical beds.

However, once again medical progress outpaced what the hospital was able to provide in terms of facilities and almost from the time the extended unit reopened, the number of high-dependency beds was insufficient for the work being undertaken and the needs of the hospital as a whole. The staff of the unit did their best to cope with an ever-increasing throughput of patients for a number of years. In 2002, plans were drawn up for a new HDU, which would be located in the courtyard of the hospital adjoining the east wing. This unit was built on metal stilts (30 metres high) and opens on to Level 3.[17] The building of the unit was not without drama. It took place over a stormy weekend and during the storm one of the segments hit a tree near the OPD, when it was being lifted by the crane over the archway into the courtyard. All the segments of the unit and some other buildings at ground level were in place within 24 hours. The staff were heard to say that the unit swayed in stormy weather until it was anchored to the floor below when the transit unit was built.

Basic in construction it may have been, but the prefab building[18] provides space for nine post-cardio-thoracic surgery, high-dependency patients (or CTHDU, as they are referred to). Opened by An Taoiseach Bertie Ahern on 29 March 2004, this dedicated CTHDU facility had an enormous impact on the provision of care and treatment for cardiac surgical cases. It also played an essential role at the beginning of the lung transplant programme and also the artificial heart mechanical bridge to transplant development.[19] In 2013 this section will be moved to level 6 of the Whitty building. The cardio-thoracic ward will move to the north block, the high dependency unit and the heart–lung surgical ward will both be located in the south block of the new building.

While some space problems were being alleviated on Level 3,[20] the need for beds to admit patients from the overcrowded emergency department continued to worry those dealing with emergency admissions. After the cardiac high-dependency unit was opened, permission was granted in June 2005 to build a 33-bed 'transit ward' facility, underneath the CTHDU, into which patients from the emergency department could be admitted temporarily until ward beds could be made available. The reason for the transit ward was clear – to alleviate the chronic overcrowding in the emergency department – and it was put in place along with a series of other interim measures, including efforts to try to reduce the number of delayed discharge cases. The unit was quickly built and opened in December 2005, making twenty-five of the beds available to the emergency department, including a six-bed clinical decision unit and two isolation beds.[21] Unfortunately, the impact of the transit ward was to be shortlived, as the lack of long-term accommodation in the community for discharged patients had a knock-on effect, delaying the transfer of patients from the transit unit to the wards. In 2007, it was obvious that the purpose it was meant to serve was not achievable and so it was turned into a regular ward (and renamed St Michael's Ward) for elective surgery, where patients await surgery.

A Grand Plan

The story of the proposed children's hospital to be built on the Mater campus is by now past history. On 6 June 1989, the boards of management of the Mater and the Children's Hospital Temple Street received a letter from the Minister for Health confirming a 'formal agreement to relocate the paediatric services provided by the Children's Hospital (Temple Street), in a new purpose-built hospital, on the Mater site'.[22] It was obvious that the three organisations involved, the Department of Health, Temple Street Children's Hospital and the Mater Misericordiae Hospital, were about to move into relatively unknown territory. On 18 February 1998, the size of the task ahead was outlined in a memorandum of understanding regarding the relocation of the Children's Hospital to the Mater campus. Apart from a profile of each of the hospitals, it outlined some significant considerations, such as:

- The objectives, especially the potential for co-operation with a view to enhancing patient care
- The services, primary, secondary and tertiary referral services
- Proposed governance, cross-representation on two boards of management
- Ethos and ethical codes
- Integration of services, some of which would be 'shared services'
- Delivery of paediatric services
- Management structures
- Budget arrangements
- Interim arrangements, in the years before the relocation of the hospital.

In 1998, a project team was set up and in due course, plans for a proposed new adult and children's hospital were drawn up.[23] The following year, the Sisters of Mercy and the Sisters of Charity (who ran Temple Street Children's Hospital) established a joint initiative to oversee the entire development, which they called the Mater and Children's Hospital Development (MCHD) Limited. Planning permission was duly received and the sod was turned for two new 'enabling buildings' on Eccles Street – the hostel and the Centre for Nurse Education. The construction of both of these buildings commenced immediately and they were completed and ready for use by the end of 2005.

A National Children's Hospital

It was hoped that the main hospital development would be able to commence in 2006. However, just as it was about to go to tender, it was announced that the proposed children's hospital would not be going ahead on the Mater campus. The HSE, notwithstanding the publication of a report, 'Children's Health First' (McKinsey 2006), which had recommended the Mater site, had decided that it would be more appropriate to build a large *national* children's hospital, which would incorporate all three existing children's hospitals in Dublin.[24] With this announcement came a recommendation to 'co-locate the National Paediatric Hospital with a leading adult academic hospital'. Consequently, the overall Mater plan was thrown into disarray.

The HSE invited all the Dublin academic teaching hospitals to submit proposals to locate the new National Children's Hospital on their campus. In total, six submissions were made to the HSE and in June 2006, it was once again proposed to locate the new hospital on the Mater site. The Sisters of Mercy agreed to gift two hectares of land[25] at the Mater, to facilitate the children's hospital development 'unencumbered and at no cost to the state'.[26] This site, when cleared of existing buildings, would also be able to accommodate a new maternity hospital in a 'tri-located' facility.

On 9 June 2006, the government approved the decision to build the National Children's Hospital on the Mater Campus and consequently ushered in a time of turbulence for the Mater. An intense media discussion on the suitability of the Mater location ensued. Generally it was felt that the hospital would be difficult to reach in an emergency because of traffic congestion in the area. Nonetheless, in May 2007 the HSE established a development board for the National Children's Hospital. They immediately set to work to draw up a framework brief. The hospital design which was ultimately drawn up consisted of a 16-storey building with 441 beds. This subsequently became a controversial plan because of the height and scale of the building.

As public discussion continued, in May 2011 the Minister for Health set up a review group of international experts to assess the plan and its location. They endorsed the plan to locate it on the Mater site. The National Children's Hospital Development Board applied for planning permission in July 2011. By then, the design and the proposed location for the hospital had become exceedingly controversial and was being opposed by a number of interested parties. A public hearing was opened by An Bord Pleanála in October 2011. The proposed building on the Mater site was considered to be too intrusive on the skyline of the city and to be in conflict with statutory planning regulations in this regard, and so planning permission was refused on 23 February 2012.

It seemed like the end of the road for the Mater plans. Once again an invitation went out for proposals to host the new National Children's Hospital on a new site. In the meantime, the Sisters of Mercy agreed to cede the original (19th-century) hospital building to the State to create the space required for research and teaching which a national paediatric hospital would be expected to provide. These facilities had previously formed part of the original design submitted to An Bord Pleanála in 2011, but were included within the building itself.

The space that was being offered for the proposed National Children's Hospital.

A New Adult Hospital

Following the 2006 choice of the Mater as a suitable site for a national paediatric hospital, the plans for the original joint adult/children's hospital needed to be modified to provide for a stand-alone new adult hospital. Planning approval for this was granted in 2008. In the meantime, plans for the Metro North underground rail system[27] were being drawn up. To facilitate both the children's hospital and the adult hospital, an underground station was included as part of the Metro line to Dublin Airport.[28] In February 2008 the government gave approval for work to commence on two stations – the Mater and Dublin Airport – but in November 2011, Metro North became another victim of the recession, being deferred indefinitely. Formal approval from the HSE to proceed to tender for the building of the adult hospital was received in July 2007. Construction commenced immediately and the building was ready for use in 2012.[29] This building development and the massive engineering project that went with it has produced some interesting structural statistics:

1.5 million accident-free man-hours during its construction
90,000 tons of concrete
5,000 tons of steel
2,500km – total distance of cable run (power/data)
27,000m – floor area of linoleum, e.g. 4 football pitches

(Taken from: *Mater Campus Hospital Development*, February 2012)

The €284 million development includes the following:
- A large, state-of-the-art emergency department
- Thirteen outpatient clinics
- Twelve operating theatres
- Radiology department
- A total of 120 beds – all single rooms (en-suite)
- Catering and waste management departments
- New energy centre
- A basement car park (444 spaces)
- A heliport at roof level for emergency cases.

This magnificent building is called the Whitty Building, after one of the great women of the Mercy Order, and it brings full circle the history of the hospital. In 2012, just as in 1861, a new hospital is open to care for the sick of Dublin and beyond. The new outpatients, catering and technical services departments were launched by the Minister for Health, Dr James Reilly, on 27 April 2012. It is expected that the next two of the planned three phases will be completed by May 2013.[30]

Understandably, the move from the old hospital to this new facility requires a substantial amount of planning, which is the preserve of the Soft Landing Steering

The Whitty Building taking shape, 2010.

Group. This group will oversee the safe, smooth transfer of patients, staff and equipment to the new hospital at all stages.

The Soft Landing Steering Group consists of the following members:[31] Brian Conlan, Chief Executive; Una Cunningham, Local Programme Manager of Clinical Care; Mary Day, Director of Nursing and Head of Operations; Kevin Finnan, Finance Manager; Deirdre Hyland, Head of Information Management Services; Martin Igoe, Head of Non-Clinical Support Services; Dr Brendan Kinsley, Chairman, Medical Executive; Laura Magahy, MCO Projects–MCHD Project Director; Professor Conor O'Keane, Clinical Director; Caroline Piggott, Director of Finance; Sean Paul Teeling, Head of Nurse Planning.

To ensure that change happened smoothly, in 2010 a systematic plan was put in place using a business philosophy known as *Lean 6 Sigma* thinking[32] to examine various processes required for a project of this magnitude and importance and a number of staff had Lean training. These staff would become part of the Lean countdown process organisation structure[33] which set out the framework required to facilitate a methodical approach to the transfer of patients and staff to the new hospital.

The new hospital will provide the people of Ireland, and north Dublin in particular, with the latest in patient care facilities. The glass-fronted entrance, with a large 'welcome' sign on it at present, leads into a spacious, brightly lit concourse from which an escalator, wide stairs and glass lift are available to take people (patients/visitors), to 'Hospital Street' on the first floor. On this level, patients attending the outpatients department can avail of a self-check-in facility (like an airport) after which they can then relax in the coffee bar while monitoring a VDU screen for their name to appear.

When the original hospital opened in 1861 its main entrance was on Eccles Street. That entrance has served generations of patients, visitors, staff, and on occasions, those who made their way into the history of the Mater for all the wrong reasons.[34] The year 2012 saw the hospital's main entrance moved to the North Circular Road, beginning a new chapter for the Mater. However, the value system that led the Sisters of Mercy in the mid-19th century to build the largest hospital in Ireland to meet the needs of the sick and socially disadvantaged prevails. Just as at that time the sisters were anxious to improve the standards of patient care and to ensure that everyone who crossed the threshold of the Mater would be treated with dignity, so it is the case today, and on into the future.

Another symbol, which cannot go unnoticed, is a large ornate granite Corinthian capital stone from the original hospital, positioned to the right of the main entrance to the Whitty Building. It is one of two unearthed in 2004 between the hospital and 38 Eccles Street and during excavations for the new hostel building;[35] it is possible

The launch of the Whitty Building in 2012. The Minister, Dr James Reilly, is flanked by Mary Day, acting CEO. John Morgan, Chairman of the Board of Directors, is second from the right.

John Morgan addressing invited guests at the opening of the Whitty Building.

that they were originally intended as part of an ornamental cupola (to include a clock and bell tower) which was to have been built above the front door at the Eccles Street entrance. Due to lack of funds, this part of the building was not completed and so the two pieces of beautifully carved Wicklow granite were deeply buried in the grounds. Already, this piece serves as a link with the 1861 development, sitting like a 'stone of Jacob' and used as a resting point and impromptu picnic table by the weary[36] on their way in or out of the hospital.

1   Recurrent outbreaks of smallpox, the slow recovery from it and the social stigma attached to it led the Sisters of Mercy to feel that they should do something to meet the needs of those suffering from infectious diseases, especially smallpox, cholera, diphtheria and tuberculosis, by building a fever hospital. Their proposal was stymied by the local population who lived in fear of these diseases.
2   The new telephone system opened on 26 September 1987 and the pharmacy on 21 May 1988.
3   Originally the telephone exchange was operated from a small wooden cubicle on the right-hand side of the entrance to the Pillar Room. It had space for one operator, who plugged each call into a small machine as it came in. It was a manual exchange so calls to the hospital came through the operator, who determined the required ward/department and then connected the call to that line. A slightly larger area was constructed at the opposite side of the entrance hall when new technology became available in the 1960s. It is now located in Phase 1A and there is a staff of Telephonists providing an excellent telephone service for the hospital.
4   The Pharmacy consisted of one room and was part of the 1936 outpatients department development.
5   In some wards, new needs have since reduced the number of beds in some cases.

6   The medical records department was located where the hospital mail service operates from at present. Sr M. Vincent de Paul Coleman RSM took care of all the patient records for many years.

7   Mater Misericordiae Hospital (1990), *Annual Report 1990*, p 128.

8   The National Rehabilitation Hospital is located in Dun Laoghaire, Co. Dublin.

9   This clinic was located on the North Circular Road OPD department.

10 Mater Misericordiae Hospital (2005), *Annual Report 2005*, p 40.

11 *Mater News* (2008), 'Ireland's first National Isolation Unit for Infectious Diseases Opens at the Mater Hospital', December, p 8.

12 Mater Misericordiae Hospital (2008), *Annual Report 2008*, p 4.

13 In 1992 there were only 13 ITU beds and no high-dependency beds.

14 Mater Misericordiae Hospital (1992), *Annual Report 1992*, p 57.

15 Mater Misericordiae Hospital (1993), *Annual Report 1993*, p 21.

16 The ceilings of Level 2 and Level 3 of the west wing were constructed in the 1930s when the new chapel was built in 1937 and the old chapel turned into four wards – St Cecilia's and St Agatha's wards on Level 3 and St Agnes' and St Gabriel's wards on Level 2. They were very modern for their time.

17 When this building was erected it was suggested that it would be possible to dismantle it in ten years.

18 Built as a temporary facility until the Whitty building was completed.

19 Mater Misericordiae Hospital (2005), *Annual Report 2005*, p 64.

20 Level 3 is the top floor of the original hospital building – there is also a Level 3 in Phase 1A.

21 Mater Misericordiae Hospital (2006), *Annual Report 2005*, p 5.

22 The Children's Hospital, Temple Street was founded in 1872 at 9 Upper Buckingham Street (nearby) by a group of charitable people led by Mrs Eileen Woodlock. It commenced with eight beds. In 1876 the Irish Sisters of Charity were invited to take it over, which they did on 2 July 1876. In 1879 they purchased 15 Upper Temple Street and on 17 June 1879 opened a new hospital with 21 beds.

23 Not to be confused with the Mater Adult Hospital opened in 2012.

24 Our Lady's Hospital for Sick Children, Crumlin; the Children's Hospital, Temple Street; and the National Children's Hospital, Tallaght.

25 Nearly five acres.

26 *The Irish Times*, 9 April 2012.

27 The metro scheme was part of the planned rail infrastructure for Dublin.

28 Interestingly, this was the second time it was planned to locate a public rail service through the hospital grounds. Shortly after the hospital opened a request was received to locate a rail line to the west through the grounds. It was refused as it would block all access to the hospital from the North Circular Road. This time Metro North (underground) was to be located between the hospital and the Mater Private Hospital, with a station opening into the adult hospital. It did not go ahead although part of the station connected to the adult hospital had to be built as it was an integral part of the plan.

29 Architects: Scott Tallon Walker. Builders: John Sisk & Son.

30 MCHD (2012), *Mater Campus Hospital Development*, Issue 10, February, p 3.

31 According to Prof. Conor O'Keane, 'The Soft Landing Process feeds into wider Health Service Executive plans and objectives and the Mater's ongoing commitment to deliver the best service', *Mater Campus Hospital Development*, Issue 10, February 2012, p 5.

32 Lean principles provide a generic set of management strategies used to change the culture of an organisation to bring about a defined objective. The philosophy provides a systematic approach to identifying and eliminating waste or non-value-added activities in a particular process through continuous improvement.

33 *Lean Countdown Process Organisation Structure*, organised by the Mater Campus Hospital Development.

34 See Chapter 11 (Gun Battle on the Corridor).

35 The hostel building was opened by An Taoiseach Bertie Ahern TD in September 2006.

36 Genesis 28:10–22 as follows: '*Jacob left Beersheba and set out for Haran. When he had reached a certain place he passed the night there, since the sun had set. Taking one of the stones to be found at that place, he made it his pillow and lay down where he was. He had a dream ...*'

Afterword

CELEBRATING THE MATER

The doors of the Mater Hospital opened to receive the sick on 27 September 1861. No one could have dreamt that this would be the beginning of an immense development which would serve thousands of people year after year, from Dublin and beyond, a development which would witness history as the country struggled for independence and which, over more than 150 years, would create its own history.

On 21 January 2011, President Mary McAleese arrived to the Mater at 11.30 a.m. to launch the celebrations for the sesquicentennial year. This year was to honour and look back with gratitude to the opening of the hospital 150 years previously and to the many developments at the hospital since then. There was gratitude for the Sisters of

President Mary McAleese greets the author in January 2011 at the launch of the celebrations of the hospital's 150th anniversary.

A mass to celebrate the 150th anniversary of the hospital.

Mercy, whose vision led to the building of this great institution, and to the thousands of staff who have contributed their expertise and energies to make the Mater the success it has become. There was gratitude and prayers for all the patients who passed through the doors of the hospital for treatment and care. There was gratitude to the Irish people for their ongoing support and interest in the work being done to care for patients, and in professional education and research. All of this was expressed in many memorable ways during the year: by word, art, symbols and a host of celebratory events during 2011. It will always remain a year to remember. As the President said in her speech:

> The foundations of the Mater Misericordiae Hospital are not bricks and mortar, but values–enduring, unchanging values summarised in the word love, in particular love of suffering humanity, a love expressed in compassion, concern, selflessness and care. There is an old proverb, 'Where there is no vision, the people perish.' Ireland of the eighteenth and nineteenth centuries was a bleak place of slums, virulent diseases, of low life expectancy, high maternal deaths and all the misery that comes with widespread destitution and poverty. The people were perishing when in 1831 Catherine McAuley founded the Sisters of Mercy and set in train a national and international movement which would set new standards and a new vision for healthcare and education. Catherine McAuley's vision was informed by her faith in God and by the challenge of the great commandment to love one another. She was dead ten years before the foundation of the Mater Misericordiae Hospital, but without her we would not be here today, nor would

we know the righteous pride we have today in this great Catholic teaching voluntary hospital which has served the sick so consummately well in generation after generation.... The Mater Hospital's foundations are the very embodiment of all that is good, selfless, decent and kind about Ireland. This simple site made its own history of care no matter what the times, tides, economic fortunes or misfortunes. It has always kept its focus on the thing that does not change: the need the sick have for help. Here it has been given generously and carefully to levels of excellence that allow us to gather this day in both pride and hope.

Now, 153 years after the vision of Catherine McAuley was realised, the Mater continues to care for the sick of Dublin and beyond and to face the complex challenges of the 21st century with the pride and hope expressed by the President. It also continues to express, daily, the values contained in its mission statement.

● *Sr Gerard Egan and Sr Helena O'Donoghue at the anniversary celebrations.*

● *A fun day to mark the anniversary.*

265

● *The staff walk organised to celebrate the 150th anniversary.*

● *Staff pose with their children at the fun day.*

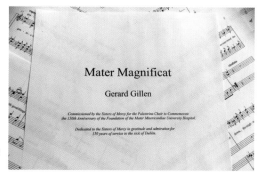

● *Sheet music for the Magnificat, which was composed to mark the occasion.*

Mission Statement

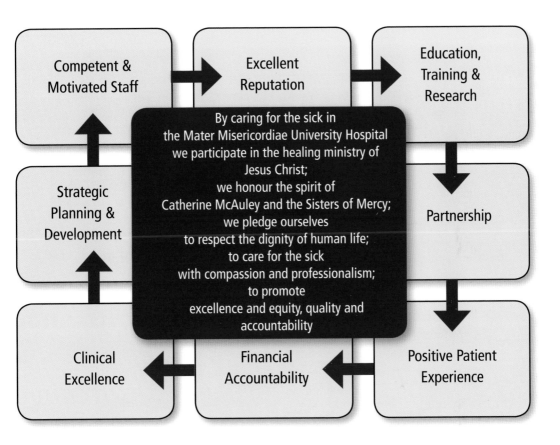

A montage of staff photos from throughout
the Mater's busy year.

Index

Note: Locators that are annotated with **i** contain photographs or illustrations. Locators that are annotated with **n** indicate that the reference appears in the notes at the end of each chapter.